FOREVER LOVED

Exposing the Hidden Crisis of
Missing and Murdered
Indigenous Women and Girls in Canada

Funded by the Government of Canada
Financé par la gouvernement du Canada

Demeter Press
140 Holland Street West
P. O. Box 13022
Bradford, ON L3Z 2Y5
Tel: (905) 775-9089
Email: info@demeterpress.org
Website: www.demeterpress.org

Demeter Press logo based on the sculpture "Demeter" by Maria-Luise Bodirsky <www.keramik-atelier.bodirsky.de>

Printed and Bound in Canada

Front cover artwork: Alyssa M. General, "Thunder Destroys the Horned Serpent," 2011, watercolour, gouache, ink, 8 x 10 feet.

Library and Archives Canada Cataloguing in Publication

Forever loved : exposing the hidden crisis of missing and murdered indigenous women and girls in Canada / edited by Memee Lavell-Harvard and Jennifer Brant.

Includes bibliographical references.
ISBN 978-1-77258-020-4 (paperback)

1. Indigenous women--Violence against--Canada. 2. Women--Violence against--Canada. 3. Girls--Violence against--Canada. 4. Missing persons--Canada. 5. Murder victims--Canada. I. Lavell-Harvard, D. Memee (Dawn Memee), 1974- author, editor II. Brant, Jennifer, 1981-, author, editor

HV6250.4.W65F64 2016 362.88082'0971 C2016-902834-8II.

FOREVER LOVED

Exposing the Hidden Crisis of Missing and Murdered Indigenous Women and Girls in Canada

EDITED BY
D. Memee Lavell-Harvard and Jennifer Brant

DEMETER PRESS

This book is dedicated to all our stolen sisters
who have been taken from us far too soon without a trace.
We carry you in our hearts, and you will never be forgotten.

To the families and children who have lost a loved one and
struggle to carry on, we walk by your side and will continue
to do this work to bring awareness, action, and change.

With this work, we hold your hand to bring honour and respect
to the beautiful spirits of our women and girls
who will be forever loved.

Table of Contents

Acknowledgements

Saying thank you cannot convey the depth of gratitude to all those who made this collection possible. Many thanks go to Demeter Press and Andrea O'Reilly, for having the vision, faith, and the fortitude to see this project through to fruition.

Thank you to the mothers, grandmothers, aunties, sisters, and daughters who are leading the struggle, and the fathers and brothers who are on this journey with us keeping the memories alive. Whether you are leading the vigils, or walking the streets after dark searching for yet another missing sister, you are strength and optimism personified, and you are our inspiration.

Thank you to the authors who put into words a reality that cannot be imagined unless you have experienced it first hand, as this is the story of every mother's worst fear.

Thank you to the Elders, those grandmothers who guide us in our work, every day in every way, to make sure we are walking with good hearts and good minds. We thank you for your guidance, your prayers, and your wisdom. You have kept us on the right path and lifted us up when we thought we could go no further.

Thank you to our mothers, Jeannette Lavell and Cathy Winter, to Jameson Brant, and to our community Grandmothers and Aunties. You taught us what it meant to be Indigenous women; to be strong, resilient and proud of who we are, to never give up hope even when things seem truly hopeless. Most of all thank you to our children: Autumn, Eva, Brianna and Jayden and Quinten. On the days when this struggle gets too hard, when we feel like we cannot face another day with another story of loss and tragedy, on those days when the experts tell us we have to learn to distance ourselves, we carry on because we have you! Because we were given the gift of these precious lives, and we will continue to do everything in our power to keep you safe even if it means we must change the world.

Introduction

Forever Loved

D. MEMEE LAVELL-HARVARD AND JENNIFER BRANT

> *To be born poor, an Indian, and a female is to be a member of the most disadvantaged minority in Canada today, a citizen minus. It is to be victimized and utterly powerless, and to be, by government decree, without legal recourse of any kind.*—Kathleen Jamieson (92)

IN *MOTHERS OF THE NATIONS: Indigenous Mothering as Global Resistance, Reclaiming and Recovery*, Lavell-Harvard and Anderson declare that Indigenous[1] women are entitled to claim a victory:

> After centuries of persecution and oppression, the simple fact that we are still here, as proud Indigenous mothers, at the heart of our families, communities, and nations, signifies the strength of our resistance. Whether this resistance has been overt, as our sisters engage in constitutional challenges or human rights demonstrations, or covert, as we silently reconnect with the land and teach our children the ways of our ancestors, our efforts have ensured the continued survival of our people. (1)

This book may be positioned as an expression of both overt and covert resistance as we contribute to the continued survival of our people in all aspects of our work as Indigenous women, mothers, grandmothers, and community members. In a country where the tragedy of more than twelve hundred missing and murdered Indigenous women and girls has been denied, obscured, or simply ignored by those with the power and resources to prevent the appalling rates of violence (not to mention the fiduciary responsibility and legal obligation to do so), the personal is indeed political. Simply being born Aboriginal and female, in a nation built on the oppression of Indigenous peoples, and the subjugation of women, engenders the very real likelihood of being subjected to the most severe forms of violence and becoming yet another homicide statistic, even without engaging in so-called high-risk activities (Boyer).

In October 2004 Amnesty International released a report titled *Stolen Sisters: A Human Rights Response to the Discrimination and Violence against Indigenous Women in Canada* in response to the appalling number, over five hundred, of Indigenous women who are victims of racialized and sexualized violence. Tragically, since this initial report, the numbers have continued to rise. Noting that Indigenous women are eight times more likely to die as a result of violence, the most recent RCMP report documents 1,181 missing or murdered Aboriginal women and girls between 1980 and 2012. Another thirty-two were identified this year, 2016, with more distressing cases being reported every month. After conducting an extensive investigation here in Canada, the United Nations Committee on the Elimination of Discrimination against Women issued their report in March of 2015 condemning Canada, unequivocally declaring the ongoing failure to protect Indigenous women and girls to be "grave human rights violation" (UNCEDAW).

The Legal Strategy Coalition on Violence against Indigenous Women documents fifty-eight separate reports that have outlined over seven hundred recommendations to address the increase in racialized and sexualized violence against Indigenous women. Yet the recommendations continue to be largely ignored. Although these reports may educate the Canadian public on the extent of the problem, the reality of violence is all too familiar and resonates within the hearts of Indigenous communities. This can no longer be ignored. This is not just an Aboriginal problem, or a women's issue, it is a national tragedy and a national shame. The stories of our stolen sisters deeply affect the lives of all Indigenous peoples in Canada. These are the stories of our sisters, mothers, daughters, aunties, and grandmothers. We hear and read about our missing sisters in the venues that connect us across Turtle Island. At almost every Indigenous conference we attend, there is yet another moment of silence. Our intent is to honour those missing sisters and their families, to honour their lives and their stories so that they are no longer reduced to "just another sad statistic" or, worse yet, "just another Indian."

The failure of the government to effectively respond to this issue has resulted in a national grassroots movement to call for a national public inquiry. Not only did the Conservative government of Canada fail to respond, but Stephen Harper dismissed the crisis altogether when he stated that the issue of missing and murdered Indigenous women is "not really high on his radar." The deliberate refusal to even acknowledge that there is an issue has been evidenced over and over in the lack of follow through on recommendations from numerous reports. Calls for action have been ridiculed to the extent of papers being thrown on the floor in the House of Commons as opposing parties have debated the need for a national public inquiry. The complete disregard from the federal level not only exacerbates the problem but sends out a clear message that devalues the lives of Indigenous women and girls; such apathy is, in fact, an integral part of the problem. As both the Inter-American Commission and The United Nations have pointed out, the disproportionate violence against our women is not the result of individual criminal acts (although the acts are indeed criminal and often deeply disturbing) but rather a reflection and function of the longstanding disregard for the lives of the original occupants of this territory, which has served the colonial project since contact.

To understand the severity of the tragedy facing Indigenous women today, the history of settler colonialism must be understood, a process deliberately and openly designed to eradicate the so-called Indian problem in North America by simply eliminating the "Indians" themselves. Indeed, our very existence as Indigenous women poses a symbolic and physical threat to the dominant colonial society (Eberts). In her exploration of the connection between the raping of the earth and violence against women, Andrea Smith explains how, as "bearers of a counter-imperial order" the strength and authority of Indigenous women is a significant threat, our very existence denying the inevitability of patriarchy (15). Moreover, in this context, our role as the givers of life becomes a liability, as it is the Indigenous woman's ability to produce future generations and ensure the continuance of her people that threatens the entire colonial project (Smith 79). This reality is evident in the Cheyenne proverb that claims "a nation is not conquered until the hearts of its women are on the ground. Then it is done, no matter how brave its warriors or strong its weapons." The deliberate targeting of Indigenous women was clearly, therefore, an integral part of the larger historical effort to destroy Indigenous nations. Our very reproductive rights as Indigenous women and our ability to mother are the biggest threats to the colonial project. This is evidenced by the sustained efforts to destroy that ability through forced sterilizations, residential schools, and child welfare apprehensions; all of which are aimed at eliminating the ability of Indigenous women to physically birth the nation and mother their own children. This has always been the means by which Indigenous women and families have been targeted in an attempt to conquer our nations. The issue of missing and murdered Indigenous women and girls in Canada today must be understood within the context of these genocidal efforts.

Not only is the presence of Indigenous peoples a symbolic threat to the national narrative—serving as a persistent and most unwelcome reminder of a sordid and dishonourable past, given the fact that much of the natural resources are on crown lands and/or disputed territories—but Smith explains how the continued existence of Indigenous nations simultaneously poses a very real contemporary threat to the economic base of the capitalist state: "As the ability of Native women to reproduce the next generations of Native peoples continues to stand in the way of government and corporate takeovers of Indian land, Native women become seen as little more than pollutants which may threaten the wellbeing of the colonial body" (Smith 107). The destruction and elimination of Indigenous women either physically or symbolically (through legislative acts) clearly benefits the colonial state.

Although the "era of Indian massacres" has thankfully passed, according to Smith, the underlying colonial ideologies that promoted the systematic state sponsored extermination of Indigenous women and children remain, and the "wholesale rape and mutilation of indigenous women's bodies continues" (27) continues. In a nation founded on the suffering and violent oppression of Indigenous peoples generally, and the targeting of Indigenous women specifically, it is not surprising that racist and sexist beliefs coalesce and harden, which continues to encourage the persecution of our women and to justify a lack of response or concern. Whether it is the individual police officer who fails to respond when a young Indigenous girl goes missing, having already labelled her as a runaway or an addict, or the RCMP report that effectively blames the victims for their own demise, highlighting the 'high risk lifestyle' of many Aboriginal women, the racist and sexist attitudes continue to put our women and girls in danger. Indigenous women and girls do not freely choose hig-risk lifestyles. It is in fact the lack of real choice that forces them into unsafe situations. Our women are born "at-risk" in First Nation communities, with no housing, no clean water, no healthcare, no education or employment, living in Third World conditions in the middle of one of the richest countries in the world. They disappear while hitchhiking or walking home along remote highways because there was no other alternative, no other transportation. As Andrea Smith has argued, the very concept of free choice does not "take into consideration all the social, economic, and political conditions that frame the so-called choices that women are forced to make" (99).

The violence must be understood as a sociological phenomenon buried under layers of colonial abuses that continue to directly target Indigenous women and girls. For Indigenous women and girls "centuries of persecution and oppression" are certainly not a thing of the past. In a country where the subjugation and elimination of Indigenous nations was, and arguably still is, the intended outcome of government legislation, policy, and practice, our survival is, in fact, an act of political resistance. For Indigenous women, rather than indicating an acquiescence to patriarchal dictates and gendered expectations, the birthing and raising of children symbolizes a revolutionary act, a grassroots rebellion against a system that would see the eradication of the "Indian problem" accomplished through the elimination of the Indians themselves. However, participating in this particular rebellion requires a strange form of parental schizophrenia, unimagined by even the most paranoid "helicopter" parent. Knowing full well that our children are indeed at-risk of a violent end, much more so than other children in Canada, and that we cannot always be there to protect them (as the families of the many missing and murdered women and girls know only too well), we must educate our girls about the very real dangers that exist and, simultaneously, encourage them to go out and reach their potential, lest they give in to fear and despair or hopelessness. We must educate our boys to honour and respect girls and women, and to walk with them as we collectively advocate for the elimination of racialized and sexualized violence.

As we write this chapter, the community of Attawapiskat has just declared a state of emergency after a number of youth suicides have swept across the community. In response, Idle No More activists are occupying Indian and Northern Affair Canada to demand the abolishment of the Indian Act of Canada. Others have noted that the whole country should declare a state of emergency for its treatment of Indigenous peoples. This issue of missing and murdered Indigenous women and girls, though understood as a human rights issue, rests within this larger colonial context and must be understood, as several of the contributors in this collection have pointed out, as a sociological phenomenon. Canada must revisit and reconcile its treatment of Indigenous peoples generally and Indigenous women specifically.

As Brenda Anderson articulates in an earlier book that comes from the 2008 Missing and Murdered Indigenous Women Conference held in Regina, Saskatchewan: "Within these profoundly disturbing accounts, we see the interplay of sexism and racism within the context of a country traumatized by practices of assimilation, residential schools and cultural genocide. A country cannot be considered healthy if any of us are comfortable with that reality." The issue of missing and murdered Indigenous women and girls attests to the ill health of this country and the continued trauma inflicted on the Indigenous people of this land.

This book began in support of the call for immediate response and action into the human rights travesty of missing and murdered Indigenous women and girls in Canada. With the recent change in government, however, Prime Minister Justin Trudeau has followed through on his promise to call a national inquiry and has articulated that "Indigenous women's lives matter." Thus, this book is both timely and, of course, long overdue. The work involved in putting this book together has been an emotionally arduous process, as the issue is close to our hearts. It is important to note that some of the chapters will be very troubling and difficult to read as sensitive material is exposed. The intention, however, is not to re-victimize but rather to bring awareness to these horrific injustices. People need to understand the severity of this issue, as it is the silence that has allowed it to continue for so long. We all need to hear the truth and to destroy the myths and the lies that blame our women and girls for their own victimization.

The essence of *Forever Loved* is expressed throughout the chapters in its honouring of our missing sisters, their families, their lives, and their stories. We offer this book in the hopes that it will provide some healing for the families affected and that it will offer lessons to non-Indigenous allies and supporters so that we can work together towards a nation that supports and promotes the safety and well-being of Indigenous women and girls. Simply put, this book demands the value of Indigenous women and girls as we come together to work towards effective and immediate action.

OUTLINE OF THE BOOK

We begin section one titled "Violence Against Indigenous Women and Girls: A Sociological Phenomenon" with Wendee Kubik and Carrie Bourassa's chapter, which outlines the repeated calls for action and provide a historical timeline of completed inquiries and recommendations (many completed prior to the release of Amnesty International's report in 2004) that have largely been ignored. As they note, "By ignoring the structural components of violence against women, it is not only allowed to continue but simultaneously encouraged through lack of accountability." Kubik and Bourassa conclude by linking the violence against Indigenous women and girls to Canada's colonial past and the continued racism, sexism, poverty, and health disparities experienced by Indigenous communities today, and they question Canada's claims as a democratic country that values equality and fairness.

In chapter two, Jessica Riel-Johns offers her understanding of racialized and sexualized violence by describing the dismantling of Indigenous matrilineal societies as a deliberate attack on Indigenous nations. As she articulates, violence against Indigenous women is a form of cultural genocide. Like Kubik and Bourassa, she questions Canada's claims as a fair and democratic country and presents her vision for a nation in which Indigenous women and girls can feel safe. Jessica ends with her personal narrative as an Indigenous woman and mother to four girls.

In chapter three, previously published in *Well-being in the Urban Aboriginal Community*, Patricia O'Reilly and Thomas Fleming document the investigative failures in the Lower Eastside Missing Women Case in Vancouver. They offer a critical analysis of the relationship between the police agencies involved and the victim's families and note the need for a serious evaluation of police attitudes towards Aboriginal women and their families. They conclude by offering recommendations for effective police responses in dealing with serial murder and missing women cases.

In chapter four, previously published in *Restoring the Balance: First Nations Women, Community, and Culture*, Anita Olsen Harper begins by outlining the traditional roles of men and women in pre-contact Indigenous societies and then describes the shifting demographics and contemporary realities of Indigenous women through an understanding of the *Indian Act*. She provides an outline of the Sisters in Spirit Campaign and describes its role in addressing the racialized and sexualized violence against Indigenous women in Canada. She draws attention to the resilience of Indigenous women and highlights the power and courage of those who share their stories of grief and healing. Her chapter ends with a narrative from a mother who shares her story of strength and the power of spirit.

Section two, "The Ongoing Erasure of Indigenous Women" includes three chapters that consider legislative and media responses to missing and murdered Indigenous women cases. These responses contribute to a narrative of victim blaming, which reduces the lives of Indigenous women to the demonizing descriptors that ultimately perpetuate and justify the violence against them.

In chapter five, Caroline Fidan Tyler Doenmez documents the

case of Cindy Gladue and describes the Canadian justice system as "one of the institutional frameworks in which Indigenous women frequently struggle to be afforded adequate protection and representation." Caroline describes the trial as a second violation that dehumanizes Cindy's death and sexually exploits her body through "an act of bodily dismemberment that perpetuated, not prevented, violence against Indigenous women." Caroline ends this chapter by drawing attention to the ways Indigenous communities reclaimed Cindy's body and, in doing so, restored her dignity and humanity.

In chapter six, Josephine L. Savarese contributes to a deepening understanding of the need to acknowledge the broader social, cultural, and political contexts as well as the wider institutions that give rise to violent behaviour. Her chapter examines Indigenous women's erasure and resistance in New Brunswick by describing acts of violence that occurred in two unrelated cases: the criminalization of Mi'kmaq land defender Annie Clair and the murder of Hilary Bonnell. Savarese describes the "factors that prohibit Maritime Indigenous women from realizing inclusion and citizenship, which, thereby, increases the likelihood of victimization." She also examines how an understanding of erasure might deepen if we were to make Indigenous women's diminished participation in social and political life clearer focal points in collections on missing women. By connecting the two cases, Savarese reveals Canada's violent treatment of Indigenous women in all facets of life through structural racialized and sexualized violence.

Isela Pérez-Torres is a Mexican journalist currently living in asylum in Spain, where she continues to draw attention to the violent deaths of Indigenous women in Mexico. In chapter seven, she outlines the "tenacious control of information exercised by the dominant elites in Ciudad Juárez" to discribe how this control contributes to continued violence for Indigenous women and impunity for violent offenders. She draws attention to the discourse of blame that targets victims and families. Her chapter sheds light on the acceptance of violence and fear tactics that silence the media. She writes about two cases in which mothers of victims who have spoken out about the violence have been murdered, whereas other victims' families have been exiled to keep them silent. She ends by noting the ethical responsibility of the media to refuse to be silent and offers her story as a lesson for Canadian journalists to continue working to bring justice to victims and families.

Section three, "Education, Awareness and Action" begins with Rosemary Nagy's work on transnational advocacy. In chapter eight, she draws attention to the global push from advocacy groups that have called on Canada for a national response to the disproportionate rates of violence against Indigenous women. She outlines Canada's shameful history of Indigenous human rights protection by making note of the country's response to transnational advocacy in the case of *Lovelace v. Canada* of 1984 and Canada's delayed and "selective endorsement" of the United Nations Declaration on the Rights of Indigenous People in 2010. As she points out, "Indigenous and women's rights groups, NWAC and FAFIA in particular, have successfully built insider-outsider coalitions that have resulted in sustained pressure on Canada over the last seven years to better respond to the missing and murdered women."

In chapter nine, Brenda Anderson describes the importance of education as a tool of inspiring change, empathy, and hope for the future. She offers a reflection of her experience teaching a women's and gender studies course on missing and murdered Indigenous women worldwide . She notes that this is the most difficult course that she teaches because students learn the painful history and contemporary realities of femicide. Her class moves through and beyond feelings of guilt to action by bringing awareness campaigns to campus and contribute to the push for a national response.

Chapter ten documents an interview with film director Nick Printup to showcase the pedagogical lessons presented in his film *Our Sisters in Spirit.* By presenting the stories of families along with the voices of academics and politicians working to put an end to the racialized and sexualized violence of Indigenous women and girls in Canada, the film serves as a call to action that inspires all to take part in an informed national dialogue. This chapter is presented in honour of the families who shared their stories and continue to advocate for justice.

Section four "Taking a Stance: Resistance and Sisterhood" includes three chapters that showcases the work of frontline workers, activists, and educators, who are all working to promote social justice for Indigenous women and girls. In chapter eleven, "Sisterhood on the Frontlines: The Truth as We Hear It from Indigenous women front line workers from the Vancouver Rape Relief and Women's Shelter," is by a feminist collective that operates a rape crisis centre and offers transition housing in Vancouver. Their experiences as frontline workers are presented to give voice and dispel the myths often presented in media accounts on missing and murdered Indigenous women and girls in Canada through a "critical examination of the power imbalances between men and women, between white people and Indigenous peoples, and between the wealthy and the poor." The authors highlight the importance of feminist solidarity with Indigenous women and note that "Non-Indigenous feminists must use their relative privileges of race and class to fight for substantive equality for Indigenous women."

Chapter twelve is presented as part of a broader collaborative strategy working to make visible the important and overlooked grassroots work of Indigenous women, families, and communities. It presents the narratives shared by the authors at the "Visualizing Justice" conference at the University of Winnipeg in 2015. The authors note:

> These voices form an important and vital piece of Indigenous grassroots knowledge to rethink how the families and communities are central to addressing the endemic, racialized, and gendered violence experienced by Indigenous women in Canada. Each presentation not only paints a picture of the struggles and challenges faced by the women, families and communities, but also reminds us of the important work that they carry out, the knowledge they share, and the many ways they give. (8)

In chapter thirteen, "Personal Political Pedagogy with respect to #MMIW," Maxine Matilpi describes her action-oriented pedagogy as one that involves creating space for stories, a space that might inspire a desire for action, and deep engagement. She also draws attention to the need for reciprocity in the learning exchange as she walks her students through an emotionally charged dialogue. Her chapter ends with an expression of ceremony and showcases an Indigenous pedagogy as a transformative and healing exchange.

Section five "Voices of Healing: Narrative and Poetry" includes poetry, spoken word pieces and a narrative piece. All pieces are creative expressions written by Indigenous women in honour of the love we collectively carry in our hearts for our stolen sisters.

The book ends with a dialogue between Dawn Memee Lavell-Harvard, Gladys Radek, and Bernice Williams discussing their own work from the grassroots to the prime minister's office, as well as perspectives on the crisis facing our women, potential strategies for initiating change, and our hope for a brighter future.

As Brenda Anderson has articulated: "To understand the connections between colonialism, racism, and sexism, we need to hear personal stories from around the world and in our own backyards. We also need to keep our theoretical maps of these worldviews and paths to justice accessible, understandable and responsive to all communities" (8). We offer this book by including a balance of academic contributions along with personal stories and poetry. In an effort to present a diversity of voices and respect the stories of all who have contributed, each chapter expresses the viewpoints and experiences of the individual authors. Understanding the issue of missing and murdered Indigenous women and girls in Canada involves us all and change takes place within the spirit of this dialogue. This book is a call for awareness and action, one that involves solidarity between women and men, Indigenous and non-Indigenous. It presents a vision of healing, plants seeds of hope and expresses our love for all missing and murdered Indigenous women and girls in Canada.

We intentionally did not write a conclusion as we urge readers to become part of a informed national dialogue. The book exposes the hidden crisis and it is now time for action. It is up to everyone to put an end to violence and work together to ensure Canada is a safe place for Indigenous women and girls.

NOTE

[1]Throughout the book the terms Indigenous, Aboriginal, First Nations, and Native are used interchangeably depending on the intention of the author in a particular context. Although Indigenous

is more commonly used in international contexts, Aboriginal is the term recognized within the Canadian constitution (which includes First Nations, Metis and Inuit). Even though many of the terms used to describe or define us have specific political associations, some of them are also terms that we have become familiar with. The terms will also rest within the terminology of the inquiry, report, or organization of reference. Using the terms interchangeably not only connects the women of the many varied Nations across Canada, and in some cases across the globe, but it also captures the complexity of our lived experiences.

WORKS CITED

Anderson, Brenda, A. "The Journey from Awareness to a Conference to a Book ... and Beyond." *Torn from Our Midst: Voices of Grief, Healing, and Action from the Missing Indigenous Women Conference, 2008*. Eds. Brenda A. Anderson, Wendee Kubik, and Mary Rucklos Hampton. Regina: University of Regina Press, 2010. 1-16. Print.

Boyer, Yvonne. *Understanding the Policy behind the Inquiry: Where Do We Go from Here?* Policy Brief. Johnson Shoyama Graduate School of Public Policy. University of Regiona. March 2016. Print.

Eberts, Mary. "Victoria's Secret: How to Make a Population of Prey." *Indivisible: Indigenous Human Rights*. Ed. Joyce Green. Halifax: Fernwood Publishing, 2014: 144-158. Print.

Lavell-Harvard, M. D., and K. Anderson. "Introduction: Indigenous Mothering Perspectives." *Mothers of the Nations: Indigenous Mothering as Global Resistance, Reclaiming, and Recovery*. Eds. Memee D. Lavell Harvard and Kim Anderson. Bradford, ON: Demeter Press, 2014. 1-11. Print

Jamieson, Kathleen. *Indian Women and the Law in Canada: Citizens Minus*. Ottawa: Advisory Council on the Status of Women, Indian Rights for Indian Women, 1978. Print.

Smith, Andrea. *Conquest, Sexual Violence and American Indian Genocide*. Cambridge, MA: South End Press, 2005. Print.

I.

VIOLENCE AGAINST INDIGENOUS WOMEN AND GIRLS:

A SOCIOLOGICAL PHENOMENON

1.
Stolen Sisters

The Politics, Policies, and Travesty of Missing and Murdered Women in Canada

WENDEE KUBIK AND CARRIE BOURASSA

IN 2004, AMNESTY INTERNATIONAL in partnership with the Native Women's Association of Canada (NWAC) released a report documenting how the economic and social marginalization of Aboriginal women in Canada has led to a significant higher risk of violence against them. *Stolen Sisters: A Human Rights Response to Discrimination and Violence against Indigenous Women in Canada* tells several stories about Aboriginal women and girls who went missing or were murdered in Canada. This groundbreaking report also documents how the violence was often met with official government indifference and systematic prejudice from various police forces. Prior to the *Stolen Sisters* report, government commissions and official inquiries—such as the Manitoba Justice Inquiry, the 1996 Royal Commission on Aboriginal Peoples, and a number of United Nations human rights bodies—had already noted these problems. In addition, many of these previous inquiries and commissions presented concrete recommendations for reforms.

Since Amnesty International's 2004 report was released, several other investigations have been undertaken. Numerous recommendations have been presented to various governments and government bodies recommending measures to be taken to end these deaths and ameliorate the dire circumstances causing many Aboriginal women to go missing. However, the numbers of missing and murdered women continues to rise (Human Rights Watch, *Those Who Take Us* 7). In this chapter, we offer a historical timeline relating to missing and murdered women, a critical analysis of why this continues to happen, and an explanation as to why Canada's federal Conservative government ignored the issue.

HISTORICAL OVERVIEW

In March of 2004, in tandem with Amnesty's Stolen Sisters report, the NWAC launched the Sisters in Spirit (SIS) campaign to raise awareness of the high rates of violence perpetrated against Aboriginal women in Canada. In November of 2005, the federal government acknowledged the problem of violence against Aboriginal women and signed a five year contribution agreement with the NWAC to address this racialized and sexualized violence. Sisters in Spirit received five million dollars over five years and with this money, instigated research and recommended a number of actions to address some of the violence against Aboriginal women (Hughes 208). The main goals and objectives of the Sisters in Spirit initiative were to:

> 1. reduce the risks and increase the safety and security of all Aboriginal women and girls
> in Canada.
> 2. address the high incidence of violence against Aboriginal women, particularly racialized, sexualized violence, that is, violence perpetrated against Aboriginal women because of their sex and Aboriginal identity; and
> 3. to increase gender equality and improve the participation of Aboriginal women in the economic, social, cultural, and political realms of Canadian society. (Hughes 209)

Two other events had a significant impact during this time period. The first was the Robert Pickton case in Vancouver, and the second was the continuing reports of missing or murdered Aboriginal women and girls along northern British Columbia's Highway 16 between Prince George and Prince Rupert (referred to as the "Highway of Tears"). Robert Pickton, a Port Coquitlam pig farmer and Canada's most notorious serial killer, was charged with the murder of women in more than twenty-six cases (although he confessed to an undercover officer that he killed forty-nine women in total).

Pickton was convicted with the second-degree murder of only six of the twenty-seven women (twenty of the charges were stayed by the crown), and in 2007, he was sentenced to life in prison with no possibility of parole for twenty-five years. The Pickton murder case, and the numerous incidents of missing and murdered women along Highway 16, brought a great deal of public attention to the violence Aboriginal women face. Because of these ghastly occurrences and the resulting media focus, knowledge about missing and murdered women, particularly Aboriginal women, became forefront in the media.

There were numerous calls for action, and connections were made to the root causes—the reasons why these murders and disappearances were occurring. The government was criticized, not only about this issue but about a number of other problems facing Aboriginal people (e.g., inadequate housing on reserves, poverty, unemployment, and health issues). The government's reaction was to point out the funding that was given to the Sisters in Spirit initiative.

However, when the Sisters in Spirit's five year funding agreement ended in 2010, the Conservative government of Canada informed the NWAC that it would no longer fund Sisters in Spirit, and the NWAC was also told that since under the Status of Women's Community Fund, no research, policy development, or advocacy could be funded, there would be no further consideration of funding for the Sisters In Spirit initiative (Barrera; Jackson). Like Sisters in Spirit, a number of other non-profit women's and advocacy groups lost funding and many disbanded.

In the March 2010 federal budget, the Conservative government allocated ten million dollars to combat violence against Aboriginal women. The money was purportedly to address the disturbingly high number of missing and murdered Aboriginal women and to take action so that law enforcement and the justice system would meet the needs of Aboriginal women and their families (Canada, Department of Finance). This sounded hopeful; however, the federal government subsequently clarified that the ten million dollars would be spent over two years, and instead of directing funds to Aboriginal women's organizations it would be distributed as follows: 4 million for the Royal Canadian Mounted Police (RCMP) to establish a National Police Support Centre for Missing Persons; 1.5 million to Public Safety Canada to develop community safety plans to improve the safety of Aboriginal women within Aboriginal communities; 2.15 million to the Department of Justice Victims Fund; and 1million to support the development of school and community based pilot projects (FAFIA 14).

The allocation of funds was decided without consulting the NWAC, and it was not specifically designed to address violence against Aboriginal women, nor would it address the more serious forms of violence, such as murder. The Conservative government felt that there was no need for Sisters in Spirit to continue its research or maintain a database of information on missing and murdered Aboriginal women because the RCMP would receive funds to collect information on all missing persons (not just Aboriginal). There was no mention of any of the underlying issues that contribute to the high rates of violence against Aboriginal women and girls (e.g., poverty, racism). With the funding for Sisters in Spirit ended, the NWAC established a new program entitled "Evidence to Action." The new three-year project would receive 1.89 million dollars in funding from the Status of Women fund for violence prevention beginning in February, 2011. However, in a clear effort to silence growing criticism on this issue, one of the conditions of this new money was that the NWAC could no longer conduct any research into missing and murdered Aboriginal women (Jackson).

In September of 2010, the government of British Columbia established the Missing Women Commission of Inquiry into the facts, decisions, and police investigations involved in the Pickton case. The attorney general of British Columbia provided funding for one lawyer to represent some of the families of women murdered by Robert Pickton but did not provide funding to any of the civil society groups granted standing by the commissioner. As a result, many of the groups that could have provided expert testimony on root causes and systemic issues were unable to participate in the Inquiry's fact-finding process because they simply could not afford to.

In March of 2011, the House of Commons and the Standing Committee on the Status of Women (composed of members of parliament from all parties) released an interim report on violence against Aboriginal women. This report recognized the need for a comprehensive approach to eliminating violence against Aboriginal women and girls. The Canadian Feminist Alliance for International Action (FAFIA) noted that this report was particularly significant because it recognized that "poverty, racism, Canada's colonial history and systemic police failures are root causes of the violence and contributing factors to it" (19). Between April 2010 and February 2011, the Committee heard from over 150 witnesses from across Canada and, subsequently, concluded that "it is impossible to deal with violence against Aboriginal women without dealing with all of the other systems which make women vulnerable to violence and make it difficult for them to escape violence" (17). The Standing Committee found that poverty was repeatedly cited by witnesses as a root cause of the violence against Aboriginal women (18). Meanwhile, parliament was then prorogued for the 2011 election, and in April, the Conservative Party of Canada was re-elected. The Standing Committee on the Status of Women was reconstituted with only two of the previous members who had heard the testimony of the Aboriginal women and civil society organizations (19).

On December 12, 2011, the newly composed Standing Committee issued a final report on violence against Aboriginal women. This report completely abandoned the root cause approach that had previously identified poverty as one of the main causes of the violence experienced by Aboriginal women. The Conservative government refused to even consider implementing a national action plan to address the disappearances and murders or deal with the underlying causes of the violence against missing and murdered Aboriginal women.

Because of the government's lack of action, FAFIA, an alliance of more than eighty Canadian women's organizations, took up the case of the murdered and missing women. One of its central goals was to ensure that Canadian governments respect, protect, and fulfill the commitments that they have made to women as a signatory to international human rights treaties and agreements, including the United Nations' Convention on the Elimination of all Forms of Racial Discrimination. In December 2011, the

United Nations Committee on the Elimination of Discrimination against Women announced that it was opening an inquiry into missing and murdered indigenous women in Canada. Previously in 2008, the committee had called on the government "to examine the reasons for the failure to investigate the cases of missing and murdered aboriginal women and to take the necessary steps to remedy the deficiencies in the system" (Human Rights Watch, "Canada: Abusive Policing").

The Canadian Feminist Alliance for International Action submitted that Canada was in violation of Article 2 of the *Convention on the Elimination of Racial Discrimination.* In January 2012, a submission to the United Nations Committee on the Elimination of Racial Discrimination was prepared by Shelagh Day of FAFIA and Sharon McIvor, which outlined their case ("CEDAW"). In October 2012, the Convention on the Elimination of All Forms of Discrimination against Women (CEDAW) committee initiated an inquiry under Article 8 of the United Nations' Convention on the Elimination of Discrimination against women. "FAFIA and NWAC requested this Inquiry because violence against Aboriginal women and girls is a national tragedy that demands immediate and concerted action," said Jeannette Corbiere Lavell, then President of NWAC ("CEDAW").

During this same time period, Human Rights Watch, the New York-based international non-governmental organization that conducts research and advocacy on human rights, also began investigating the incidents of missing and murdered women. On February 13, 2013, Human Rights Watch released an eighty-nine page report titled *Those Who Take Us Away: Abusive Policing and Failures in Protection of Indigenous Women and Girls in Northern British Columbia, Canada.* This report documents not only the ongoing failure of police to protect Indigenous women and girls but also the violent acts perpetrated by police officers themselves. At the time, Human Rights Watch stated that the RCMP failed to properly investigate a series of disappearances and suspected murders of Aboriginal women. As a result, Human Rights Watch called for the Canadian government to establish a national commission of inquiry into the murders and disappearances of Indigenous women and girls, including the examination of the impact of police misconduct in communities along Highway 16, the "Highway of Tears." Human Rights Watch stated:

> With leadership from indigenous communities, [the government must] develop and implement a national action plan to address violence against indigenous women and girls that addresses the structural roots of the violence as well as the accountability and coordination of government bodies charged with preventing and responding to violence. (*Those Who Take Us* 15)

Human Rights Watch is very clear that "unless the systematic problems of poverty, racism and sexism, the underlying social and economic problems, are dealt with we will continue to have missing and murdered women" ("Canada: Abusive Policing"). "The threat of domestic and random violence on one side, and mistreatment by RCMP officers on the other, leaves indigenous women in a constant state of insecurity," argues Meghan Rhoad, women's rights researcher at Human Rights Watch, as she questions, "Where can they turn for help when the police are known to be unresponsive and, in some cases, abusive" (Human Rights Watch, "Canada: Abusive Policing").

Worldwide, according to the UN Secretary General in combination with the United Nations Declaration on the Rights of Indigenous Peoples (UNDRIP), national strategies are needed to end violence against Aboriginal women and girls (NWAC). On International Women's Day March 8 2013, NWAC in their media release again requested a national inquiry for the missing and murdered Aboriginal women and girls. Also on this day, the Federation of Saskatchewan Indian Nations renewed their own call for a national public commission of inquiry. Opposition parties and Aboriginal leaders, such as Shawn Atleo, then national Chief of the Assembly of First Nations, called for a public commission inquiry into the missing and murdered Aboriginal women and girls in Canada.

In April 2013, Canada's provincial Aboriginal affairs ministers said that a national inquiry is needed to examine why Aboriginal women are seven times more likely to die of violence than other Canadian women (Editorial, "No to Inquiry"). On April 17 2013, nine of Canada's provinces called for a national inquiry. The provinces also asked that Ottawa consult with them, the territories, and Canada's five national Aboriginal organizations to set the terms of reference for an inquiry (Paul). Parliament, at this time, agreed to appoint a special committee on the matter of missing and murdered Aboriginal women but resisted calls for a national inquiry. Then on May 1, 2014, the RCMP released statistics that indicated nearly 1200 Aboriginal women had been murdered or had gone missing in Canada in the past thirty years; about 1000 murder victims, and approximately 186 disappearances (LeBlanc). RCMP Commissioner Bob Paulson stated "I think there's 4 per cent of aboriginal women in Canada; I think there's 16 per cent of the murdered women are aboriginal, 12 per cent of the missing women are aboriginal. So clearly an overrepresentation" (LeBlanc).

Conservative Prime Minister Steven Harper in 2014 continued to dismiss the calls for a national inquiry and argued that the deaths should be viewed as individual crimes and not as a a "sociological phenomenon" (Singh), thus denying any link between the violence and poverty, racism, the colonial past, lack of housing, and the dire living conditions that Aboriginal people in Canada face everyday. In August of 2014, the outcome of a meeting between provincial premiers and national Aboriginal groups was the decision to hold a National Roundtable on Missing and Murdered Indigenous Women and Girls. This Roundtable was held in Ottawa in February 2015. It included the Assembly of First Nations, the Congress of Aboriginal Peoples, the Inuit Tapiriit Kanatami, the Métis National Council, and the Native Women's Association of Canada as well as federal Aboriginal Affairs Minister Bernard Valcourt, Status of Women Minister Kellie Leitch, and representatives from each of the provinces and territories. The basic outcome was a commitment to keep talking and to begin nationwide prevention and awareness campaigns. There was, however, agreement to hold another meeting at the end of 2016 (Smith).

Also in February of 2015, the Legal Strategy Coalition on Violence against Aboriginal Women, a national coalition of advocacy groups including Amnesty International, released a critical report of the RCMP's own report *Missing and Murdered Aboriginal Women: Operational Overview*." The report concluded that the federal government had ignored most of the more than seven hundred recommendations contained in fifty-eight reports on violence against Aboriginal women and girls in Canada. Forty of these studies were from the federal government. The study also shows that only a handful of the seven hundred recommendations had been acted on. Numerous groups continued to call for a national inquiry into missing and murdered Aboriginal women. The Conservative government steadfastly refused to call an inquiry and stated that there have already been numerous reports documenting the issues. Although this is true in terms of numerous reports, there has been very little concrete action on any of the recommendations contained in those reports.

Although the RCMP's report is factual in highlighting that Aboriginal women are a marginalized population who experience higher rates of violence, unemployment, substance abuse, and are overrepresented in the sex trade, there were concerns with how these facts were reported. In what amounts to clear victim blaming, pointing to the supposedly high-risk lifestyles, the often dire circumstances faced by many Aboriginal women were presented as risk factors. Similarly, by positioning the homicides as a result of relationship violence, highlighting the fact that Aboriginal women, for the most part, knew their perpetrators, the report blames not only the victims but also Aboriginal men and Aboriginal families. The report fails to point out that the risk factors are linked to much deeper systemic issues, including the history of colonization and the resulting pervasive poverty in most communities. The Native Youth Sexual Health Network (NYSHN) notes that the risk factors raised in the report, such as alcoholism-drug abuse, sex trade work, and intimate partner violence are all linked to the lack of safe access to transportation and safe houses and the continued legacy of settler colonialism, racism, discrimination, and stereotyping (Hodge). Moreover, colonization has not "ended" and continues in new forms through Indian Act policy and legislation.

In fact on October 7, 2015, despite several Aboriginal women having gone missing along the "Highway of Tears," Bob Zimmer (Conservative incumbent in Prince George-Peace River riding) said that the violence was a result of unemployment. He stated that "One of the major drivers of missing and murdered aboriginal women is lack of economic activity or, simply put, a lack of a job" ("Conservative MP Says"). He went on to say that many women do not want to leave the reserve and that puts them at risk because little employment can be found on the reserve, which yet again blames women for their own victimization.

What is of particular concern is how Indigenous women and men are being stigmatized through the reporting of high rates of intimate partner violence. The 2014 RCMP report indicates that 62 percent of the murders of Indigenous women and girls reported by the RCMP were acts of domestic violence committed by a spouse, former spouse, family member, or intimate partner (Benjamin and Hansen). What was not highlighted in the report or in the media was that this rate is significantly lower than the rate of domestic violence reported in the general population as 74 percent of the murders of non-Aboriginal women are committed by intimate partners and family members (Benjamin and Hansen). Although the report demonstrates that most female homicide victims had a previous relationship to the perpetrators, Amnesty points out that Aboriginal women were more likely than non-aboriginal women to be murdered by a casual acquaintance (including, neighbours, employers and what police call "authority figures"), a fact that was ignored. Of note, in the twenty-two year period covered by the RCMP report, acquaintances are responsible for the murder of three hundred Aboriginal women and attacks by strangers account for almost 10 percent of homicides—eighty-one murders of Indigenous women or girls (Benjamin and Hansen).

Although no one is denying that intimate partner violence (IPV) is an issue in Indigenous communities, these are not unique situations. IPV occurs in homes across Canada, yet in the RCMP report, Indigenous women are stigmatized and marginalized. As Amnesty International notes:

> It's generally understood that the majority of acts of violence against women and girls are committed by someone from the same ethnic group or background. As many commentators have pointed out, the unique significance that the government is attaching to the Indigenous identity of many of the perpetrators of violence against Indigenous women

> and girls is part of a wider social narrative that places the responsibility for violence against Indigenous women and girls solely on Indigenous communities themselves. (Benjamin and Hansen)

Although the RCMP commissioner office has the ability to release comparative figures so that Aboriginal people are not further stigmatized and marginalized, it has done this to date.

UNDERLYING STRUCTURAL PROBLEMS TO BE ADDRESSED

Calls for change and action have been reiterated time and time again since the first Amnesty paper, *Stolen Sisters*, was published in 2004. The focus for change has been on the structural components that cause and enable violence against women. To help stop violence against Aboriginal women these factors must be addressed. Amnesty International's 2009 report, *No More Stolen Sisters*, notes that poverty, racism, Canada's colonial history, and systemic police failures are both the root causes of the violence and the contributing factors to it (2). By ignoring the structural components of violence against women, it is not only allowed to continue but simultaneously encouraged through lack of accountability. Two facets of the problem have been identified by Aboriginal families and non-government organizations, including NWAC, Amnesty International and the Canadian Feminist Alliance for International Action: the failure of police to protect Aboriginal women and girls from violence and to investigate promptly and thoroughly when they are missing or murdered; and the disadvantaged social and economic conditions in which Aboriginal women and girls live, which makes them vulnerable to violence and unable to escape from it (Canadian Feminist Alliance for International Action).

These two issues have been highlighted by United Nations treaty bodies, including the Committee on Economic, Social and Cultural Rights in 2006 and the Committee on the Elimination of Racial Discrimination in 2007. Canada accepted the underlying principles in these recommendations; however, the United Nations Committee on the Elimination of Discrimination against Women (CEDAW) in reviewing Canada's compliance, acknowledged that although a working group had been established, there were still many cases of murdered or missing Aboriginal women that had not been fully investigated (Canadian Feminist Alliance for International Action).

CEDAW recommended that Canada "develop a plan for addressing the particular conditions affecting aboriginal women, both on and off reserves," which include "poverty, poor health, inadequate housing, low school-completion rates, low employment rates, low income and high rates of violence" ("CEDAW"). Canada was to report back in 2009 and did so; however, FAFIA, the British Columbia CEDAW group, and Amnesty indicated that Canada had taken no adequate action.

ANALYSIS: COLONIAL, RACIST, AND SEXIST ATTITUDES STILL OCCURRING

It has been more than a decade since *"Stolen Sisters: A Human Rights Response to Discrimination and Violence against Indigenous Women in Canada"* was released by Amnesty International and NWAC. The issue of missing and murdered women has been at the forefront in the news, and awareness has been raised across Canada. Pressure has been put on governments, agencies, and police forces to deal with this massive problem. The government of Canada has taken a few steps to address the murders and disappearances, but the persistence of the violence indicates a need for comprehensive plan of action.

The federal Conservative government did agree to establish a parliamentary committee to study the issue, but Aboriginal women's lives remain at risk, in part because of the failure of Canadian officials to implement critical measures needed to reduce the marginalization of Aboriginal women in Canada. Systemic poverty, economic, social, and health problems among Aboriginal populations have, time and again, been demonstrated and linked. One of the most recent examples of this was the poverty and inadequate housing recently reported on the Attawapiskat reserve in northern Ontario. This was one of the reasons for the hunger strike of Theresa Spence and the start of the Idle No More Movement. Canada's Conservative government has demonstrated time and again, a lack of will to make the changes that would stop these incidents from occurring. Neo-liberal policies have cut funding and curbed the voices calling for action and change. There have been changes in mandates of organizations and government policy so that the focus can only be on what the government agenda has deemed acceptable. Why has there been so much resistance to addressing this problem by the federal Conservatives? It is widely understood that the roots of the ongoing patterns of violence experienced by too many Aboriginal women in Canada are to be found in the processes and dynamics of colonialism. In the case of Canada, there was a dual process of colonialism, first involving European powers and then internally by the Canadian state. The situation of Aboriginal people in these processes varies: in some cases, they were incorporated into commercial networks only to be cast aside at the whim of unfavourable market conditions, whereas, in other cases, they were deemed irrelevant or even problematic to economic development and were treated accordingly (Daschuk; Carter).

A patriarchal gender order accompanied and informed the activities of the European external colonizers and the internal colonization of the Canadian state. Patriarchy is a gender order in which men are dominant and masculinity tends to be esteemed. Within patriarchy, major social institutions, practices, and ideological frameworks support, legitimize and facilitate male and masculine domination and the oppression and exploitation of women and many other men; femininity is, moreover, devalued.

The role of racism in the operation and justification of colonialism has been well documented, as have the intersections of racism and patriarchy. The fact is that having lost their land, political independence, cultural and social institutions and entire way of life, many Aboriginal people in Canada face increasing rates of poverty, unemployment, inadequate housing, and declining heath statuses. To avoid the negative effects inherent in racist patriarchal colonialism, the federal governments in Canada would have to engage in systematic, deliberate sustained alliances with First Nations to support mutual actions and policies that address and redress the deleterious impact of centuries of racist patriarchal colonialism. This did not happen under the Conservative government. In order to address the multiple root causes of the high rates of missing and murdered Aboriginal women, the federal Conservative government would need to spend money to rectify numerous issues. This would not resonate with its traditional base of conservative voters, who would not see it as a good investment. The current manifestation of the ideology of extreme individualism is marked by a denigration of the common good.

In October 2015, a federal election brought the liberal government of Justin Trudeau to power. Trudeau had campaigned on promises to call an inquiry into the missing and murdered women and on a promise for more funding to First Nations for health and education. On December 8, 2015, the federal government called for an inquiry and cross-country consultations have been initiated with First Nations groups, organizations, and families. The federal budget brought down on March 22, 2016, did include funding for Aboriginal communities and a renewed relationship with Aboriginal peoples, so there is hope for change.

CONCLUSIONS

Over the past years, the political will to implement change and address the structural problems and violence Aboriginal women face in Canada has been lacking. The roots of this violence are very much linked to Canada's colonial past, the racism perpetrated against First Nations, Metis and Inuit people, the resulting poverty, food insecurity, and the sexism and misogyny that women, particularly Aboriginal women, experience. During the time of Steven Harper, there was a lack of political will to address the problems facing marginalized groups, particularly Aboriginal women, because by conservative logic, it is not up to the government to fight racism, sexism, poverty, health disparities, inadequate housing, or even to support NGOs that might address these issues. The role of the government was seen as supporting and reinforcing the operation of the market and ensuring that private individuals were left free to fend for themselves. This system resulted in over twelve hundred missing or murdered Aboriginal women.

Canada claims to be a democratic country that values equality and fairness. Clearly, for equality to exist the persistent underlying causes of inequality need to be addressed. People who advocate for justice need to be allowed to speak. For the past twelve years, the

Native Women's Association of Canada (NWAC) has designated October 4 as a day to remember and honour the lives of the many missing and murdered Aboriginal women and girls in Canada as well as to offer support to families who have been tragically touched by the loss of a loved one to violence. In 2014, there was a record breaking 264 Sisters In Spirit Vigils registered across Canada with most major media outlets covering the stories. Walk 4 Justice, which has carried out a walk across Canada each summer since 2006 to talk with Aboriginal families and communities about missing women, believes that there are many cases of missing and murdered Aboriginal women and girls that have gone undocumented by police or media. The large number of missing and murdered women has very deep roots in the structures of our society, deep roots that must be addressed in a systemic manner so that justice can prevail. This call has been echoed by the United Nations as well as numerous international and global human rights organizations. Until the murders stop, the shame is Canada's.

WORKS CITED

Amnesty International. *Stolen Sisters: A Human Rights Response to Discrimination and Violence against Indigenous Women.* Toronto: Amnesty International Canada, 2004. Print.

Amnesty International. *No More Stolen Sisters: The need for a Comprehensive Response to Discrimination and Violence Against Indigenous Women in Canada.* Toronto: Amnesty International Canada, 2009. Print.

Barrera, Jorge. "Need for 'Action' behind Funding Cut to Sisters in Spirit: Cabinet Ministers' Letter." Aboriginal Peoples Television Network News (APTN), 1 Dec. 2010. Web. 22 Apr. 2016.

Benjamin, Craig and Jackie Hansen. "The Need for Accurate and Comprehensive Statistics on Missing and Murdered Indigenous Women and Girls." Amnesty International, 15 Apr. 2016. Web. 22 Apr. 2016.

Canada. Department of Finance. *Budget 2010, Chapter 3.4 Supporting Families and Communities and Standing Up for Those Who Helped Build Canada.* Government of Canada, 4 Mar. 2010. Web. 22 Apr. 2016.

Canadian Feminist Alliance for International Action (FAFIA). *Disappearances and Murders of Aboriginal Women and Girls in Canada*. FAFIA, 2012. Web. 22 Apr. 2016.

Carter, Sarah. *Capturing Women: The Manipulation of Cultural Imagery in Canada's Prairie West*. Montreal-Kingston: McGill-Queen's University Press. 1997. Print

"CEDAW Looking at Canada's Missing and Murdered Women." Indian Country Today Media Network, 14 Dec 2011. Web. 22 Apr. 2016.

"Conservative MP Says 'Kack of a Job' Cause of Missing and Murdered Indigenous Women." *CBC News*, 8 Oct. 2015. Web. 22 Apr. 2016.

Daschuk, James. *Clearing the Plains: Disease, Politics of Starvation, and the Loss of Aboriginal Life*. Regina: University of Regina Press. 2014. Print

Editorial. "No to Inquiry." *Winnipeg Free Press*, 20 April 2013. Print.

Hodge, Jarrah. "Victim-Blaming in Coverage of RCMP Report on MMIW." *Rabble*. N.p., 22 May 2014. Web. 22 Apr. 2016.

Hughes, Judy. "The Sisters in Spirit Initiative: Native Women's Association of Canada." *Torn from our Midst: Voices of Grief, Healing and Action from the Missing Indigenous Women Conference*. Eds. B. Anderson, W. Kubik, and M. Rucklos Hampton. Regina, Saskatchewan: Canadian Plains Research Center, 2008. 208-218. Print.

Human Rights Watch. *Those Who Take Us Away Abusive Policing and Failures in Protection of Indigenous Women and Girls in Northern British Columbia, Canada*. New York: Human Rights Watch, 2013. Print.

Human Rights Watch. "Canada: Abusive Policing, Neglect Along 'Highway of Tears.'" Human Rights Watch, 2013. Web. 22. Apr. 2016.

Jackson, Kenneth. "Stephen Harper's Longest War: Missing and Murdered Indigenous Women." Aboriginal Peoples Television Network News (APTN), 9 Sept. 2015. Web. 22 Apr. 2016.

LeBlanc, Daniel. "List of Missing, Killed Involves 1,200 Cases." *Globe and Mail* 2 May 2014: A10. Print.

Native Women's Association of Canada (NWAC). "NWAC Observes

International Women's Day." Native Women's Association of Canada, 17 May 2013. Web. 22 Apr. 2016.

Paul, Alexandra. "Provinces agree to Press for National Inquiry into Missing Aboriginal Women." *The Globe and Mail,* 17 Apr. 2013. Web. 22 Apr. 2016.

Singh, Jakeet. "The Ideological Roots of Stephen Harper's Vendetta against Sociology." *Toronto Star,* 26 Aug. 2014. Web. 22 Apr. 2016.

Smith, Joanna. "Hope and Frustration." *Toronto Star* 28 Feb. 2015: A1. Print.

2.
Understanding Violence Against Indigenous Women and Girls in Canada

JESSICA RIEL-JOHNS

> *The situation that we are in today is such that our women and children aren't respected as they used to be. It is not the fault of the men. It is because of the layers of influence we have had from another culture. We are in a state of confusion and we are trying to work our way out of it. People are calling it healing. Well, whatever it is, we are trying to find our balance, and when we find the balance, we will know it because the women won't be lost. They will be respected and taken care of and so will the children.*
> —Kim Anderson (*A Recognition* 13)

WHEN ONE THINKS about what life is supposed to be like in Canada according to its claims as a fair and democratic country, a society where everyone is considered equal and citizens peacefully co-exist should come to mind. Most importantly, these claims should represent a country where all women and girls can feel safe. Unfortunately, this is not true for the Indigenous women and girls of Canada. Rather, this grand narrative of an equal society blinds us to the hidden, ugly truths within this "great multicultural" country.

I only learned of Amnesty International's No More Stolen Sisters campaign during a class I took at Brock University as part of the Gidayaamin program in 2011. I had never heard of this systemic issue prior to the course. I was just starting a journey of discovery of my own cultural identity, and I was completely taken aback when I learned about the issue of missing and murdered Indigenous women and girls. It was not something that was publicly known at the time but has thankfully gained much more media attention with the recent coverage of the launch of a national public inquiry. It was disheartening to learn the extent of the discrimination and violence against Indigenous women in Canada. Amnesty International has indicated that Indigenous women between the ages of twenty-five and forty-four with Indian status are five times more likely than other women of the same age to die from violence. According to The Ontario Native Women's Association, Indigenous people make up 4.3 percent of Canada's population and are six times more likely to be victimized than any other women in Canada. Although my understanding was that Indigenous women were being targeted for reasons unknown, which I will explore throughout this chapter, many have argued that poverty, drug and alcohol dependency, and sex work play a factor into why Indigenous women are missing and murdered; Canadian society has overlooked these factors and has ignored their systematic nature.

My attempt in the advocacy work that I now do is to provide a deeper understanding of the racialized and sexualized violence experienced by Indigenous women as a contemporary sociological phenomenon rooted in the history of Canada. I write this chapter, as an Indigenous woman, who wishes to examine the historical perspective on the racialized and sexualized victimization of Indigenous women and girls in Canada. I write this with respect to all our Stolen Sisters and families in mind in hopes that justice will prevail and that this systematic issue can be looked at more closely and be better understood.

DISMANTLING MATRILINEAL SOCIETIES

Racialized and sexualized violence against Indigenous women in Canada is a systematic issue, resulting in alarming rates of missing and murdered Indigenous women. Although women in general have been devalued throughout Canadian history, it is important to recognize the effects that colonization has had on Indigenous women specifically. Patriarchy has had a significant effect on Indigenous women. As Noel notes, "since early settlers have migrated to North America, the patriarchal values have pushed out decades of Indigenous matriarchal values. Indigenous women were powerful in their communities and there was no battle of the sexes" (77). Noel points out that "In European eyes, gender relations were hierarchical; dominance was all too often integral to male honour, making a powerful woman a rival to be disarmed" (78). In Indigenous communities before colonization, men and women had various roles in their communities that were understood to be equalitarian. The patriarchal division between women's work and men's work was non-existent. Rather, within Indigenous communities, men and women worked together as a unit for their community. Within Haudenosaunee societies, matrilineal understandings can be dated back to the creation story, in which Sky Woman exemplifies the power of women (80). Today, these teachings inform cultural practices and teachings about the reciprocal roles between men and women. Moreover, within Indigenous ideologies, women are revered for the power they hold to sustain and give life (Anderson, *Life Stages*). The ability to cleanse themselves through their monthly cycles is also understood as a time of women's power and is highly respected. The power of Indigenous women filters through all aspects of life. The accounts of early Western explorers describe the considerable amount of power and influence Indigenous women had on their people (Portman and Garrett). These powerful roles stood in contrast to the newcomers view on a women's place in society. Winona Stevenson compares the roles of European and Indigenous women during the colonization period:

> Where European women were fragile and weak, Aboriginal women were hard-working and strong; where European women were confined to affairs of the household, Aboriginal women were economically independent and actively involved in the public sphere; where European women were chaste and dependent on men, Aboriginal women had considerable personal autonomy and independence—they controlled their own sexuality, had the right to divorce, and owned the products of their labour. (55)

The very strength of Indigenous women stood in contrast to the role of settler women and was, therefore, a threat to the development of a patriarchal society. Thus, Indigenous women were poorly treated and demonized as settler women were taught to fear Indigenous women. This strategy, referred to as systemic violence by Andrea Smith, is explained in the following passage:

> The relatively egalitarian nature of Native societies belies patriarchy's claims to normality, and thus it is imperative for a patriarchal society to thrive to destroy egalitarian societies that present other ways of living. The demonization of Native women, then, is part of white men's desires to maintain control over white women. (78)

This often quoted Cheyenne proverb speaks to the deliberate attack on Indigenous women as way to conquer the entire nation: "A nation is not conquered until the hearts of its women are on the ground. Then it is done, no matter how brave its warriors or strong its weapons."

The dismantling of the matriarchal society is one of the first acts of racialized and sexualized discrimination against Indigenous women. As Acoose explains, "This male dominated Eurocentric view of the "Indian" or the "Native" has almost totally effaced from history the lives of Indigenous women" (62). This history of patriarchy and colonization, which has led to the racialized and sexualized discrimination of Indigenous women, must be acknowledged as the foundation for the contemporary violence against Indigenous women in Canada. Moreover, the erasure of their presence was deliberate to the development of the Canadian nation.

POLITICAL AND LEGAL DISCRIMINATION

Canada's history of racialized and sexualized discrimination is entrenched in legislated policies that have specifically targeted Indigenous women. These policies, enforced by the Canadian government through the Indian Act, are indeed forms of violence against Indigenous women. Specifically, under section 12 (1) (b) of the *Indian Act* of 1867, Indian status could be removed, which was used to target Indigenous women. Under this section, Indian status women who married non-status men lost their status and all rights associated with it, including access to community resources (Harry). Not only was this legislation assimilatory in intent and nature, but it also placed Indigenous women in a vulnerable situation, as it cut family and community ties. Moreover, as this act was aimed at the erasure of Indigenous women, its connection to the sociological phenomenon of missing and murdered Indigenous women and girls in Canada is evident. Thus, Canada's hidden history of legislated policy has affected the welfare and well-being of Indigenous women in Canada and is undoubtedly related to the racialized and sexualized violence experience by Indigenous women today.

The *Indian Act* enforced the removal of women from the centre of their community to lessen the amount of power that they held; the rights of Indigenous women were removed and a more patriarchal worldview enforcing male power was instilled. Historically, this power has slowly taken away Indigenous women's authority in their community and has disrupted matrilineal ways of life. Beverly Jacobs describes this disruption in her community in the following:

> Once the *Indian Act* was passed, the responsibilities of our men and women changed drastically. As a result of being confined to a reserve, our traditional men and women lost their responsibilities in using their strengths, either physically or mentally. Women were thought of as property by our O:gweho: we men who became acculturated into believing that they had to think like white men. The entitlement to status under the *Indian Act* itself enabled that to happen, wherein the male would gain status and his wife and his children would gain his status. (113)

Moreover, the *Indian Act* denied Indigenous woman the right to vote in a band election and to hold positions in political office, and to speak at public meetings (Shepard, O'Neil, and Guenett). Women's roles in Indigenous communities have been removed, stripped, and left bare because of colonization. Moreover, Indigenous women continue to be abused by new and complex forms of gender discrimination in the *Indian Act* (Palmater).

Indigenous women are discriminated against for being both Indigenous and women. To be an Indigenous woman in Canada is to experience marginalization, oppression, and colonization, which can be felt through many generations of Indigenous women. As the above attests, racialized and sexualized discrimination is not something new to Indigenous women. Historically, when an Indigenous woman was forced to assimilate to Western society, the power of that woman diminished, as the loss of status has shown. Western society is based on a patriarchal worldview, and, thus, Indigenous woman have faced discrimination, ignorance, bigotry, and violence. Patriarchy involves stripping away the very nature and beauty of Indigenous womanhood, leaving women stripped of who they are supposed to be in their community and vulnerable to the violence experienced in settler spaces.

THE ONGOING SEXUALIZATION OF INDIGENOUS WOMEN

Indigenous women have been sexualized by men since settler contact. As Acoose articulates, dominant stereotypes of Indigenous women include the Indian princess-squaw binary. These two very opposing, but equally dangerous, categories both sexualize and romanticize Indigenous womanhood. This type of sexualization is an issue and a concern when it comes to missing and murdered Indigenous women in Canada. Acoose argues that these stereotypes, embedded in Canadian literature, have led to an acceptance and normalization of violence against Indigenous women. Moreover, Emma LaRocque states that "the dehumanizing portrayal of the squaw and the oversexualization of Native females such as in Walt Disney's Pocahontas surely renders all Native female persons vulnerable" (12). The sexualization of Indigenous woman portrayed as either the Indian princess or the "dirty squaw" is seen in literature, historical texts, video games, movies, and music (Acoose). These notions have resulted in harmful stereotypes, which have become accepted throughout all levels of society and entrenched within dominant ideologies that target racialized women, leading to the high rates of missing and murdered Indigenous women. This is a sociological phenomenon that has been happening since colonization and is deeply entrenched within the settler mindset. Violence against Indigenous women has been imprinted on our women through the experiences of our ancestors and still continues today in this supposedly "fair and democratic" society. In other words, the layers of violence against Indigenous women must be understood as intergenerational as well as a contemporary daily lived experience.

In a fact sheet exploring the root causes of violence against Indigenous women, the Native Women's Association of Canada (NWAC) states that the National Council of Welfare discusses "the history of colonization has burdened our nation with a continual 'passing down of various loads or degrees of post-traumatic stress. Generation after generation, so that we wind up with this entire burden of our people as they exist today.'" The connection between colonization and intergenerational trauma is apparent in many forms of traumatic experiences that occurred at residential schools has been related to the violence, abuse, alcoholism, that plague many Indigenous communities. Intergenerational trauma also manifests in the prevalence of high suicide rates and other mental health issues, related to the loss of cultural identity. These issues are related to the racialized and sexualized violence experienced by Indigenous women at the hands of both Indigenous and non-Indigenous men. Moreover, it has contributed to Indigenous women's vulnerability to violence.

Honouring Indigenous Women's Strength and Resiliency

Indigenous women endure many traumatic experiences in life, but alongside this trauma, they also display strength and resiliency. For example, the leadership roles of Indigenous women have not been completely dismantled, which is evident in their will to keep advocating for a return to their rightful place in society. The following words shared by Nongom Ikkwe during a brief submitted to the Royal Commission on Aboriginal Peoples in 1993 attest to the importance of Indigenous women reclaiming their roles as leaders in their communities:

> Our people will not heal and rise toward becoming self

> governing and strong people both in spirit and vision until the women rise and give direction and support to our leaders. That time is now, the women are now actively participating in insuring the empowerment of their people. Life is a daily struggle as women, as mothers, as sisters, as aunties and grandmothers. We are responsible for the children of today and those of tomorrow. It is with pure kindness and our respect for life that allows us to gladly take up this responsibility to nurture the children, to teach of what we know, from what we have learned through trial and error. (qtd. in "Highlights from the Report of the Royal Commission on Aboriginal Peoples" 7)

In this long journey, Indigenous women have fought to have their status renewed in society and to regain their identity. Many women have shared their stories and visions of healing through academic papers, novels, poetry, and other forms of writing and advocacy work. In these forms of writings, Indigenous women have had their story heard and have created awareness within society about the trauma that they have endured throughout colonization, including the residential schools, the eugenics movement, and the Sixties Scoop. Indigenous women may not have the voice in society that they once had, but putting a pen to paper is the most powerful weapon that can be used to educate and to bring awareness to these pressing issues. In this way, Indigenous women are working through their collective trauma to offer healing and restore balance within their communities.

Today, Indigenous women, men, families, and communities continue to pursue active roles in Canada. Alongside them, various movements across Canada have been actively requesting an inquiry into missing and murdered Indigenous woman by advocating through social media, protests, Indigenous woman's literature, art, petitions, and other grassroots movements to pressure the federal government for an inquiry. Moreover, media outlets, such as CBC news, are finally starting to provide extensive coverage on this issue as well as a space for Indigenous women to have their voices heard. For example, in an opinion piece entitled "Missing and Murdered: What It Will Take for Indigenous Women to Feel

Safe," Big Canoe and Massimo draw attention to a recent study released by the Legal Research Strategy Coalition that looked at over fifty-eight studies and recommendations from those studies. They note that Canada's failure to protect Indigenous women's lives is evident in its unwillingness to follow through on the aforementioned reports:

Shockingly, researchers found that only a few of over 700 recommendations in these reports have ever been fully implemented. This report demonstrates that the government's stance that MMIW is not a sociological phenomenon is wrong. This report demonstrates decades-long inaction by the government to even start to adequately address the systemic and structural violence against indigenous women and girls. (Big Canoe & Massimo)

As they articulate further in the article, Indigenous issues were not high on then Prime Minister Stephen Harper's radar and this apathy towards Indigenous women's lives filtered into the social institutions designed to protect them:

> The police have failed to adequately prevent and protect Indigenous women and girls from killings, disappearances and extreme forms of violence, and have failed to diligently and promptly investigate these acts.... Every Canadian needs to pay attention and listen to what the federal government is saying or doing, but also, more importantly, what they are not doing. Every Canadian needs to make their own commitment to action that addresses systemic violence against Indigenous peoples. (Big Canoe and Massimo)

These reports provide evidence of the continued oppression that Indigenous women and girls face. Fortunately, with the persistent of Indigenous women, such as Big Canoe and Massimo, who are taking leading roles in the push for action, the demand for a national public inquiry has been heard. The newly elected Prime Minister of Canada Justin Trudeau has followed through on his promise of launching a national public inquiry in missing and murdered Indigenous women, and this is surely the result of

Indigenous women who demanded their voices be heard.

It is my hope that this national public inquiry will present an understanding of the historical issues that I have noted throughout this chapter. The racialization and sexualization of Indigenous women is deeply rooted in the development of Canada as a patriarchal and colonial society. Moreover, Indigenous communities continue to be underfunded, and families there are living in Third World conditions. Reserves in northern communities do not have access to resources that most Canadians have access to. These poor living conditions must not be left out of the discussion of Indigenous women's vulnerability to violence. Moreover, the continued racialization and sexualization of Indigenous women in Canada today must be acknowledged. The history of Canada, in its treatment of Indigenous women, is a shameful one, which is long and unsettling. It is a history that Canada can no longer ignore. To understand the present experiences and the extent of violence Indigenous women face in their daily lives, all Canadians should know this history and work towards the development of a nation in which all women and girls are safe.

PERSONAL NARRATIVE

As I noted earlier, I first learned about missing and murdered Indigenous women in the Gidayaamin Program at Brock University in 2011. The instructor was talking about Amnesty International's No More Stolen Sisters campaign. I sat there listening intently because I had not heard of this campaign and was unaware of the extent of the issue. After class, I went home and immediately read the website in its entirety and signed the petition. I was shocked that this was happening and nothing was being done. As a mother to four girls, I thought of them and thought to myself "what if it happened to one of them?" I thought about how I could make a difference and bring this issue to light. I then thought what if that had been me. It could have been me. I am not removed from the violence that targets Indigenous women, nor are my daughters. As a teenager, I put myself at risk when I ran away from home at sixteen years old with another friend who was having trouble at home. Looking back, I had no reason to leave home other than

I was easily persuaded to do things that I knew I shouldn't do. My home life was great, but I was looking for an adventure. This adventure led me to hitchhike from Sault Ste. Marie to Toronto. What if I had gotten into a vehicle with someone and had never made it back home? I now as a mother realize the hurt my mother must have felt. She had no idea that I had left, where I had gone, or how I gotten to Toronto. I must have put her through so much stress and worry. I remember calling her and hearing the hurt in her voice. I have felt this as a mother myself when my daughter ran away from home when she was fourteen. As a mother, I wondered if she was okay, where she was, and a million other questions. These are questions that would flood through the mind of any mother. Every time there is a documentary, news story, or photograph shown on social media of another missing sister, I think of that mother and family.

I started to write about missing and murdered Indigenous women in my academic classes, and soon after, I was presenting on this important systemic issue because I wanted to be a voice for those who do not have one. I wanted to help to educate people on how important this is to communities and as a country. I was invited to co-present on the issue of missing and murdered Indigenous women at the Niagara Social Justice Forum held at Brock University in 2015. We had almost one hundred people attend the presentation, and the co-ordinator of the forum had to move our session into a larger room. Although I was terrified to speak in front of such a large audience at the time, I wanted to do it for all missing and murdered women. I did not want them only to be a statistic; I wanted them to be known as a real person—a grandmother, a mother, a sister, an aunt, a daughter, a niece, a granddaughter, a cousin, or a friend. These women lived real lives, and they are not a number. They have names. They have stories. They matter.

I had seen the call for this book and thought this is something that I wanted to do to continue to work for these women, to be that voice alongside others who have done so much for missing and murdered Indigenous women. So I sat at my computer and decided to write from the heart and then move on from there. I work to educate people on this issue and bring an understanding to the magnitude of missing and murdered Indigenous women. I just presented again this year at the 2016 Niagara Social Justice Forum at Brock University. This year, our presentation was on Building Solidarities, but I still felt the need to update what has happened over a year time on missing and murdered women and how we can form allyship from the presentation from the year before. I discussed the inquiry, grassroots movements, missing and murdered Indigenous men, and how to be an ally with the families. I will continue to advocate and educate for my sisters and their families with a good heart and a good mind. My heart goes out to the families affected by this issue and who have lost a loved one. My hope is that they will find the answers that they deserve so to bring some healing and peace, and that justice will be served. I will carry you all in my heart and continue to do this work and be that voice along with others who contribute to the voice for justice and reconciliation. You are Forever Loved.

Kakikaa Sagi'aaganii

WORKS CITED

Acoose, Janice. *Iskwewak-Kah'Ki Yaw Ni Wahkomakanak: Neither Indian Princesses nor Easy Squaws*. Toronto: Canadian Scholars' Press. 1995. Print.

Amnesty International. *Stolen Sisters: A Human Rights Response to Discrimination and Violence against Indigenous Women in Canada*. Toronto: Amnesty International Canada, 2004. Print.

Anderson, Kim. *Life Stages and Native Women: Memory, Teachings and Story Medicine*. Winnipeg: University of Manitoba Press, 2011. Print.

Anderson, Kim. *A Recognition of Being: Reconstructing Native Womanhood*. Toronto: Canadian Scholars' Press, 2000. Print.

Canada. Indigenous and Northern Affairs Canada. "Highlights from the Report of the Royal Commission on Aboriginal Peoples." Indigenous and Northern Affairs Canada. Government of Canada, 1996. Web. 16 Apr. 2016.

Laboucan-Massimo, Melina, and Christa Big Canoe. "Missing and Murdered: What It Will Take for Indigenous Women to Feel Safe." Canadian Broadcasting Corporation, 18 Mar. 2015. Web. 16 Apr. 2016.

Jacobs, Beverley. "International Law/The Great Peace." MA. University of Saskatchewan, 2000. Print.

LaRocque, E. "The Colonization of a Native Woman Scholar." *Women of the First Nations: Power, Wisdom, and Strength*. Eds. C. Miller and P. Chuchryk. Winnipeg: University of Manitoba Press, 1996. 11-18. Print.

Harry, Katrina. "The Indian Act and Aboriginal Women's Empowerment: What Front Line Workers Need to Know." Battered Women's Support Services (BWSS), 2009. Web. 16 Apr. 2016.

Native Women's Association of Canada (NWAC). "Fact Sheet: Root Causes of Violence Against Aboriginal Women and the Impact of Colonization." NWAC, 2015. Web. 16 Apr. 2016.

Noel, Jan. "Power Mothering: The Haudenosaunee Model in Lavell." *"Until Our Hearts Are on the Ground": Aboriginal Mothering, Oppression, Resistance and Rebirth*. Eds. Jeannette Corbiere Lavell and Memee Lavell-Harvard. Bradford, Ontario: Demeter Press, 2006. 76-93. Print.

Ontario Native Women's Association. "Missing and Murdered Aboriginal Women: Fact Sheet." Ontario Native Women's Association, 24 Sept. 2014. Web. 11 Mar. 2015.

Palmater, Pamela. *Beyond Blood: Rethinking Indigenous Identity*. Saskatoon: Purich Publishing, 2011. Print.

Portman, Awe Agahe Tarrell, and Michael Tianusta Garrett. "Beloved Women: Nurturing the Sacred Fire of Leadership from an American Indian Perspective." *Journal of Counselling and Development* 83.3 (2005): 284-291. Print.

Shepard, Blythe, Linda O'Neill, and Francis Guenett. "Counselling with First Nations Women: Considerations of Oppression and Renewal." *International Journal for the Advancement of Counselling* 28.3 (2007): 227-240. Print.

Smith, Andrea. "Not an Indian Tradition: The Sexual Colonization of Native Peoples" *Hypatia* 18.2 (2003): 70-85. Print.

Stevenson, Winona. "Colonialism and First Nations Women in Canada." *Scratching the Surface: Canadian Anti-Racist Feminist Thought*. Eds. Enakshi Dua and Angela Roberts. Toronto: Women's Press, 49-82. Print.

3.
"Only the Silence Remains"

Aboriginal Women as Victims in the Case of the Lower Eastside (Pickton) Murders, Investigative Flaws, and the Aftermath of Violence in Vancouver

PATRICIA O'REILLY AND THOMAS FLEMING

> *The effects of past discrimination have resulted in the poor socio-economic situation applicable to most Aboriginal women, but it is also attributable to the demeaning image of Aboriginal women that has developed over the years. North American society has adopted a destructive and stereotypical view of Aboriginal women.* (Chartrand et al)

THE STATUS OF ABORIGINAL WOMEN within Canadian urban culture can be characterized on one hand by desperation and despair, and on the other hand, as largely invisible to the average Canadian. The first group's interaction with street cultures is characterized by illegal and legal drug abuse, poverty, violence, involvement in the sex trade, health issues, frequent interaction with agencies of social control and treatment programs in a "revolving door" of jail, court, and release. This chapter focuses on individuals drawn from street life and the sex trade, specifically the victims of Robert Pickton. However, we believe it is important to balance our subject matter with a clear recognition that the victims in this case are a specific group of Aboriginal women; they should not form for the reader an overarching portrait of urban Aboriginal women in general. The integration of Aboriginal women into the major urban landscapes of Canada has reflected the general trend of off-reserve residence. Approximately 71 percent of Aboriginal people reside off-reserve, with 59 percent residing in large cities or smaller urban centres (Dickson-Gimore 75). A broader view of the lives of the overwhelming majority of Aboriginal women in the urban landscape is provided by The Urban Aboriginal Task Force study from 2007 and Howard-Bobiwash's research on women's class struggles in Toronto during the period between 1950 and1975.

As early as 1974, in a chapter concerning Aboriginal immigration to the major cities of Canada, Frideres concluded that although the federal government was encouraging persons to acculturate into urban centres, the "municipal governments are not prepared to extend or continue this help (with migration) and there is continual conflict" between the various levels of government (100). Thus, Aboriginal people found themselves in an environment in which they were "more exposed to alien ways of thought and direct discrimination" (100). In this analysis, Frideres found that there was a "compartmentalization of whites' activities" creating the well-understood condition of "two solitudes," in that there is a lack of communication across barriers (100). The end result was the production of a loosely tethered existence for some urban Aboriginals and a high degree of transiency. However, the overwhelming majority of Aboriginal persons, whose lives are lived within the "mainstream" do not live risky lifestyles, nor are they involved with the criminal justice system (see Urban Aboriginal Task Force).

Other researchers have commented on the problems Aboriginal women, and Aboriginal peoples in general, have when integrating into urban communities (Abbott; Balakrishnan and Jurdi). More recently, Voyageur has provided an excellent overview of the multitude of barriers that Aboriginal women face in Canadian society. Although Frideres's work is important, it does not specifically address the issue of Aboriginal women caught in this alien world and the effect this has on their social capital and "life chances" (Dahrendorf). Fleming's work on homeless street youth and homeless persons is instructive in providing depth to our understanding of how some Aboriginal women have little in the way of social capital to spend in a major city environment, and how their life chances are severely affected by their sense of alienation in the urban interstices (*Down and Out in Canada*).

Members of the second group of Aboriginal women mentioned above—those who are largely "invisible" to most Canadians—are individuals who live and work in cities with little or no awareness or acknowledgement of their Aboriginal status by the community.

The overwhelming majority of these women live "normal" lives, as do the majority of Canadians, generally unnoticed and unrecognized by wider society. Some reach the heights of professional or artistic achievement. In other words, their lives and accomplishments contribute positively to Canadian society and Aboriginal society.

It is women drawn from the first group described above who are partially the concern of this chapter. Our focus in this chapter is on police investigative failures in the Robert Pickton serial murder case (referred to as the Missing Women Investigation), with respect to the following: Aboriginal women victims of his crimes; the treatment of the families of these murder victims by investigators and government during and after the discovery of multiple bodies at the Pickton farm; and the aftermath of the crimes, specifically the value, or lack of value, of a public inquiry into the disappearances and deaths of the women. Our chapter develops a critical analysis of the investigative failures in the case, which we link with the status of many of the victims as Aboriginal women and sex-trade workers. We argue for more informed approaches to dealing with serial murder victims and their families through recognizing the vulnerability of Aboriginal women working in the street sex trade in the urban context and acknowledging the unique nature of dealing with Aboriginal peoples (Chartrand et al.). We conclude with some recommendations for the conduct of future investigations of linked missing persons and/or serial murder cases.

THE PICKTON MURDERS: BACKGROUND

From the early 1980s until 2002, women were disappearing from Vancouver's Lower Eastside. This area is well known as a "stroll" for sex workers (Lowman, "Violence," "Prostitution Law"), and as a location where drug use, drug dealing, and violent street crimes are a part of everyday life. The women who were disappearing were all known sex workers who had issues with heavy drug use (Rossmo, "Criminal Investigative Failures in the Missing Women"). During the 1990s, the rate of disappearance and the number of missing women began to escalate. A number of concerned groups, among them Aboriginal family coalitions, believed that there was a serial murderer at work, and called on Vancouver Police Services to focus their investigation into the disappearances in this direction. Although various groups expressed concerns, the police steadfastly refused to seriously consider that a serial killer might be operating in the area.

This was more than disconcerting given that a Vancouver police detective, Kim Rossmo, had prepared a report in 1999 that concluded that the majority of the missing women were *dead*, not *missing*. Senior management in the Vancouver Police Department refused to accept the conclusions of Rossmo's report or have him play a significant role in the investigation, even though he had recently become the first detective in Canada to receive a PhD in criminology, specializing in geographic profiling of serial offenders (LePard). Although Rossmo was an internationally recognized expert in serial murder cases and the inventor of geographic profiling, he was effectively demoted for his efforts, as his unit was closed down. He subsequently sued Vancouver Police Services for wrongful dismissal but did not prevail. At the time of his case in 2001, police spokespersons still denied the existence of a serial killer. Six months later, in February 2002, the RCMP executed a search warrant for another matter at the farm of Robert Pickton, and in the course of the search, pieces of identification and purses belonging to some of the missing women were discovered. Rossmo wrote that these same pieces of evidence had been viewed four years earlier by an RCMP constable investigating another complaint at the farm (*Criminal Investigative Failures* 33).

After a missing woman's identification was positively identified at the Pickton farm, a large scale investigation of the property ensued. During the initial stages, as the magnitude of the forensic investigative challenge was comprehended, it was determined that a full-scale archaeological dig of the farm would be required to recover possible relevant personal possessions, bone fragments, clothing, and DNA linked to victims. It was apparent to investigators that Pickton had disposed of his victims by feeding their remains to his pigs. His intent was to destroy anything that could possibly be used to identify the women's remains. However, although the pigs ingested the flesh and crushed the bones of the victims, they also left behind bone fragments that were used to establish the identity of victims by matching DNA to established records or to their family members.

Pickton was not fastidious in his disposal of identification cards or other personal items. Identification cards show a high degree of resistance to disintegration even when buried so that readable information can be gleaned from them for decades. The dig at the farm involved forensic identification officers from the RCMP and other agencies, scientists, and anthropology students. The cost of the dig, which lasted more than a year, was estimated to be $70 million; the dig itself involved the collection one hundred thousand exhibits (Rossmo, *Criminal Investigative Failures* 33). This estimate does not include all of the other costs associated with the prosecution of the Pickton case. It is not unreasonable to argue that more than $200 million was spent to convict Pickton.

After more than a year of investigation, twenty-six individuals had been identified from materials found on the farm, with a twenty-seventh distinct victim remaining unidentified. Pickton was tried in six cases and was found guilty of second degree murder in all of them. Crown prosecutors wisely chose to pursue those six cases because solid evidence existed regarding the identity of the victims, which was most likely to result in conviction. Although the families of the remaining twenty victims initially believed that the Crown would pursue court cases in relation to these individuals, Pickton's life sentence, the cost of the cases to that point, and the possibility that the weakness of several of the remaining cases might result in acquittal in those cases made pursuing prosecutions risky and potentially damaging to victims' families. It could well be suggested that not prosecuting these cases—even for very compelling reasons, including the costs involved and the possibility of acquittal in some cases—left families without closure and perhaps with lingering doubts about the role that police investigative flaws might have possibly played in the murders of their loved ones. It is significant to note that eleven of the thirteen identified missing women who were murdered after 1999 (and after Rossmo's report) were victims of Pickton.

ABORIGINAL SEX-TRADE WORKERS AND POLICE

Despite assurances to the contrary, police in Canada have often failed to provide Indigenous women with an adequate

> standard of protection. (Amnesty International 2)

> My Aboriginal sisters are not perfect victims in the eyes of the police and the courts, especially when they're considered vagrant, addicted and sex workers. (Thompson 1)

One of the enduring issues that arises out of the Pickton cases in relation to his victims is why the police efforts did not reflect the same commitment to resources and solution as other missing persons cases. The response of the Vancouver Police Department to the rising number of missing women on Vancouver's Lower Eastside can be put in perspective when we consider the existing research on victim selection and police response that has been generated over the past quarter-century. Serial murderers have demonstrated propensity to select certain groups of individuals as their preferred targets (Leyton; Hickey, *Serial Murderers* 4th ed.). In general, they are drawn to victims who have, or appear to have, little ability to defend themselves from physical attack or kidnapping. Thus, persons who are small in stature are more preferable as victims than larger individuals. Male serial killers who select female victims have much in common with rapists. Serial murderers hunt for victims who show obvious signs of alcohol or drug intoxication; who place themselves in isolated areas largely immune from police observation or other individuals who might intervene in a suspicious altercation; or who pursue "risky" lifestyles, of which street sex work is one of the most dangerous (Fleming, *Serial and Mass Murder*; Hickey, *Serial Murderers* 4th ed.; Leyton). As criminologists Cohen and Felson demonstrate in their classic article on routine activities theory, when individuals' daily routines put them at risk of victimization, they are more likely to fall prey to crime. As Hickey relates serial murderers' motivations can also include a desire to "destroy those who symbolize what they fear or loathe including gays, the homeless, prostitutes, the elderly, and the infirm" (Hickey, *Serial Murderers* 4th ed. 259). Research conducted by Jenkins as well as Kim Egger ("Preliminary Data" 8) has shown that cross-cultural and historical analysis of serial murder victims identifies that the same groups are victimized again and again.

However, there are clearly other reasons why these specific groups—to that we have added Aboriginal women (Fleming and O'Reilly, "History Repeats Itself;" "The Value of Victims")—are repeatedly targeted by serial killers. The answer lies in the police response, or more specifically the lack of police response, to the murders of persons in the above-mentioned groups. Although homicide detectives should be recognized for their dedication, commitment, and service, there is ample evidence arising from the study of serial murder cases to argue that social class, race, sexual preference, age, occupation and residence status play a significant role in determining what level of police resources will be invested in the solution of a homicide.

Murders in everyday life, as opposed to serial murders, pose considerably less investigative challenges to detectives (Leyton). Serial murders typically involve strangers as perpetrators and victims are selected at "random" with little or no evidence to connect the offender with the victim. When there is no pattern in the murders committed by the serial killer, investigators may believe they have a series of unrelated homicides committed by several perpetrators. Alternatively, they may erroneously focus on one suspect, when two serial murderers are at work in their community. There is little doubt that the murder of a mother of small children who is of middle- or upper-class status will receive more investigative attention from police than the murder of a street sex worker, since considerable political, legal and media pressure would be brought to bear if a solution to the first case were not forthcoming (Rossmo, "Criminal Investigative Failures in the Missing Women"). Sherry Lewis, then executive director of The Native Women's Association of Canada, illuminated the systemic nature of discriminatory treatment of Aboriginal women victims of crime when she commented on the Highway of Tears case, in which five Aboriginal woman had disappeared over a number of years beginning in1988, and said that "one non-Aboriginal woman goes missing and all of a sudden there was a media frenzy" (d'Entremont, 2004).

Not all of Robert Pickton's victims were Aboriginal, but over half were. We have deliberately chosen not to separate the victims in our discussion, contending that all victims are of equal importance; however, our focus is more specifically those who were Aboriginal. The victims' "three-prong status" as Aboriginal women, substance abusers, and sex-trade workers placed them in categories demonstrated in research into serial murder investigations to cause investigative inertia (S. Egger, *The Killers among Us*; Fleming and O'Reilly, "The Value of Victims). This failing was not unique to this investigation, as extant research clearly demonstrates, but that does not diminish its total unacceptability.

Several prominent serial murder cases in the United States involved members of the above-stated victim categories and defied solution for lengthy periods of time, sometimes years or even decades. Included in this list are the cases of Ted Bundy, Dennis Rader (The BTK killer), Gary Ridgeway (the Green River Killer), John Wayne Gacy, and Jeffrey Dahmer. Dahmer's selection of African American gay men as his victims ensured his immunity from suspicion. On one occasion, police returned to Dahmer's apartment a fourteen-year-old boy who had been seen running down the street naked. Police dispatchers were recorded laughing at and belittling reports of this incident when they came from African Americans, evidencing their racist attitudes. Rather than observing the boy's sheer terror or finding a qualified interpreter to question him, the intervening officers believed Dahmer when he told them that he and the boy were lovers. Minutes after police left Dahmer murdered the boy.

One of the predominant theories to explain why serial killers choose individuals from certain groups as victims is that they view them as "less dead" (S. Egger, *The Need to Kill*). Serial killers view victims as less than human, not deserving of life, which requires them to dispatch the victim. They are "less dead" because they are viewed as less than alive, less than human. Serial killers who choose to victimize sex workers may do so because they view themselves as carrying out a service to society by ridding the streets of those individuals whom they believe are a blight on the community. Such "mission-oriented" killers see themselves in heroic terms as saviours of society, although there is no evidence that Pickton fit into this analytic category (Holmes and Holmes). It is much more reasonable to assume that as an individual familiar with policing, he recognized that sex workers were a lower investigative priority and much easier prey, since their disappearance might not be noticed for a considerable period of time. As Steven Egger argues, "These groups lack prestige and in many instances are unable to alert others to their plight. They are powerless given their situation in time, place or their immediate surroundings" (*Serial Murder* 2). Norris and colleagues assertion that "the quantity and quality of law enforcement the citizens receive, both as victim and suspect reflects the underlying pattern of social stratification in society" (qtd. in Dickson-Gilmore 75) is instructive. Furthermore, if one accepts that this will produce a pronounced lack of societal reaction, reflecting both the status of the Pickton victims and their race, then agitation for police action will not be forthcoming. Both institutional and investigative inertia appear to have plagued the Missing Women Investigation. As Hickey instructs, "victims of [serial] crime are often perceived as losers ... victims get what they deserve" (*Serial Murderers* 4th ed. 303).

The *Missing Women: Investigation Report*, prepared by Deputy Chief Constable Doug LePard of the Vancouver Police Department, argues to the contrary. It acknowledges that there were "poisoned" relations with some victims' families, but, in the end, the Vancouver Police Department did not investigate the missing sex workers' cases any differently than it would have had the victims been women from an upper-class neighbourhood. This is in contrast to clear evidence from numerous serial murder cases around the world (S. Egger, *Serial Murder*, *The Killers among Us*; Hickey, *Serial Murderers* 5th ed.) that this is a repetitive trend:

> Bias against sex-trade workers was not the reason for the deficiencies in the Missing Women investigation. However, barriers to reporting marginalized persons as missing ... poisoned relations with families of some of the missing women. These factors did compromise the investigation by creating, at the least, a lack of trust in the VPD [Vancouver Police Department]. (Lepard 325)

Street sex workers inhabit a very dangerous world punctuated by violence, drug use, and risky lifestyles (Comack and Seshia; Lowman, "Violence"; Shaver). They are at once visible, plying their trade on the street, and invisible to others in the community, who either do not frequent this type of area or who ignore street persons when they encounter them, a common phenomenon (Fleming, "Policing Serial Murder"; Davis and Shaffer). Sex workers are often viewed in negative terms by members of the wider community for engaging by choice in an activity that is fraught with risk. Victims are often blamed for their victimization. In this light, it can be argued that victims have precipitated attacks on themselves. Hickey states that "prostitutes were far more likely to be targets than any other group of victims" (*Serial Murderers* 4th ed.260).

Street sex workers are vulnerable to attack because they enter the vehicles of "johns" or customers, and accompany them to alleyways, back parking lots, private residences, and other isolated locations. Drug addiction provides a tool that serial killers can use to lure victims to remote locations—their so-called "killing ground"—with a promise of drugs. The Vancouver Police argued that the women were "transient," and their absence could be explained by theories other than that of a serial killer (LePard 324). However, if the families of the missing women reported them missing, and expressed fears that they were dead, why would the Vancouver Police dismiss their concerns and offer alternative theories about where they were and what they were doing (for example; in another city working in the sex trade)?(Rossmo, "Criminal Investigative Failures in the Missing Women").

Incidentally, the ploy of serial killers luring victims with the promise of alcohol or drugs is not new by any means. In 1827, the Scottish serial murders Burke and Hare lured their victims back to their rooms to kill them by befriending them and promising them liquor. The liquor they gave their victims was meant to stupefy them, rendering them defenseless so they could be suffocated.

It was only after the arrest of Pickton and the issuance of a study by Amnesty International on violence against Aboriginal women (*Stolen Sisters: A Human Rights Response to Discrimination and Violence against Indigenous Women in Canada*) that the victims became visible (Culhane). It is a reflection of the kind of public interest that serial killers elicit that average people know the name of and are familiar with Robert Pickton about whom countless news articles and a book have been written, whereas they are almost totally unfamiliar with the identity of his victims.

INVESTIGATIVE FAILURES IN THE PICKTON CASE

> Virtually every interjurisdictional serial killer case including Sutcliffe...Ted Bundy and the Green River Killer in the United States and Clifford Olsen (sic) in Canada, demonstrate the same problems and raise the same questions. And always the answer turns out to be the same-systemic failure. Always the problems turn out to be the same, the mistakes the same, and the systemic failures the same. (Campbell 2)

> Most of these problems (in the Missing Women Case) are systemic and [identifying them] could help lead to improvements in policing. (Rossmo qtd. in Kines and Bolan)

To inform our discussion of investigator interaction with tbe Aboriginal families of Pickton's victims, we have provided an analysis of why the Missing Women Investigation did not move forward based on the groups from which the victims were drawn. In this section, we wish to address the systemic errors that played a significant role in the investigative errors that plagued this case, which then acted as a catalyst for prompting victims' family members to perceive that their concerns were not being addressed by either the Vancouver Police Department or the RCMP. Given the extensive inquiry conducted by Justice Campbell into the problems encountered in the Bernardo-Homolka serial murder case, why did systemic errors once again prevent an effective investigation from being conducted?

Previous studies have identified a series of recurring issues in the investigation of serial murder cases that either prolonged the period that the murderer continued to operate or otherwise resulted in a flawed investigation. These issues—adapted from the work of Steven Egger (*The Need to Kill*) and others (Hickey *Serial Murderers* 4th ed.; Jenkins; Leyton)—include:

> 1. A lack of commitment on the part of the police service(s) to the idea of a serial murderer operating in their jurisdiction
> 2. Recurring problems co-ordinating serial murder investigations as a result of misdirection and the lack of a clear major-case management model.

3. Problems inherent in managing a large number of cases and the data they produce.
4. Detective inexperience in serial murder cases given their rarity.
5. Internal issues in police investigations caused by cognitive biases and organizational traps (Rossmo, *Criminal Investigative Failures* 9-34).

We will provide a brief analysis of each of these issues. Serial murders, as we have indicated, are rare events in Canadian society. From 1981 to 2011, Canada has experienced three cases of "mega murder" (Ashburner and Soothill; Soothill et al.) or, in other words, serial murder cases that generated an enormous number of media accounts over a long period of time (Fleming, "Policing Serial Murder," *Serial and Mass Murder*). The Olson, Bernardo-Homolka, and Pickton cases dominated media coverage, in terms of the number of reports concerning their cases. Some twenty thousand news items in Canada were generated in relation to Bernardo and Homolka, either individually or together, from the time of their arrest in 1993 to 2007 (Fleming *Serial and Mass Murder*).

Given their rarity, police chiefs and senior management are naturally reluctant to declare that a serial killer is at large, since this type of announcement has immediate ramifications and is met with high public expectations that an arrest will be forthcoming. The lack of relationship between most serial killers and their victims can result in frustrating, extremely expensive investigations that yield few or no results while sapping major resources from other policing priorities. The Toronto case of Jane Doe in 2004—a woman who was the victim of a serial rapist and who sued the Board of Commissioners of Police—demonstrates the extreme dangers that can be created when police do not inform the public that a serial predator is operating in a particular area. Although the decision to announce such an investigation is difficult, we argue that the safety of potential victims should be the priority when making decisions as to how to proceed in these cases. Later in this chapter, we will return to this topic with regard to the Missing Women Investigation to illustrate that even when research pointed to an overwhelming likelihood that the women were dead, police still did not accept this possibility and argued that "were there a dead body, no doubt the information would have been treated differently" (LePard 332). However, analysis of existing serial murder cases would have demonstrated that serial killers develop "dumping grounds" and, as a result, no bodies may be found for a considerable period of time extending over months, years, or even decades (Fleming"Policing Serial Murder"; Leyton; Hickey, *Serial Murderers* 4th ed.). Surely, the non-discovery of bodies could not have prevented police from considering the possibility that a serial killer was operating when so many women were missing.

The second factor connects to co-ordinating serial murder investigations. The co-ordination of a serial murder investigation, especially one that involves two distinct police jurisdictions, is a complex undertaking at best. The fact that Pickton picked up his victims on the Downtown Eastside of Vancouver but murdered and disposed of them in the suburb of Port Coquitlam meant that his crimes were committed in two different police jurisdictions, because of the RCMP's mandate to police provincially in British Columbia. Since the two police services involved in the missing women case did not accept the possibility that a single serial murderer was responsible for the disappearance of the women, it is clear that the co-ordination of efforts and resources between the two was unlikely to occur. There is little evidence in either the report of the Vancouver Police Department (Lepard) or the RCMP (Williams and Simmill) that a co-ordinated effort existed with regard to the cases, although there is some evidence that they exchanged information. As Lepard has commented, "The bigger lesson is we need better communication amongst police;" he also cited training and staffing issues inside both the Vancouver Police Department and the RCMP ("Pickton Investigation to Be Reviewed by B.C."). It is interesting to note that the RCMPdid not become involved in the case until 2001 and that shortly thereafter the case was solved (not, however, as a result of a serial murder investigation).

As Kim Rossmo states, "Police ignored Canada's most prolific sex murderer for over three years because they did not want to believe, despite evidence to the contrary, that a serial killer was responsible for the missing women in the Downtown Eastside" (Rossmo, *Criminal Investigative Failures* 33). Rossmo conducted a statistical—and epidemiological—style analysis of women reported missing between 1995 and 1999. LePard's (100-101) observations of this study are worth considering:

> Using a variety of sources of data, [Rossmo] found that the number of women who had gone missing in the previous 30 months was significantly higher than what could be expected by chance. Further, he found it was statistically unlikely that any more than two of the Missing Women would be found. He reported that if the women had met with foul play, the fact that none of their bodies had been found made the separate killer theory unlikely. He stated that "the rarity of serial murder, even in high risk population groups, makes the separate, multiple predator option improbable." Finally, he found that "the single serial murder [sic] hypothesis (that would include partner or team killers) was the *most likely explanation* for the majority of these incidents." (LePard 101, emphasis added)

The fact that the women had disappeared from a geographically small area made the results of his analysis even more significant. By way of comparison, if there had been a similar number of persons diagnosed with a deadly disease in such a small area, it would have been cause to declare an epidemic. Interestingly, Rossmo is reported to have drafted a press release in September 1998 that would have alerted the public to the possibility that a serial killer was responsible for the disappearances on the Downtown Eastside (Kines and Bolan).

The third factor relates to the management of the data generated by the high number of cases of missing women. The large amount of data—which includes reports, investigations, interviews, tips, suspects and so on—associated with these cases poses a significant investigative challenge for detectives. This was particularly true in this case, since the serial murder theory had not been accepted. In fact, as late as July 2001, when Rossmo sued the Vancouver Police Department for wrongful dismissal, police spokespersons still denied the existence of a serial killer in the cases. The resources needed to conduct a proper investigation eluded police services until shortly before Pickton's arrest, but were available in excess *after* his arrest. Rossmo suggested that police management's insistence on treating the case as "a missing persons inquiry instead of a serial murder investigation" (Kines and Bolan) meant that "they didn't have the resources for this type of case." He also noted that an arrest was made shortly after resources were dedicated to the case (Kines and Bolan).

The fourth factor hindering serial murder investigations in general (not only the Pickton case) is detectives' lack of experience with this type of case. Information gleaned from previous inquiries and academic research literature suggests that there is little effort to educate investigators about the challenges of serial murder cases. At one point, the Vancouver Police Department did send representatives to meet with investigators from the Green River serial murder case in the United States (Lepard). We have argued elsewhere that there is a pressing need to find appropriate channels to pass on lessons learned in previous serial murder investigations, and to educate detectives in the complexities of these cases (Fleming and O'Reilly, *History Repeats Itself*).

Finally, Rossmo has developed an insightful analysis of the cognitive biases and organizational traps that can occur in any major crime investigation, which we believe is of significant value when applied to understanding some of the flaws that occurred in the Pickton investigation ("Criminal Investigative Failures in the Missing Women"). His analysis provides the compelling argument that detectives may fall into a series of thinking traps that reinforce their own theory of a case, "while ignoring or refusing to search for contradicting evidence" (Rossmo, *Criminal Investigative Failures* 17). Thus, if detectives initially viewed these cases as missing women cases, they were more likely to ignore alternative theories, such as the one suggested by Rossmo's statistical report. Rossmo also relates that detectives "often fail to account for the absence of evidence" (*Criminal Investigative Failures* 18). This is relevant to our analysis of the failed investigative efforts in the Pickton case because the issue of the lack of either sightings of the missing women or an in-depth review of evidence that suggested they were dead (aside from Rossmo's report) would naturally affect investigative approaches. One would have to ask what effort was expended in looking for a possible dump site for their bodies, since the missing women were not considered homicide victims by investigators.

Several other factors are illuminated by Rossmo's excellent analysis of systemic issues that plague law enforcement institutions, including what he terms "inertia, momentum, and roller coasters" (*Criminal Investigative Failures* 23). Inertia stems from the inherent nature of police services, as agencies are highly bureaucratic and demonstrate what he refers to as "an unwillingness to change, evolve or act" (*Criminal Investigative Failures* 23). This is particularly relevant to our interest in how the missing women and their families were ignored, since in this model "marginalized victims" are not prioritized by police. In addition, as Rossmo points out, "when a response finally does occur, it is often insufficient" (*Criminal Investigative Failures* 23). Contrast this inertia with the treatment of a series of garage robberies that occurred in a well-to-do neighbourhood in Vancouver. The police board authorized a $100,000 reward in this case but refused to do so in the case of the missing women. Vancouver's mayor at the time, Philip Owen, did not accept a serial killer theory, as this statement of his illustrates:

> There's no evidence that a serial killer is at work.... No bodies have been found.... I don't think it is appropriate for a big award for a location service." He (the mayor) scoffed at claims by relatives of the missing women that the prostitutes had close ties to their families and wouldn't just vanish from the streets. "That's what they say," Owen said, "some of these girls have been missing for a year. All of a sudden ...it becomes a major event." (Phillips qtd. in Rossmo, *Criminal Investigative Failures* 31)

A month later when the city finally agreed to put up the reward, it did so reluctantly and had the provincial government pledge 70 percent of the reward (Rossmo *Criminal Investigative Failures* 32).

Another factor that can send an investigation in the wrong direction is organizational momentum that is highly resistant to change. To understand this concept, consider the difficulties that would confront a police agency announcing that it was incorrect in its assumptions about a case and was redirecting its efforts in a completely different direction. This would certainly be the catalyst for the media, politicians, and the public to question the expertise of the investigators and the competency of senior management. Lepard notes that managers did not want to make such an announcement to the media, since they did not trust it or view it as an investigative tool, a serious flaw that has had a negative effect on past cases, including the Bernardo investigation (Campbell). As history has demonstrated, the media can co-operate with police and play an important role in assisting investigations, but it can also wreak havoc with detectives' investigative efforts if there is no fair and consistent media policy (Campbell). As Rossmo (*Criminal Investigative Failures*) and others (S. Egger *Serial Murder*; *The Killers among Us*; Hickey, *Serial Murderers* 5th ed; Keppel and Birnes) have shown, it is a Herculean undertaking to change suspects or the predominant theory being used to explain a crime internally, because of some investigators' resistance to considering other possibilities, and externally, because of concerns about possible negative public perceptions of the police service and its capabilities.

The reluctance of police investigators to consider other suspects once an investigative strategy has begun to focus on a particular individual (a prime suspect) has been a significant factor in wrongful conviction cases across North America. This is known as the roller-coaster effect. In Canada, the cases of Guy Paul Morin (Makin) and Robert Baltovich (Finkle) are two of the most well recognized examples. Other secondary suspects are unlikely to reemerge later in an investigation if they have been discarded early in the process, according to Rossmo (*Criminal Investigative Failures* 24). As he points out, cold-case detectives working a crime years later, with no attachment to the predominant (incorrect) theory or to suspects identified in an earlier investigation, are often able to identify the true perpetrator of the crime because the detectives come to the file without bias or the sense that they must strictly adhere to the original investigation's overarching theory.

"IN HARM'S WAY": VIOLENCE AGAINST ABORIGINAL WOMEN, POLICE APPROACHES, AND THE FAMILIES OF VICTIMS

These acts of violence may be motivated by racism, or may

> be carried out in the expectation that societal indifference to the welfare and safety of Indigenous women will allow the perpetrators to escape justice. (Amnesty International 5)

In the previous sections of this chapter, we have provided an analysis of the systemic and other factors that can stall or misdirect a serial murder investigation. We have also tried to demonstrate the politics of neglect that led both the police and decision makers to fail to consider the possibility that the missing women were dead and to devote sufficient resources to the investigation. In this section of the chapter, we will argue that, consequentially, they treated the victims and their families as though they did not matter.

It is no coincidence that the families of Robert Pickton's victims, both Aboriginal and non-Aboriginal, began to question the commitment of both the Vancouver Police Department and the RCMP to solving the cases of their missing loved ones or to considering the possibility of a serial killer operating on the Lower Eastside, given the issues we have raised thus far. In 2002, Karin Joesbury brought a civil suit against the RCMP in relation to the death of her daughter, Andrea Joesbury (Williams and Simmill 25). In response, the RCMP commissioned two officers, Inspector R. J. Williams and Staff Sergeant K. W. Simmill, to undertake a review of the case and to produce a document "for the purpose of current and anticipated civil litigation" (Williams and Simmill). The RCMP mandate also took into account the possibility that other victims' families might come forward with civil claims.

The Joesbury family contended that the RCMP had failed in its duty to investigate information regarding Pickton's farm in Port Coquitlam over the period 1983 to 2002; that the RCMP had identified the possibility that a serial killer was responsible and had not engaged in a proper investigation; and, finally, that the RCMP did not communicate with other police forces, which would have "assisted in detecting Robert Pickton's activities" (Williams and Simmill 2). The RCMP s response indicates that it perceived no difficulties in communicating and working with the Vancouver Police. The authors of the report argue that this was a project of great "magnitude" and attached "the daily log" to the report to bolster this claim. Williams and Simmill (23) indicate that new policies on missing persons were being developed as the report was being prepared. In the end, they conclude: "from a global perspective covering the elements outlined at the beginning of this report, we are of the opinion the RCMP acted appropriately and followed up investigative leads, with respect to Robert Pickton" (23). The reviewers admit that there was "delay in action" regarding the Pickton case, but they claim that this was "caused by many other high profile investigations" (23). They view it as "unfortunate that the Coquitlam Detachment's priority pressures precluded this file from receiving *continuous unlimited resources and commitment*" (Williams and Simmill 26, emphasis added). This raises the question: what case could be of higher priority than one in which dozens of women had disappeared from the streets of Vancouver in one small area? It also reveals senior management's concern about the costs involved in launching an effective investigation. Given that the document was prepared by the police to defend against possible civil suits, it buttresses a positive view of their own conduct and cites resource issues and other priorities to explain shortcomings in the investigations. However, as we will note in a later section of the chapter, in reviewing the police investigations covering the 1999 to 2002 period, the Oppal Inquiry will have access to an enormous budget. Given the existence of the Campbell Inquiry (1996), extensive research by academics cited throughout this chapter, and the experience of the Olson case, we question whether inquiries have a significant effect on future serial murder investigations, given the usual time lag between cases. We contend that police investigators could benefit from consulting with recognized academic experts in the field of serial murder inquiry to avoid some of the pitfalls encountered in the Pickton case. We will return to this topic in our conclusions. What is most puzzling is the concluding statement of the RCMP review document: "although this was a complex review, with very unique circumstances based on our experience and from the interviews conducted, it is suffice to say nothing would have changed dramatically if those involved had to do it over again" (Williams and Simmill 27). Where does this conclusion leave us? Certainly one might expect that those involved could reflect on the issues that prevented an earlier identification and arrest of Pickton, rather than bolstering their view that nothing would change if it had to be done again. Others have also questioned the "thoroughness "of a review that runs twenty-seven pages in length in comparison to the LePard Report, which was prepared for the Vancouver Police Department and fills 405 pages. Perhaps, we can view the report merely as a document meant to defend a position in a civil case, and for which, like the Pickton investigation itself, the resources could not be found to produce a more useful and instructive document.

In 2004, Amnesty International released *Stolen Sisters,* a report on violence against Aboriginal women in Canada. This was a response to the concerns of Aboriginal families over the violent victimization of Aboriginal women across Canada. This violence can take any one of a number of forms. In our introduction, we alluded to the very difficult plight that faces Aboriginal women entering an urban environment from a reserve setting and to the racism, discrimination, and violence that play a part in the everyday lives of far too many. In its discussion of the Pickton case, the Amnesty International report suggests that the delay in identifying a single serial killer was involved in the disappearances of so many women. It also states, "police and city officials had long denied that there was any pattern to the disappearances or that women were in any particular danger" (23).

The case of serial murderer John Martin Crawford, who was convicted of the killings of three Aboriginal women, is instructive in terms of how these women, and Indigenous women victims of homicide in general, are reduced into the previously discussed category of the "less dead." As he received an award from The Institute for the Advancement of Aboriginal Women, Warren Goulding, who wrote a book on the Crawford case, commented, "I don't get the sense the general public cares much about missing or murdered Aboriginal women. It's all part of this indifference to the lives of Aboriginal people. They don't seem to matter as much as white people" (Purdy).

The Aboriginal Justice Inquiry and Implementation Commission also expressed this sentiment, arguing that Indigenous people are "over-policed" but "under protected" (Chartrand et al). More disturbing perhaps is their view that "many police have come to view Indigenous people not as a community deserving protection, but a community from which the rest of society must be protected" (Chartrand et al.). As Travis has noted, the media has done little to raise public concern about missing or murdered Aboriginal women, since it "either just 'didn't care' or reduced victims to implicitly guilty, drug-addicted prostitutes." According to Travis, the delays in the police investigating into the missing women's cases reflected the view that they were "social outcasts.... The prevalence of drug addicts and prostitutes among the missing—not to mention Native—rendered them inconsequential."

This raises another issue—the reluctance of Aboriginal peoples to engage with the police. As the 2004 Amnesty International report argues "many Indigenous people feel that have little reason to trust police and as a consequence are reluctant to turn to police for protection" (80). Moreover, street sex workers have the added burden of engaging in a profession in which some of their activities (solicitation and communication) are subject to charge and arrest. CBC Associate Producer Audrey Huntley, who has documented cases of missing Aboriginal women, found that Aboriginal families of victims "most of the time felt that they hadn't got the attention [of officials]. They were met with a lot of indifference on the part of the police" (Travis). The Supreme Court recently agreed to hear an appeal of a case launched by Lower Eastside sex-trade workers in 2007. The case challenges current laws, which they claim subject sex workers to an increased risk of violence, since they are reluctant to call police when they encounter violence because it will result in arrest (Wyld). They argue that sex workers are denied the fundamental right to security of the person guaranteed under Canada's Charter of Rights and Freedoms.

The Aboriginal Justice Inquiry of Manitoba, which convened in the 1990s, found that underlying sexist and racist stereotypes about Aboriginal women were pervasive in society. Moreover, the inquiry commented that "sexism and racism contributes [sic] to the assumption in the part of perpetrators of violence against Indigenous women that their actions are justifiable or condoned by society" (qtd. in Amnesty International, 12). The researchers who completed the Amnesty International report found that numerous studies that explored Canada's approach to policing "concluded that Indigenous people as a whole are not getting the protection they deserve" ("Solutions"). Of particular significance to this argument are the reports by Aboriginal families that "police failed to act promptly when their sisters or daughters went missing, treated the family disrespectfully, or kept the family in the dark about how the investigation—*if any*—was proceeding" (Amnesty International 12, emphasis added). Moreover, incidents were reported to the researchers that were disturbing in light of the inertia of the investigation into the missing women in the Pickton case: "despite the concern of family members that a missing sister or daughter was in serious danger, police failed to take basic steps such as promptly interviewing family and friends or appealing to the public for information" (Amnesty International 12).

Overall, police have responded to criticism of the Missing Women Investigation in two ways. First, they have suggested that they acted appropriately but were constrained by lack of resources and conflicting priorities; they have placed blame on individual police officers. Second, they have suggested that responsibility for the investigation lay with others. The LePard Report argues that the Vancouver Police Department had a responsibility to apply pressure at a management level to the Coquitlam RCMP, with whom, in its opinion, the legal responsibility for the investigation fell. However, Vancouver Police did not accept that murders had been committed, claiming that if there had been "compelling" evidence of murder it would have applied more resources to the investigation. LePard's report suggests that "the investigation was plagued by a failure at the VPD's management level to recognize what it was faced with" (LePard 4 of summary). LePard also suggests that responsibility for the failed management of investigation lay with those high-level positions in the Coquitlam RCMP and the Provincial Unsolved Homicide Unit.

LePard's report puts forth the "bad apple" theory and suggests that just a few officers were responsible for the poor overall performance of the department. At the same time, it attempts to lessen criticism of the investigators and management by refocusing the blame on Pickton: "While there were individual police officers whose performance was lacking, the true villain in this tragedy is the suspect" (323). This is curious given the Campbell Inquiry's (1996) finding that failed serial murder investigations reveal systemic errors. Richard Ericson's classic study of detective work *Making Crime: A Study of Detective Work* also supports the notion that it is the bad barrel rather than the bad apple that must be examined. Although it is easy to place blame on individual police personnel—who are nameless, retired, or deceased—to find a long-term solution, it is more crucial to look at the system that created an environment in which such mistakes could be made. It is suggested that the failures in this case were partially the result of inadequate resources, including a lack of sworn officers and civilian support staff (Lepard 325); this argument also resounds in the Williams and Simmill report. We raise the issue of whether the problem is lack of resources, or the failure to use existing resources to their best advantage, which appears to be reflected in Rossmo's insider account of the investigation ("Criminal Investigative Failures in the Missing Women"). There is a candid admission that "VPD management failed to exploit Detective Inspector Kim Rossmso's talents when needed most but this scarcely excuses the refusal of upper-level officers to consider the ramifications of his 1999 report" (LePard 328).

In the end, the LePard report concludes that "the investigation of Pickton prior to February 2002 was inadequate and a failure of major case management" (316). However, one must remember that Pickton was *arrested* in that month; therefore, the investigation, despite its cost and thoroughness, was to *recover* evidence from his farm and other sources sufficient to identify his victims and convict him of murder. It appears that enormous resources suddenly became available for forensic evidence gathering only when the enormity of Pickton's crimes was realized and public and political interest became focused upon the case. In contrast, when women were disappearing from the Lower Eastside, neither the Vancouver Police Department nor the RCMP raised an alarm to find the resources to *prevent* more women from disappearing. Given their experience with the Olson serial murder investigation in the late 1970s and early 1980s, the results of the Campbell Inquiry and Rossmo's statistical analysis of the disappearances, both police agencies should have considered making a request for the resources needed to meet the investigative challenges. However, as LePard notes, the media strategy on the disappearances "was being driven—or at least influenced—by managers who either didn't believe in the serial killer theory, or felt that publicly acknowledging *a serial killer would only create more problems, or both*" (329, emphasis added).

LIMITING VOICES AND LIMITING SCOPE: THE OPPAL INQUIRY AND ABORIGINAL PEOPLE

> The critical difference is racism. We are born to it and spend our lives facing it. Racism lies at the root of our life experiences. The effect is violence, violence against us, and in turn our own violence. (Chartrand et al, 1999)

> My Aboriginal sisters are not perfect victims in the eyes of the police and the courts, especially when they're considered vagrant, addicted and sex workers. (Vancouver Rape Relief and Women's Shelter qtd. in Thompson)

As previously discussed, as early as 2002, Kim Rossmo and Doug McKay-Dunn, a retired inspector, called for an inquiry into the problems with the Missing Women investigation. In fact, Rossmo is cited as saying that, "any effort to delay an inquiry until after the current criminal investigation is 'clearly a stalling tactic'" (Kines and Bolan). Nine years passed before an inquiry was launched in January 2011. Several critical problems with this inquiry have been raised by Aboriginal Chiefs, Elders and Aboriginal peoples.

First, the scope of the inquiry is limited to police actions over a defined historical period, 1999 to 2002. This limitation has been the subject of considerable criticism from Aboriginal leaders and others (Keller). Although Commissioner Oppal later recommended a wider scope for the inquiry, broadening it into a "study and hearing commission" as we shall learn, access to resources prevents Aboriginal groups from being heard in an effective way.

Chiefs have also questioned the appointment of Mr. Oppal, who has "many ties to the Liberals," and formerly served as Attorney General of British Columbia (Mulgrew). Stewart Phillip, president of the Union of British Columbia Indian Chiefs, questioned why the government of British Columbia did not consult with "Aboriginal and women's organizations about the terms of reference" (Mulgrew). Given that Mr. Oppal was part of the government, some have questioned the appearance of his appointment: "There is a perception there may not be independence there.... Perceptions, whether reality or not, cause concern" (James qtd. in Mulgrew). Given the Aboriginal status of many of the victims, and the importance of the issues surrounding violence against Aboriginal women in British Columbia, we question why co-commissioners were not appointed from the ranks of Aboriginal Chiefs and Elders. This would have gone a long way to ensuring that Aboriginal voices were acknowledged. From an Aboriginal justice perspective, consultation with Aboriginal Chiefs, Elders and victims' families should have been undertaken by the government of British Columbia before it appointed a commissioner, regardless of his excellent credentials. Excluding Aboriginal Chiefs and Elders as decision makers sends the inappropriate message that those from the dominant culture can evaluate the facts surrounding the issues, make decisions, and render judgments without the participation of Aboriginal persons as equal judges or commissioners.

Although the Oppal Inquiry will listen to various groups and individuals through the medium of community forums, it does not have a specific mandate to address wider issues of violence against Aboriginal women in the province, including the thirty-two unsolved murders on the Highway of Tears. Stewart Phillip criticizes the community forums, since "there is no obligation to document the information and comments brought forward at public sessions" (Matas). In his opinion, they will little effect the outcome.

A major—but perhaps not unexpected—blow to the Aboriginal community occurred when the government of British Columbia denied funding to Aboriginal groups and sex-trade workers to cover their legal costs in relation to the inquiry. The solution offered by Mr. Oppal appears to be "finding lawyers willing to work for free" (Keller). Although the inquiry argues that people will be heard despite not having funding, we question how these groups can make *effective* presentations on substantive issues when they either have no access to legal representation or are dependent on the pro bono generosity of lawyers. Given the complexity of the issues and the resources necessary to draw up submissions and factums, what lawyer or firm could responsibly hope to do an adequate job against the massive legal representation and financial resources of the government funded agencies at the centre of the inquiry? Although we acknowledge the significant amount of quality work done pro bono by lawyers in Canada, we are also aware of the enormous financial costs and personal commitment of time and resources required to do a satisfactory job representing groups who want to make submissions. We contend that it is unrealistic to assume that pro bono representation will adequately ensure that all voices are heard. David Eby, executive director of the British Columbia Civil Liberties Association, reflects on the fundamental inequity between government agencies and the affected: "There are lawyers on the government's side representing everyone from the RCMP to the VPD to the criminal justice branch, who are basically saying that there were no problems or if there were problems, they've been fixed—and *they've all got full government funding*" (Keller, emphasis added).

The decision not to provide funding appears even more ominous given the RCMP's own suggestion that there is little doubt that "it attempted to exhaust all investigative avenues relative to the suspect" (Williams and Simmill) and that the Vancouver Police directed responsibility to the RCMP Coquitlam detachment and the Provincial Homicide Unit. It also supports Rossmo's 2002 comment regarding delaying tactics being used in bringing forward the inquiry. It can be suggested that refusing to provide funding to Aboriginal groups hardly provides an even playing field and will, in fact, severely limit their ability to bring forward issues for consideration, which ensures that silence envelopes their concerns. As Sahajpal notes, "By not allowing these advocacy groups to have their voice heard, the tragedy continues," and for us, only the silence remains.

RECOMMENDATIONS

The objectives of this chapter were to provide an analysis of flaws in the police investigation into the Lower Eastside Missing Women Case and to further our understanding of police attitudes towards

Aboriginal victims and their families. We hope it is evident that there must be a serious evaluation of police action, and lack of action, in this investigation. This evaluation should be conducted by independent researchers recruited from outside of the policing agencies responsible for this investigation. In our opinion, the direct involvement of Aboriginal leaders and Elders as both equal adjudicators and investigators is absolutely critical to the success and acceptability of its results and recommendations for Aboriginal peoples. We also argue that there is a need for change to police investigative protocol in possible serial murder cases to avoid the major pitfalls and traps that thwarted this investigation. Specifically, given the analysis in this chapter, we recommend:

Police officers and civilian staff receive training that will permit them to deal with the families of Aboriginal victims of crime in respectful manner, taking their concerns seriously and reporting back to them in a timely manner.

Police make use of academic researchers and resources to further their knowledge of bodies of existing research on investigative issues and specific offender patterns to avoid the investigative traps that plagued this investigation (Rossmo, *Criminal Investigative Failures;* Fleming and O'Reilly, ""Kept in the Dark").

In light of the Amnesty International's report (2004), issues of racism in police dealing with Aboriginal victims and families of victims should be further investigated by researchers. The results of this research should be conveyed to the chiefs of police nationally for immediate ameliorative action.

Nationally, homicide detectives should have regular opportunities for networking and education on serial crimes, which could be accomplished through conferences. This would allow them to be informed about research and investigative experience and techniques as well as potential pitfalls in investigations. In this way, direct investigative experience could be handed down through generations of investigators.

Our genuine belief is that these recommendations, if acted on, would have a positive impact on future investigations of serial crimes and lift the veil of silence.

The recent report of the Truth and Reconciliation Commission has made an important contribution to exposing the extreme hardships that our First Peoples have suffered through countless generations, and although we remain sceptical, it has shown a way forward to a more promising future. Certainly, the events chronicled in this chapter give thought to the need for a reconstituting of police approaches to the issue of Missing and Murdered Indigenous Women and a recasting of police relations with First Nations peoples. We do not expect this to be an easy or short process. In this. we echo the sentiments of Justice Sinclair who stated from the Truth and Reconciliation Commission that "Reconciliation is about forging and maintaining respectful relationships."

Originally published in Well-Being in the Urban Aboriginal Community, *Ed. David Newhouse, et al., Toronto: Thomson Educational Publishing, 2012. Reprinted with permission.*

WORKS CITED

Abbott, Karen L. "Urban Aboriginal Women in British Columbia and the Impacts of Matrimonial Real Property Regime." *Aboriginal Policy Research: Setting the Agenda for Change, Volume II*. Eds. Jerry P. White, Paul Maxim, and Dan Beavan. Toronto: Thompson Educational Publishing Inc., 165-181. Print.

Amnesty International. *Stolen Sisters: A Human Rights Response to Discrimination and Violence Against Indigenous Women in Canada*. Toronto: Amnesty International Canada, 2004. Print.

Armstrong, Janice. "RCMP Respond to the Release of VPD's Review of Missing Women's Investigation." *Royal Canadian Mounted Police*. Government of Canada, 2010. Web. 20 Aug. 2015.

Ashburner, E., and Soothill, K.L. (2002). Understanding Serial Killing: How Important Are Notions of Gender. *Police Journal* 73 (2002): 93-99. Print.

Balakrishnan, T. R. and Rozzett Jurdi. "Spatial Residential Patterns of Aboriginals and Their Socio-economic Integration in Selected Canadian Cities." *Aboriginal Policy Research Vol. IV*. Eds. Jerry P. White, Susan Wingert, Dan Beavon and Paul Maxim. Toronto: Thompson Educational Publishing Inc. 2007. 263-274. Print.

Campbell, Justice Archie. *Bernardo Investigation Review*. Toronto: Government of Ontario. Government Printing Office, 1996. Print.

Chartrand, Paul, Wendy Whitecloud, Eva McKay, and Doris Young. *The Aboriginal Justice Implementation Commission Volume I*. Manitoba: Manitoba Statutory Publications Office, 1999.

Cohen, Lawrence E., and Marcus *Felson*. "Social Change and Crime Rate Trends: A Routine Activity Approach." *American Sociological Review* 44.4 (1979): 488-608. Print.

Comack, Elizabeth, and Maya Seshia, (2010). "Bad Dates and Street Hassles: Violence in the Winnipeg Street Sex Trade." *Canadian Journal of Criminology and Criminal Justice* 52.2 (2010): 203-214. Print.

Culhane, Dara. (2003)."Their Spirits Live within Us: Aboriginal Women in Downtown Eastside Vancouver Emerging into Visibility." *The American Indian Quarterly* 27.3 (2003): 593-606. Print.

Dahrendorf, R. *Life Chances*. Chicago: University of Chicago Press. Print.

Davis, Sylvia, and Martha Shaffer. "Prostitution in Canada: The Invisible Menace or the Menace of Invisibility?" *Walnet*. N.p., 21 Dec. 1994. Web. 19 Apr. 2016.

D'Entremont, Deidre. "Seeking Justice for Canada's 500 Missing Native Women." *Cultural Survival*, 2004. Web. 19 Apr. 2016.

Dickson-Gilmore, J. "Aboriginal People in Canada: Culture, Colonialism and Criminal Justice." *Diversity, Crime and Justice in Canada*. Ed. B. Perry. Toronto: Oxford University Press. 2011. 75-89. Print.

Doe, J. *The Story of Jane Doe: A Book about Rape*. Toronto: Random House. Print.

Egger, Kim. "Preliminary Data Base on Serial Killers from 1900-1999." *The Killers among Us: An Examination of Serial Murder and Its Investigation*. Ed. S. Egger. Upper Saddle River, NJ: Prentice Hall, 1999. 38-73. Print.

Egger, Steven. *Serial Murder: An Elusive Phenomenon*. New York: Praeger, 1990. Print.

Egger, Steven. *The Killers Among Us: An Examination of Serial Murder and its Investigation*. Upper Saddle River, NJ: Prentice Hall, 2001. Print.

Egger, Steven. *The Need to Kill: Inside the World of the Serial Killer*. Upper Saddle River, NJ: Prentice-Hall, 2003. Print.

Ericson, Richard. *Making Crime: A Study of Detective Work*.

Toronto: University of Toronto Press, 1993. Print.

Fleming, Thomas. (1993)."Policing Serial Murder : The Politics of Negligence" (1993). in L. Visano and K. McCormick (eds.) *Understanding Policing*. Toronto: Canadian Scholars' Press, 323-346. Print.

Fleming, Thomas. *Down and Out in Canada: Homeless Canadians*. Toronto: Canadian Scholars Press, 1993. Print.

Fleming, Thomas, ed. *Serial and Mass Murder: Theory, Policy and Research*. Toronto: Canadian Scholars Press, 2006. Print.

Fleming, Thomas, and Patricia O'Reilly. "History Repeats Itself: Recurring Errors in Canadian Serial Murder Investigation." Presentation at The Western Society of Criminology Conference. Honolulu. 4-6 Feb. 2010. Print.

Fleming, Thomas, and Patricia O'Reilly. "The Value of Victims: Police Treatment of Victims' Families in the Lower East Side Missing Women (Pickton) Case" The Critical Criminology Conference. 2010. Print.

Fleming, Thomas and Patricia O'Reilly. "Kept in the Dark: Reforming Police Practices in Communicating with Aboriginal Families in the Aftermath of the Case of the Lower East Side Missing Women (Pickton) Case." Fostering Biimaadiziwin: A National Research Conference on Urban Aboriginal Peoples. 2011. Print.

Frideres, J. *Canada's Indians: Contemporary Conflicts*. Toronto: Prentice Hall, 1974. Print.

Goulding, Warren. *Just Another Indian : A Serial Killer and Canada's Indifference*. Calgary: Fifth House, 2001. Print.

Hickey, Eric. *Serial Murderers and Their Victims*. 4th ed. United States: Wadsworth, 2006. Print.

Hickey, Eric. *Serial Murderers and Their Victims*. 5th ed. United States: Wadsworth, 2010. Print.

Holmes, Ronald, and Stephen Holmes. *Serial Murder*. 3rd ed. London: Sage, 2010. Print.

Howard-Bobiwash, Heather. "Women's Class Strategies as Activism in Native Community Building in Toronto, 1950-1975." *American Indian Quarterly* 27.3-4 (2003): 566-582. Print.

Truth and Reconciliation Commission of Canada. *Honouring the Truth, Reconciling for the Future: Summary of the Final Report of the Truth and Reconciliation Commission of Canada. Truth and Reconciliation Commission of Canada*. TRC, 2015. Web. 19 Apr. 2015.

Jenkins, P. *Using Murder: The Social Construction of Serial Homicide*. New York; Aldine de Gruyter, 1994. Print.

Keller, James. "Province Denies Funding for Sex Workers, Aboriginal Groups at Pickton Inquiry." *The Globe and Mail*, 24 May 2011. Web. 19 Apr. 2016.

Keppel, R. D., and W.J. Birnes. *Analysis of Modus Operandi and Signature Characteristics of Killers*. Boca Raton: Taylor and Francis, 2009. Print.

Kines, Lindsay, and Kim Bolan. "Two Former Police Officers Join Call for Investigations." *The Vancouver Sun* 16 Mar. 2002. Print.

LePard, Doug. *Missing Women: Investigation Review*. Vancouver: Vancouver Police Department, 2010. Print.

Leyton, Elliot. *Hunting Humans: The Rise of the Modern Multiple Murder*. Toronto: McClelland and Stewart, 2005. Print.

Leyton, Elliot. *Men of Blood: Murder in Everyday Life*. Toronto: McClelland and Stewart, 2005. Print.

Lowman, John. "Violence and the Outlaw Status of (Street) Prostitution in Canada." *Violence Against Women* 6.9 (2000): 987–1011. Print.

Lowman, John. "Prostitution Law Reform in Canada." *Toward Comparative Law in 21st Century*. Ed. The Institute of Comparative Law in Japan. Tokyo: Chou University Press, 1998. 919-946. Print.

Makin, K. *Redrum the Innocent*. Toronto: Penguin, Print. 1998.

Matas, Robert. "In Aftermath of Pickton Case, B.C.'s Missing Women Commission to begin inquiry." *The Globe and Mail*, 18 Jan. 2011. Web. 19 Apr. 2016.

Mulgrew, Ian. "Oppal to Head Pickton Inquiry." *vancouversun.com*. Vancouver Sun, 28 Sept. 2010. Web. 19 Apr. 2016.

Norris, C., N. Fielding, C. Kemp, and J. Fielding. "The Status of this Demeanour: An Analysis of Social Status on Being Stopped by the Police." *Seen but Not Heard: Aboriginal People in the Inner City*. Ed. C. LaPraire. Ottawa: Department of Justice, 1994. Print.

"Pickton Investigation to Be Reviewed by B.C." *CBC News*, 20 Aug. 2011. Web. 19 Apr. 2016.

Purdy, Chris. "Serial Killer Who Roamed Saskatoon Met with Indifference by Police, Media: Journalist-Author Accepts Award for Book About Slain Aboriginal Women." *The Edmonton Journal* 26 Nov. 2003. Print.

Rossmo, D. Kim. *Criminal Investigative Failures.* Boca Raton: CRC Press, 2009. Print.

Rossmo, D. Kim. "Criminal Investigative Failures in the Missing Women/Pig Farm Serial Murder Case." Greenbelt, MD: The Academy of Criminal Justice Sciences. 2011. Print.

Sahajpal, Roohi. "Discrimination in B.C.? No Funding for Advocacy Groups in Pickton Inquiry." *McClung's Magazine.* N.p., 2011. Web. 19 Apr. 2016.

Shaver, F. "Prostitution: On the Dark Side of the Service Industry," *Post-Critical Criminology.* Ed. Thomas Fleming. Scarborough: Prentice Hall Canada, 1997. 42-65. Print.

"Solutions." *Amnesty International.* Amnesty International Canada, 2015. Web. 19 Apr. 2016.

Soothill, K. et al. "The Reporting Trajectories of Top Homicide Cases in the Media : A Case Study of the Times." *Howard Journal of Criminal Justice* 43.1 (2002) 1-14. Print.

Thompson, Kristen. "Everybody Failed Pickton Victims: Women's Shelter." *Metro Vancouver.* Metro, 25 Aug. 2010. Web. 19 Apr. 2016.

Travis, Heather. "Pickton Trial: Who Were the Victims?" *The Tyee.* N.p., 4 Feb. 2006. Web. 19 Apr. 2016.

Urban Aboriginal Task Force: Final Report. Ontario Federation of Indigenous Friendship Centres (OFIFC), 2007. Web. 19 Apr. 2016.

Voyageur, Cora. "First Nations Women in Canada." *Visions of the Heart: Canadian Aboriginal Issues.* Eds. David Long and Olive Patricia Dickason. Toronto: Oxford University Press, 213-235. 2011. Print.

Williams, R.J. and K.W. Simmill. *Re: Joesbury vs. Her Majesty the Queen (Project Evenhanded Request for Assistance-External Review File: 2002E-3220.* Canada: Royal Canadian Mounted Police, 2006. Print.

Wyld, Adrian. "Top Court Will Hear Prostitution Law Challenge." *CBC News*, 31 Mar. 2001. Web. 19 Apr. 2016.

4.
Sisters in Spirit

ANITA OLSEN HARPER

THE TRADITIONAL ROLES of women and men in pre-contact Indigenous societies were balanced and stable; they allowed women safety and powerful places within those societies (Sinclair). Within societies where men held political office, women were honoured and highly esteemed for their invaluable contribution to the survival of the whole nation and for their places as mothers, grandmothers, wives, daughters, aunts, and sisters. That many pre-contact Indigenous societies were both matriarchal and matrilineal ensured women's authority and legitimacy.

In what is now southern Ontario, for example, Iroquoian clan mothers had a strong political voice; they were responsible for both choosing and removing their leaders (*sachem*). They were autonomous and highly respected and although both women and men were considered equal, each exercised a great deal of personal autonomy within their societies. Other First Nation societies, even if they were patriarchal in structure, were similar to the Iroquoian system in their recognition and placing of women in high standing. Hunting and gathering peoples considered women essential and valued economic partners in the various work activities associated with seasonal cycles. In these societies, women took on domestic roles that included food preparation, making clothing, childcare and socialization, as well as significant roles in essential livelihood activities, such as tanning hides, winnowing rice, and preparing fish nets and weirs. Common understanding was that any harm suffered by women would have a negative impact on the whole nation.

Among the Anishinaawpe, women were given the responsibility of directly relating to the Earth and keeping up the Fires of Creation. They also maintained the fires that were used for cooking and heating. In servicing the community fires for ceremonial purposes, they were vigilant about ensuring that their attitudes were spiritually pure and honourable to the Creator and their mother, Earth. Both the physical and spiritual activities were recognized and esteemed by community members because for it was recognized that not all members could serve in the same capacity. Like the Iroquois, Anishinaawpe women were personally autonomous, appreciated, and treated as valued members in all aspects of community life.

The foundation of education in Anishinaawpe and Cree societies was based on women. Creation history begins with a woman descending from a hole in the sky; she needs to care and provide stewardship for Earth. As part of her work, the woman, who is known as Grandmother or Nokomis, taught the original people about the ways of keeping Earth alive and well, and this included instruction about its healing ways. Grandfather, or Mishomis, is honoured for the four directions and the ways of the Sky. This is why the Anishinaawpe still honour Earth as mother and use sweetgrass, Earth's hair, in most types of ceremonies.

At the heart of all traditional Indigenous teaching was the expectation that people would treat one another with honour and respect in all circumstances, including wife-husband relationships (Aboriginal Justice Implementation Commission). Consequently, there was very little family breakdown in most Indigenous societies. Within societies as a whole, the First Peoples held strongly to their beliefs that the Creator gave women special and sacred gifts as life-givers and caretakers, as mothers and wives, and that everything, including gender gifts and roles, was bestowed by the Creator.

The equality of women and men in pre-contact times was accepted as the voice of Creation. Although their roles and responsibilities were different, men were not considered "better" or "more important" than women, or vice versa. The fulfillment of both roles together held a balance that was necessary for meeting both the physical livelihood and spiritual needs of the entire nation. These understandings were a continuing source of strength and peace for Indigenous societies.

CHANGING REALITIES FOR INDIGENOUS WOMEN IN CANADA

The Europeans who came into Indigenous territories, lands they later called "Canada," originated from societies whose traditions, religions, and institutions were overwhelmingly in opposition to those of the First Peoples. Their societies, far from being egalitarian, were hierarchical in nature because Europeans had embedded the concept of male superiority and female inferiority into the foundations of all their social, economic, and religious institutions. This reasoning became the start of a centuries-long imposition of Eurocentric values onto Indigenous civilizations; altering the male-female balance was a significant part of their attempts to remake Indigenous people and society into what was deemed acceptable by European standards. As well, European worldviews[1] based on Christianity, identified Indigenous peoples as pagan, although it was acknowledged that they had the potential to become Christian, and, thereby, European. In response to what was interpreted as divine instruction, the newcomers saw themselves as the initiators and perpetrators of both religious change and the total reconstruction of the Indigenous people.

In British society, where many newcomers had been socialized, women were relegated to property passed first from fathers and then to husbands. The idea of women as autonomous individuals was given no credence. The Christian religion was integral to sustaining this viewpoint, as the following examples attest:

- marriage was called "taking a wife";
- wives were known as the "weaker vessel" (1 Peter 3:7); husbands were to help their wives "overcome sin" (Ephesians 5:26–27); wives were to submit to husbands (1 Peter 3:1); a woman was bound to her husband as long as she lived (1 Corinthians 7:39);
- widows and their daughters were excluded from land ownership; land was passed only to sons; and
- women could not bear arms, enter into political office, or hold contracts.

During the colonial period, Indigenous women took European

men as husbands.[2] The clergy and others in high social standing, however, did not approve of intermarriage and in retaliation, began to promulgate falsehoods about Indigenous women being promiscuous and "easily available" in a sexual sense (Kirk). These myths provided a ready and convenient explanation for European men being willing participants in these relationships. There appears to have been little effort expended towards making European men accountable for their own behaviour and marriage choices when they married Indigenous women. Mixed marriages, which rarely involved European women and Indigenous men, were frowned on also because of the perceived disastrous consequences of "civilized" Christian men marrying "pagan" women, which was interpreted as a "better" race marrying into a "lesser" one. However, Europeans ignored the motivation for these marriages, which were often initiated by the Indigenous people themselves because Indigenous societies were establishing socio-economic ties with Europeans to increase the strength of their own kinship systems. The colonial regime was, thus, paving the way for the unfair victimization of Indigenous women that prevails to this day.

Foreign settlement *en masse*, particularly the arrival of white women, further lowered the status of Indigenous women. For example, white women became the ideal wife and mother and because of their race, colour, and very identity, Indigenous women could not possibly become part of this élite.[3] Early on, race played a role in establishing a class system in which white people were superior to Indigenous people, and white women were superior to Indigenous women. Mixed marriages continued to be vilified, and Indigenous women were blamed for being the cause. To reinforce these sentiments, conscious efforts were made to alienate Indigenous women from "respectable" society. It was believed that white "ladies," being morally and racially superior, should not associate with Indigenous people, the women especially, lest they likewise became corrupt and tainted. Some historians note that the rise in the number of white women during these settlement years paralleled the increasing racism against Indigenous women.

Public opinion about First Nations people, and the women in particular, soon became expressed in concrete action. The British colonial government mandated through legislation what they called "Indian Affairs," and later, in 1876, amalgamated several of these legislative pieces into the Indian Act.[4] Under the Act, both men and women were considered minors and wards of the Crown, but the legislation was particularly harsh towards the women. Like European women of the time, they could not enter into contracts, vote, become professionals, or hold office. Men were allowed a few more rights: for example, male band members over the age of twenty-one could make decisions about surrendering lands. In 1906, the *Indian Act* was amended to state expressly that all those registered under the Act were "non-persons" under Canadian law,[5] which marginalized First Nations people from Canadian society.

The *Indian Act* also created a new system of governance for the reserves: the elected chief and council system could now not include women yet was still characterized as "democratic" by the government. Women were stripped of any formal involvement in the political processes of their nations. Furthermore, the *Indian Act* imposed male lineage and formalized male-female inequality into law by defining an Indian as any "male person" of Indian blood. A woman could not be an Indian in her own right according to the law ("Women in First Nations Politics"). There were also inequalities with respect to the legislated registration: if an Indian woman married a non-Indian man, she and her children lost their place on the Indian Affairs registry. Conversely, when an Indian man married a non-Indian woman, his wife and children all became status Indians. Up to 95 percent of all enfranchisements (loss of 'Indian status')[6] were involuntary and resulted from these provisions of the Act.

Indian agents from the Department of Indian Affairs regularly reported on reserve activities. Although their overall portrayal of Indians was derogatory,[7] depictions of women were particularly disparaging. For example, Indigenous women were described as "poor housekeepers and bad mothers"—qualities contrary to their versions of ideal womanhood. As well, various churches were recruited to help implement the residential school system, which further eroded the image and traditional roles of Indigenous women. This particularly egregious type of schooling was designed to make it difficult, if not impossible, for Indigenous parents to raise their own children. Indigenous mothers and fathers, suddenly finding themselves in a vacuum without their children, experienced deep spiritual desolation. More and more, mothers found themselves isolated, without legal protection, and, often, without their own community's support.

FROM THEN TO NOW: THE ROOTS OF SISTERS IN SPIRIT

It is, indeed, intriguing to examine the status of Indigenous women today, early in the new millennium. Have life conditions and circumstances improved over the years, and, if not, is there an explanation? Could there be a correlation to the legacy enforced by the Indian Act? First, in looking at the area of health, research has uncovered hard evidence of the poor health status of Indigenous women in Canada and of social disparities in their lives compared with other Canadian women. Data from the Canadian Population Health Initiative show that Indigenous people are the unhealthiest group in Canada and that Indigenous women experience a disproportionate burden of ill-health compared to other Canadian women. For example, Aboriginal females experience almost 3 times higher rates of gestational diabetes than non-Aboriginal females (Public Health Agency of Canada). HIV/AIDS is another area of major concern to Indigenous women. Indigenous women bear a disproportionate share of HIV/AIDS infections within the entirety of Indigenous people's infection rate. In studies of young people who use street drugs, findings show that "Aboriginal women were three times more likely than men to be HIV positive" (Mehrabadi et al.); the main cause of this has been identified as gendered experiences of trauma and sexual abuse. Factors that influence vulnerability and risk include gender inequity, colonial representations of Indigenous women, social exclusion, and biological susceptibility. Many new HIV cases result from injection drug use in the overall Indigenous population; for Indigenous women, this risk factor is six times greater than for non- Indigenous women. The Canadian Indigenous AIDS Network states that "various social, economic and behavioural issues are believed to be influencing this health concern. In addition, Indigenous women can experience a triple layer of marginalization, based on gender, race and HIV status."[8]

Poor economic prospects for Indigenous women in Canada contribute to their high rates of HIV/AIDS. Native communities, and particularly women living on reserve, are notorious for their high rates of unemployment and lack of economic opportunity. Unemployment rates of the female Indigenous labour force (17 percent) in 2001 are more than twice those of the female non-Indigenous labour force (7 percent) (Statistics Canada). Many Indigenous women—who are driven from their communities by divorce, separation, or other family-related reasons—enter into the sex trade in urban centres because it is the only way they can provide for themselves and their children. Long-term conditions of poverty and racism leave many Indigenous women with little option but to work the streets to make ends meet. A 2005 study of sex work in Vancouver revealed that 52 percent of those sex trade workers randomly interviewed were Indigenous—a significant overrepresentation compared to the proportion of Indigenous people (1.7 percent) within the general Vancouver population. Similar proportions were found in British Columbia's capital city, Victoria (Farley and Cotton).

Moreover, the social circumstances and prospects of Indigenous women are far from ideal. The International Think Tank on Reducing Health Disparities and Promoting Equity for Vulnerable Populations report says that "the colonial legacy of subordination of Indigenous people has resulted in a multiple jeopardy for Indigenous women who face individual and institutional discrimination, and disadvantages on the basis of race, gender and class (Adelson). Indigenous women recognize that racism in Canadian society and government institutions must stop in order for them to reach economic, social, gender, and racial parity. For example, regarding the widespread incidence of intimate partner violence within Indigenous communities, many women are emphatic that the broader context of institutionalized violence against all Indigenous people, regardless of gender, must first be addressed. This would include addressing all the failings within the justice and police systems, which appear to target Indigenous people, and in particular, the women.

Violence against Indigenous women is an overwhelming problem in Canada, which, for the most part, has remained ignored. Amnesty

International's 2014 *Annual Report* for Canada states that "Decades of government policy have impoverished and broken apart Indigenous families and communities, leaving many Indigenous women and girls at heightened risk of exploitation and attack." Topping Amnesty International's list of Canada's violations has always been the disproportionately high incidence and severity of violence against Indigenous women. The report, quoting numbers from Statistics Canada, also states that "the national homicide rate for Indigenous women is at least seven times higher than for non-Indigenous women."

Many people believe that revealing these findings was long overdue and that the overall Canadian consciousness is still suffering from collective (and selective) amnesia regarding violence towards Indigenous women. Educators, students, social work and health-care professionals, and Indigenous women themselves have, over the decades, begun to talk about these issues in both formal and informal discussions. They see it as one way of cultivating positive change. Many refuse to let these issues continue to be ignored and insist that the causes be identified, examined, and addressed. They continue to work at building a collective voice that asks, "How can we advocate for changes within Canadian society so it can no longer glibly tolerate, even foster, violence against Indigenous women?"

Indigenous women trail non-Indigenous women in all areas of well-being. They are in a constant struggle against factors of race, class, and gender, which are systemic within mainstream society, and they most often bear the burden of social and economic dysfunctions within their own communities.

SISTERS IN SPIRIT: THE CAMPAIGN RISES

The mid-to-late1940s saw the rise of a new social consciousness within the Canadian public. Finally, some changes regarding Indigenous-related problems would be forthcoming. A joint Senate and House of Commons committee was established in 1946 through the efforts of Indigenous advocates and their non-Indigenous allies. The committee undertook an in-depth investigation of the Indian Act, the first since its inception, which led to a series of amendments starting in 1951. Some of the more notable changes were:

- all registered Indians became Canadian citizens;
- in 1960, registered Indians were given the right to vote in federal elections;
- the Hawthorn Report of 1967 identified the First Peoples not only as Canadian citizens, but as Citizens Plus; and
- the control of federal Indian agents on reserve communities was reduced following the 151 amendments to the Indian Act. Beginning in the 1960s, Indian agents were removed from all communities across Canada.

Unemployment on reserves had always been problematic, but the change from subsistence to wage-based economies encouraged women to leave their reserves to look for employment in urban centres. Because movement restrictions had been lifted, this had become easier to do. They also sought better life opportunities through access to mainstream education. Communications were greatly improved, which led to the rise of public awareness on a number of issues. However, despite these legal and social changes, racism against Indigenous women did not abate; it continued to plague them, especially those moving to the cities.

The number of Indigenous women who suffered along their life journeys—those who may have gone missing or may have been murdered during these years—is not known. One woman stated, when she was asked about missing or murdered Indigenous women that "Indigenous women are constantly being victimized. Very little attention from police is given to missing Indigenous women. There is a mindset among many non-Native agencies that Indigenous people are nomadic and they are somewhere visiting, and not missing. This is not, and has not always been true."[9]

One case in particular drew national attention to the extent of the violence faced by Indigenous women in Canada: the racialized and sexualized murder of Helen Betty Osborne in The Pas, Manitoba. The most appalling aspect about this murder was that although Osborne was killed in 1971, a full sixteen years passed before her murderers were brought to trial. Also shocking was the fact that during those years, the towns people knew who her murderers were but did not inform the police. Furthermore, the RCMP investigation of the murder was mishandled to the extent that the province established the Aboriginal Justice Inquiry, which found that racism against Indigenous people, women in particular, was inherent within the justice system (Aboriginal Justice Inquiry of Manitoba).

The media flurry[10] associated with the Osborne case, late as it was by more than a decade and a half, served a constructive purpose in raising public awareness about what many Indigenous community members had already known for a long time: that violence against Indigenous women was readily ignored by Canada's police and public. Several other high-profile serial murder cases involving Indigenous women were to surface over the next few years.

The first began in the early 1990s when sex trade workers in Vancouver's notorious Downtown Eastside began noticing that for at least the past decade, many of their peers were simply vanishing and not heard from again. Their queries to police were largely futile, and they were beginning to believe that police were reluctant to act because most of the missing women were sex trade workers, drug addicts, and/or Indigenous. As the number of missing women kept rising, however, the media itself began to hear rumours, and the curiosity of those further outside the neighbourhood was piqued. In September 1998, a group of women, mainly Indigenous, confronted the Vancouver police and demanded that action be taken. Reporters began to ask questions, and soon the public was aware that there was, indeed, some truth about missing women in this area. In response, the joint Vancouver City Police-RCMP task force was initiated, but by this time, more than seventy women were officially missing.[11] In early 2002, nineteen years after the first woman was reported missing, Robert William Pickton was arrested and later charged with twenty-seven counts of murder. It is believed that at least one third of Pickton's victims were Indigenous. This was the largest serial killer investigation in Canadian history.

An area in British Columbia is known as the "Highway of Tears" because of the large number of Indigenous women who have gone missing or have been found murdered along this nearly eight-hundred-kilometre stretch of northern highway between Prince George and Prince Rupert. Suspicious activity began in the mid-1990s, when three fifteen-year-old Indigenous girls were found murdered in three separate instances. As the years went on, more and more young women travelling on that highway were later reported missing. The official count varies, and the unofficial count is much higher—some say at least forty went missing. Only one of these young women was non-Indigenous. The only entire family to have ever disappeared in Canada—an Indigenous family—did so in this area.

During recent years, the bodies or remains of many women have been found in rural communities near Edmonton, Alberta. Most of the victims were involved in the sex trade or drugs, or both; many were Indigenous. Project KARE was established by the RCMP in response to these murders with the main focus on the more recent deaths. Almost all sex trade workers in the Edmonton area have been co-operating with police in this initiative, which involves recording their personal information in case they become crime victims.

Although these are not, by far, the only cases in Canada regarding missing and murdered Indigenous women, it is important to note that media involvement helps concerned Indigenous groups and individuals mobilize police and other authorities into concrete action. Far too often, police simply view sex workers as unstable and disconnected from societal norms. By extension, this becomes a reason for ignoring extremely violent crimes against sex trade workers, most of whom are Indigenous (Farley and Cotton). Along with the media, non-Indigenous women's groups have given their voices as a conduit for the concerns of Indigenous women because the voices of Indigenous women by themselves are insufficient and inadequate to draw the attention required.

These are only a few examples of the extreme discrimination against Indigenous women and give reason to why Indigenous women are coming together to lobby outside groups for action to stop their loved ones from disappearing or being murdered. No longer will they tolerate being ignored by police and government authorities, who should be helping them get justice and real answers. No longer will they accept the ill-fated journeys of being pushed aside as they have been according to the dictates of the colonial forces of century-old Canadian institutions.

SISTERS IN SPIRIT: FROM CAMPAIGN TO REALITY

Many non-Indigenous organizations, particularly those involved in matters of social justice, are fully aware that Canada's justice system responds to violent crimes against Indigenous women in a vastly different way than to the same crimes against non-Indigenous women. The organizations that have helped the Native Women's Association of Canada (NWAC) in its push for the Sisters in Spirit campaign are mostly humanitarian, and include the Law Commission of Canada, Canadian Ecumenical Justice Initiatives (known as KAIROS),[12] Amnesty International, the Canadian Association of Elizabeth Fry Societies, and various groups within major churches.[13]

One KAIROS spokesperson, Ed Bianchi, stated that it first became officially involved upon learning about the increasing numbers of Indigenous women who were missing or had been murdered. He also knew that NWAC was very much involved in this specific area and that then-president Kukdookaa Terri Brown had suffered the loss of a close loved one to violent crime, one that is still unsolved. At KAIROS's next annual committee meeting, mutual networking began in this area, a relationship that is still ongoing.

Amnesty International is another organization that began working closely with NWAC. It, too, is fully aware that police respond with detailed and ongoing investigations for missing non-Indigenous women, in contrast to those for Indigenous women, which are too often treated lightly and not given proper credibility. Amnesty International was approached by NWAC President Brown, who, at the time, was in the process of pulling together a church group coalition to advocate and lobby for research funding regarding missing and murdered Indigenous women in Canada. She invited Amnesty International to be a part of this coalition as NWAC needed as many independent and credible voices as possible for support. By coincidence, Amnesty International was then launching a violence against women campaign. To the advantage of both agencies, the objectives and the timing of those objectives were closely related.

As well, Amnesty International had just hired two researchers for a project that would focus on the stories of the victims, as related by their close family members. The researchers were Giselle LaVallee and Beverley Jacobs. (In September 2004, Jacobs became NWAC's next president.) The resulting report, "*Stolen Sisters*," was released in October 2004; it raised considerable national awareness and received widespread international attention, which was encouraging. Ms. Jacobs presented an overview of the findings in 2005 to the United Nations Permanent Forum on Indigenous Issues in New York. At the time, many said that the *Stolen Sisters* report was the main reason for the federal government's approval of NWAC's funding request for the Sisters in Spirit initiative at that time.

The Sisters in Spirit campaign was also supported, both financially and otherwise, by the United, Anglican, Catholic churches, among others. The campaign ran from March 2004 to March 2005 and worked towards several distinct objectives:

- to estimate the number of Indigenous women who have died from violence, or suspected violence, and the number of missing Indigenous women in Canada;
- to put a face on every name that appeared on the lists of missing or murdered Indigenous women in the country;
- to document the life histories of all these Indigenous women;
- to draw more media attention and foster public concern regarding missing Indigenous women;
- to procure $10 million aimed at stopping violence against Indigenous women and to raise awareness of the specific issues faced by Indigenous women within Canadian society;
- to foster constructive action from all those who could make a difference in lowering the numbers of missing and murdered Indigenous women, including police, medical officials, courts, and Indigenous leaders; and
- to provide public education that would increase awareness of the underlying causes of violence against Indigenous women.

Others working with NWAC, in the meantime, did not wait for

government policy and legislative changes to address racialized and sexualized violence against Indigenous women but, instead, continued lobbying and advocacy efforts. Finally, in May 2005, the federal government announced that it would fund Sisters in Spirit in the amount of $5 million over five years. The contribution agreement between NWAC and the federal government, signed later that year, enabled NWAC to start building its internal capacity, work in collaboration with other Indigenous and non-Indigenous women's organizations, and continue advocating for the human rights of Indigenous women.

Sisters in Spirit supports initiatives that also work towards eradicating violence against Indigenous women. NWAC representatives speak at various functions to articulate the integral role of colonization to the displacement of Indigenous women and to work to educate the public about the ways in which colonization has been the root cause of missing and murdered women in Canada. The organization also strives to collaborate among all those who draw national, regional, and local attention to missing women and their grieving families, and to discuss how awareness itself can help guard against further disappearances and murders.

SISTERS IN SPIRIT: CONDUCTING THE ACTIVITIES

Because the driving motivation behind the Sisters in Spirit initiative is the eradication of violence against Indigenous women, which leads to their disappearance or murder, its overall goal is to reduce the related risks while increasing the safety of all Indigenous women in Canada. An anticipated side benefit is that gender equality will be improved; as well, the initiative expects that Indigenous women will be able to participate more fully in the various segments of Canadian society so that their economic, social, cultural, and political aspirations can be realized.

The foundation for achieving this overall goal is research. In this context, research entails the methodical and systematic collection and evaluation of information on the topic of racialized and sexualized violence against Indigenous women in Canada. It is extremely valuable in bringing about social change. Interested Indigenous community members and individual families and friends have been actively involved by providing first-hand information about the background and most recent activities of the victim. These individuals provide the Sisters in Spirit research team with a better understanding of the victim's real-life issues and experiences. The results of this research, once analyzed and placed, are used to educate others, affect public policy, promote community involvement, and, most importantly, make meaningful social change that will stop violence against Indigenous women. The process itself gives authority to Indigenous women's voices—voices that benefit all Indigenous people, women and men, by contributing to positive social changes in Canada. This type of problem solving is accomplished through what the Sisters in Spirit initiative calls its community-based research plan.

Because it is so important to preserve and maintain the various cultures of the Indigenous women involved, the entire research process is driven within a cultural framework that amalgamates cultural and ethical values. The Sisters in Spirit initiative has always captured these under the headings of caring, sharing, trust, and strength.

Qualitative information in the form of life histories, or case studies, shapes the main part of the data collection. This information is retrieved orally through a structured interview process with participating family members or friends. The goal of the process is to gain a better understanding of the circumstances, root causes, and emerging trends surrounding missing or murdered Indigenous women. Quantitative information, including statistical data and the numbers of actual missing or murdered women in Canada, is also vitally important and is included in the Sisters in Spirit research program. From this information, community action kits have been developed for use within the community agencies. These educational tools stress the importance of constantly keeping in touch with women who leave for any reason at all. Regarding the policy agenda of the Sisters in Spirit initiative, the research team has been working with participating families and the community to develop a strategy to initiate essential changes within various levels of government. A comprehensive strategic policy framework, developed for use at both the national and international levels, has been the basis for discussion on Indigenous women's human rights. The framework addresses the socio-economic, political, and legal status of Indigenous women, and the underlying factors that contribute to racialized and sexualized violence against them.

There are several objectives in the Sisters in Spirit initiative. Primarily, the initiative aim is to enhance public knowledge about the extent and global impact of racialized and sexualized violence against Indigenous women. In addition, the initiative seeks to dispel common myths and stereotypes about missing and murdered Indigenous women by presenting the realities of racialized and sexualized violence, as derived from key informant interviews.[14] Articulating the status of both Canadian and international law as they relate to either supporting or suppressing the violation of Indigenous women's human rights is another key component of the Sister in Spirit's work.

The following is a list of the benefits of the *Sisters in Spirit* initiative for Indigenous families and communities:

- Sisters in Spirit helps mobilize the caring power of community;
- Sisters in Spirit provides tools on its website to help all families of missing and murdered women navigate the justice system and other areas effectively;
- The initiative's website provides links to community organizations providing frontline service delivery in the area of violence against women, such as grieving support groups and victims' assistance;
- The Sisters in Spirit media strategy aims to reassure families that they are not forgotten and that their loved ones are presented fairly, without stereotype or prejudice;
- Sisters in Spirit research helps to validate the experience of families of missing and murdered women and to create much needed networks that promote healing and wellness;
- The Sisters in Spirit initiative targets root causes, identifies prevention strategies and risks, and assists in developing safety plans;
- In conjunction with other organizations, the Sisters in Spirit initiative works to increase trust and inspire hope that violence against Indigenous people, particularly against

Indigenous women, will end;
- The initiative helps families of missing and murdered women to have some peace of mind knowing that Sisters in Spirit is raising national awareness about their family members and the entire issue of racialized and sexualized violence against Indigenous women; and
- The *Sisters in Spirit* initiative takes into account the needs of the whole family and community.[15]

The Sisters in Spirit initiative is indebted to the participating families, for without their vision, strength, commitment, and efforts, it could not achieve its stated objectives. Indeed, without them, NWAC would not have been able to garner enough support to move the campaign into an actual initiative.

THE RESILIENCE OF WOMEN

Oriented towards the positive and not the negative, Sisters in Spirit acknowledges the resilience of many survivors and close friends of missing and murdered women. Their perceptions as survivors are valuable to all women, even to those who do not experience such trauma in their lives. The ways in which these women deal with grief and their motivation in moving forward in their lives are stories of personal power and immense courage.

A death by murder is extremely difficult to acknowledge and accept, and so is the situation of a close relative or friend who simply disappears, never to be heard from again. In a single moment, everything taken for granted about that person no longer exists, and, instead, feelings of emptiness, anguish, shock, vulnerability, helplessness, and, sometimes, guilt engulf and overwhelm the survivors.[16] The violence associated with most murders must be one of the worst feelings that survivors, especially parents, have to endure. Because the police and justice systems must be involved, the situation is exacerbated: the notorious relationship between Indigenous people and police has roots in historical practices that compound and perpetuate the damaging experiences of Indigenous people, including these kinds of experiences, within the Canadian justice system. Circumstances related to a death can further complicate matters for the family. For example, coroners decide when a body is released for burial—this may take weeks or even longer. During this time, family and friends have to wait for closure regarding the earthly remains of their loved ones. Also, because of the public nature of murder, media may be involved and its participation may be intrusive, inconsiderate, or marred by inaccurate and biased reporting.

Family members and friends dealing with murder are at risk of posttraumatic stress disorder and need coping strategies to deal with their grief. Some, particularly parents, question their spiritual beliefs because of being unable to adequately account for such extreme and drastic loss (Thompson and Vardaman). Survivors need support. Almost anyone can be involved by listening non-judgmentally and with companionship (Clegg). One survivor stated that what was not helpful was impatience and irritation about what was perceived as a lengthy grieving process; in reality, families and friends never get over the murder of a loved one. Although each person grieves in different ways, almost all experience feelings of loneliness and isolation, and find that talking about their loved one in a caring and trusting environment is very helpful to them.

Some women talk about how they also become a victim of the murder by "giving in" to grief and not progressing with their own lives. They come to understand that keeping an eye on the future is important and that they have to be determined to move ahead. One woman stated that she keeps focused by pursuing what she knows to be right, maintaining a positive attitude, having faith in God and/or the Creator, seeking and benefitting from counselling, and fulfilling her own responsibility towards her other children and her friends.

There are elements in women's lives to describe the attributes of those who successfully cope with the stress and adversity that comes from the murder of a loved one. Some things to consider are:

- the family and community environments in which the survivor was raised, especially the extent to which significant nurturing and supportive networks were present;
- the number, intensity, and duration of stressful or adverse circumstances that each woman faced, especially at an early

age, and how she was able to deal with these; and
- each woman's internal characteristics, temperament, and internal locus of control or mastery (Shapiro).

"Locus of control" refers to a person's perception of what are the main causes of life events (Graves). Simply, does a woman believe that she controls her own destiny or that it is controlled by others or by fate? There are two kinds of locus of control:

- internal—an individual believes that her behaviour is guided by her personal decisions and efforts; outcomes are contingent on what she does;
- external—the person believes that her behaviour is guided by fate, luck, or other external circumstances, such as the actions and behaviours of others; outcomes are contingent on what others do and on events outside her personal control.

These elements play a role in the extent of a person's resilience, adaptability, and ability to meet challenges (Brown and Kulig). One Indigenous educator, Eber Hampton, says this about resilience:

> The Europeans took our land, our lives, and our children like the winter snow takes the grass. The loss is painful but the seed lives in spite of the snow. In the fall of the year, the grass dies and drops its seed to lie hidden under the snow. Perhaps the snow thinks the seed has vanished, but it lives on hidden, or blowing in the wind, or clinging to the plant's propensity to progress. How does the acorn unfold into an oak? Deep inside itself it knows—and we are not different. We know deep inside ourselves the pattern of life. (31)

SISTERS IN SPIRIT: ONE WOMAN'S ACCOUNT

The following is a narrative[17] from one mother whose worst nightmares were confirmed—her daughter's DNA was found at the infamous pig farm in Port Coquitlam, British Columbia. This mother last heard from her daughter through a Christmas card in 1998. On 17 May 2002, years later, a policeman knocked on her door and told her that the search was over—the remains of one victim were positively identified as those belonging to her missing daughter. This mother was asked what kept up her strength, day by day, and what kept her from giving up on life:

It is the spirit within that keeps me going. I myself did not grow up with my mother, and I know that my granddaughters have to grow up without theirs. I can relate to their pain on, say, Mother's Day—when I was in boarding school, making things for my mother such as a card with roses or other flowers on it, they were for my mom but she couldn't get them. My stepmother was cold towards me, and when I'd come home for summers and after my dad went to work in the mornings (he maintained the roads), I would go up and spend most of my days up in the hills. I knew which berries to eat, like cranberries, raspberries, chokecherries, and Saskatoons. There was spring water there that I would drink. Back then you could drink this water.

My grandchildren were in foster care already, before their mom died. In 1998, November 18, the last time I spoke with her, she had put them into temporary care, but I told her to wait until the 20th when my practicum was over and I could take care of them. This was in Vancouver. When I did call her on the 20th, their dad had already taken them to another city on the other side of the country. My grandchildren are now in a good foster home, and once a month I talk to them. The foster mom is now okay with me having their phone number, but at first she wasn't because she was afraid that I would give it out to the dad, as she is afraid of his violence. There was a lot of trust that had to be built, and that is still going on.

That is what helps me, that they would know I love them. In spite of them not having a mother, the next step is to have a grandmother, and that is me. They are starting to build up trust with me.

When I first found out what happened to my daughter, I took time off work in 2002 and went to a psychologist. She did help me, but the greatest psychologist was my sister. I had gone, in January 2003, to visit her and she was crying. When I asked her what was wrong, she said something like, "that SOB[18] *not only took my niece, but he's taking my sister, too." This is when I woke up. I realized that he was taking me as a victim, too, and that I was letting him still be a perpetrator to my family.*

This really helped me on my healing journey; my sister is my psychologist. I had to realize that he was taking my life, as well. At first, there was a point that I didn't want to live, I wasn't suicidal, but I didn't want to ever wake up because at night, I was flying in spirit. I would get up and feed myself and do some other things, but I really wanted to go back to where I'd go at nights. I would go back to where I came from, my power place, back in the hills, where the spring was, and the fresh water was running, and where the berries were food for me.

My daughter was there, too. She was so healthy, so alive.

In the process of seeing the psychologist, I trusted her enough to tell her about where I'd fly to at nights. She said that I needed to be reprogrammed and helped me with that even though I didn't want to do that; it was my time of joy. Now I don't do that anymore as an escape. Now, it just happens and I don't always go back to those hills.

I go elsewhere, and every human being can do that, too. Going into a deep, deep meditation, I'd see my body lying there. I don't have to carry that body when I go away, but when you come back, you feel the heaviness, like a big thump. It's a beautiful light body when you go away like that, and my daughter was able to do that before she left. There were times when I used to feel her, and I would have to tell her to get back because of the "walk- in." Even though you are connected to your body with a long silver cord, another spirit can jump into your body if you stay away too long.

I had befriended a local city policeman who understood my flights, and he promised that he would find an answer to me about my daughter, as the Vancouver police weren't doing too much. He warned me that I may not get the answer I wanted, but that I would get an answer. It was a short time later, on May 17, 2002, that I heard the knock on my door from a New Westminster RCMP officer with very bad news.

I am not going to let Pickton take my life. The victimization stops here.

Through a journalist from this city, I found another lady who was in the same situation as I am—her daughter was found at the pig farm, too. We're in contact at least two or three times a week through e-mail; when I feel down, I write to her, and I feel better after I speak with her. We know we're there for each other, for support.

When that happened to my daughter, our family split up, and it's now all about my two granddaughters who are now eleven and thirteen years old. They will decide what they want to do with their mother's remains. By the time the trial is over, and after he decides to appeal, this can go on for another five years, and by then my older granddaughter will be an adult and she can make decisions.

This is really strange, something that happened to me recently. Where I work, a psychic came in who was really well-known at one time. He could tell that I had a deep pain I was carrying around with me, and I told him about it in confidence. "You're going to have to release that man," he said. "There's nothing you can do or say that can hurt him—and your thoughts are going to destroy you. Go out in the bush and the trees, walk in the water. God's punishment is a lot harsher than you can ever give." So about a week ago, I went with a friend to a nearby park and I found a place where there were trees surrounding me. There, I prayed and then went into the water to release this entity. I feel a lot better now, and when I got back to the car, my friend said that I looked so peaceful. Now I know that that man, the psychic, came into my life for a reason and that was to help me heal even more.

There is one big thing I need to say: when people and the press are so discriminating against sex-trade workers, my thoughts and feelings are that they are women with a deep, deep, great inner strength. If I lived my life half as courageously as they do, only then can I consider myself a real woman. My daughter went to work to provide for her children, but she got caught up in the drugs.

In 1995, my daughter gave me a portrait of herself when she lived in another city, and I see that she still smiles at me. She's my greatest support system, and she's in Spirit.

CONCLUSION

As Canada's most rapidly growing female population,[19] Indigenous females are still experiencing difficult social conditions and a deprived economic reality, which has plagued them over the past several centuries. This continuing historic marginalization has resulted in a shocking statistic, as related by the Toronto Metropolitan Action Committee on Violence Against Women and Children: "Up to 75 percent of survivors of sexual assaults in Indigenous communities are young women under 18 years old. Fifty percent of those are under 14 years old and almost 25 percent are younger than 7 years old" (METRAC). Violence against Indigenous women only because they are Indigenous (racialized violence) and because they are women (sexualized and/or genderized violence) has been ongoing in Canada for many generations. The Indian Act paved the way in formalizing the societal attitudes and behaviours that condone, accept, and perpetuate the marginalization of Indigenous women and, ultimately, their victimization.

Many Indigenous women become easy targets for dangerous and violent men because their poverty forces them to live in unsafe situations with few viable options. These men, themselves products of Canadian society, are aware, whether on a conscious level or not, of Indigenous women's vulnerability and their lack of a significant voice and value within society. They are also fully aware of the reticence of law enforcement agencies to take action, even very serious crimes are committed against Indigenous women. Such violent men often target a specific social class or type, those that they perceive to be the most defenceless.

It is through this adversity that Indigenous women have come together. Their need for concrete answers and a strong desire for justice have resulted in common goals and understandings. They seek allies in the non-Indigenous community, who have become aware that the type of thinking that normalizes violence against vulnerable populations, particularly against Indigenous women, is present in Canada. They recognize that immediate action is needed and that previous and current programs and policies have produced inadequate results for Indigenous women.

These are the circumstances into which Sisters in Spirit was born, originally as a campaign, then as a full initiative. Indigenous people whose female family members went missing or were later found murdered began the process by networking and building camaraderie; others—most of whom did not share this particular trauma in their lives—have joined to show their support. Together, they built a collective resolve to take constructive and immediate action that would reduce future incidents and deal firmly with those found responsible. This group, perhaps loosely joined together in a formal sense, is woven together by a deep understanding that effective strategies must target the cause of the problem, the attitude of non-Indigenous Canadians—a destructive and firmly entrenched attitude within mainstream Canada that allows and encourages the targeting of Indigenous women for extreme violence and murder. The same attitude permits Indigenous women to drift away from society and its systems without notice—sometimes for great lengths of time, times in which despair and death might have actually overtaken them. Sisters in Spirit and its allies believe that the elimination of this condescending and pejorative attitude will eradicate sexualized and racialized violence, and, indeed all types of violence against Indigenous women.

Sisters in Spirit continues its work in helping to establish and maintain networks for surviving family members and friends. It has facilitated several circle-type gatherings in which participants meet and talk in a trusting and caring environment. Many family members and friends—once so isolated because of the racialized and sexualized violence that so deeply and permanently touched their lives—are finding ways to reach out to other survivors and to give and receive encouragement and hope. The network making up Sisters in Spirit, including those women who specifically work from the NWAC, is finding creative ways to cultivate the internal resilience that rises above the suffering brought on by the murders and disappearances of loved ones.

No doubt Sisters in Spirit will continue to undergo transformations as it pursues its goals and as other groups or individuals become involved. Canada's Indigenous community has been suffering from having its women go missing or found murdered for at least 180 years,[20] and those involved in Sisters in Spirit find that the time is ripe—indeed, long overdue—to rid the country of the bigotry and cultural bias that target Indigenous people in general and Indigenous women in particular.

Originally published in Restoring the Balance: First Nations Women, Community, and Culture, *Eds. G. G. Valaskakis, M. D. Stout, and A. Guimond. Winnipeg: University of Manitoba Press. 125-148. Reprinted with permission.*

ENDNOTES

[1]This concept consists of any number of suppositions about humankind's role within the universe and the resulting exchanges of humans with other living and non-living creation. As well, a worldview holds a perception about how time passes and its bearing on all relationships. Another important element includes a concept of the essence of human nature and assigns fundamental motives to the way humans should, and do, behave. These, in turn, shape and uphold a people's ideology, which is their belief in what constitutes perfect or ideal human interchanges with one another and with nature.

[2]Sometimes men abandoned their "New World" families and returned home for good.

[3]Aboriginal women in the Fur Trade society were considered the ideal wives. They provided an essential economic link with their home and other Aboriginal nations; they were skilled labourers in the construction of the supplies necessary for survival in what Europeans called the "wilderness," and they were loving wives and mothers in a world characterized by its harshness and loneliness. Changes in the nineteenth century, however, reversed their role; sexual exploitation and racism served to increasingly alienate them from the new society developing in western Canada.

[4]These were *The Act for Civilizing and Enfranchising Indians* (1859) and *An Act for the Gradual Civilization of the Indian Tribes of* Canada (1868). The very titles of these articulate their motivation and goals.

[5]This was done by defining a "person" as an individual "other than an Indian."

[6]"Status Indians" could acquire full Canadian citizenship by severing their ties (culture, tradition, rights to land, etc.) to their home communities; the government used the Indian Act as a control while those on the Indian registry were being assimilated through

enfranchisement. The 1960 change to allow "status Indians" the right to vote in federal elections was the first time that Canada acknowledged citizenship for Indigenous people without the condition that they assimilate into mainstream society.

[7]For example, Duncan Campbell Scott, deputy superintendent of the Indian Department in 1920, stated that "I want to get rid of the Indian problem ... Our objective is to continue until there is not a single Indian in Canada that has not been absorbed into the body politic, and there is no Indian question" (Smith 38).

[8]The estimated increase of HIV infections is 91 percent during the three years between 1996 and 1999 alone. On 5 March 2004, the Canadian Aboriginal AIDS Network issued a press release, "Aboriginal Women Continue to Face Major Challenges as International Women's Day Approaches," which included these figures.

[9]Anonymous contribution. Nova Scotia Native Women's Association, *Sisters in Spirit* Promotion/Consultation Session, Millbrook, NS. 7 Feb. 2006.

10These included the works of Lisa Priest and the Aboriginal Justice Inquiry of Manitoba.

[11]Officially, the issue of a large number of sex workers missing from Vancouver's Downtown Eastside came to public attention in July 1999. This came in the form of a poster offering $100,000 from the Vancouver Police Department and the Attorney General of British Columbia for information leading to those person(s) involved. The American television program America's Most Wanted aired a segment on this shortly afterwards, but without results.

[12]KAIROS is a faith-based ecumenical movement for justice and peace; it consists of 100 communities spread across the country. Its Aboriginal component began in August 2001. See www.kairoscanada.org/e/index.asp.

[13]These include eleven churches and church organizations, including the Anglican, Catholic, United, Christian Reformed, Mennonite, Presbyterian, and the Religious Society of Friends (Quakers) churches.

[14]A "key informant" is anyone who is in a position to know the community as a whole or the specific portion that relates to the issue.

[15]These objectives are taken directly from the contribution agreement signed between Status of Women Canada and the Native

Women's Association of Canada.

[16]Amick Resnick Kirkpatrick, Fact Sheet (Medical University of South Carolina, National Crime Victims Research and Treatment Center).

[17]Telephone conversation, 14 June 2006. Name of interviewee withheld by request.

[18]The interviewee is referring to Robert William Pickton.

[19]"The Aboriginal female population grew by 20 percent between 2006 and 2011, more than four times the growth of the non-Aboriginal female population, at 4.8 percent. In those five years, among the Aboriginal female population who reported a single identity, growth was highest for First Nations (+23 percent), Inuit (+18 percent), and Métis (+17 percent) females, similar to the pattern for the Aboriginal male population" (Statistics Canada, "Aboriginal Identity").

[20]An Algonquin artist, Janet Kaponoichin, depicts the true story of an Algonquin girl who was raped and murdered by British soldiers during the building of the Rideau Canal in 1827. This painting hangs in the Maniwaki Cultural Centre in Maniwaki, QC.

WORKS CITED

Aboriginal Justice Implementation Commission. *Final Report: Chapter 13: Revenue Generation.* Winnipeg: Government of Manitoba, 2001. Print.

Aboriginal Justice Inquiry of Manitoba. *The Deaths of Helen Betty Osborne & John Joseph Harper. Report of the Aboriginal Justice Inquiry of Manitoba (Vol. II).* Winnipeg: Aboriginal Justice Inquiry of Manitoba, 1991. Print.

Adelson, N. "Reducing Health Disparities and Promoting Equity for Vulnerable Populations." Presentation at Reducing Health Disparities and Promoting Equity for Vulnerable Populations. International Think Tank, Ottawa, ON, 2003. Print.

Amnesty International Canada. *Violence against Indigenous Women and Girls in Canada: A summary of Amnesty International's Concerns and Call to Action. Amnesty International.* Amnesty, 2014. Web. 20 Apr. 2016.

Brown, D., and J. Kulig. "The Concept of Resilience: Theoretical

Lessons from Community Research." *Health and Canadian Society* 4.1 (1996): 29–50. Print.

Canada. Public Health Agency of Canada. *Diabetes in Canada: Facts and Figures from a Public Health Perspective. Chapter Six: Diabetes Among First Nations, Inuit, and Métis Populations*. Government of Canada, 15 December 2011. Web. 20 April 2016.

Canadian Aboriginal AIDS Network (CAAN). "Aboriginal Women Continue to Face Major Challenges as International Women's Day Approaches." CAAN, 2016. Web. 20 Apr. 2016.

Canadian Population Health Initiative. *Improving the Health of Canadians*. Ottawa: Canadian Institute for Health Information, 2004. Print.

Clegg, J. "Death, Disability, and Dogma." *Philosophy, Psychiatry, and Psychology* 10.1 (2003): 57-73. Print.

Farley, M. Lynne, J. and A. J. Cotton. "Prostitution in Vancouver: Violence and the Colonization of First Nations Women." *Transcultural Psychiatry* 42.2 (2005): 242–271. Print.

Graves, T. D. "Urban Indian Personality and the 'Culture of Poverty.'" *American Ethnologist* 1.1 (1974): 72–73. Print.

Hampton, E. "Towards a Redefinition of Indian Education." *First Nations Education in Canada: The Circle Unfolds*. Eds. M. Battiste and J. Barman. Vancouver: University of British Columbia Press, 1995. 5-46. Print.

Leipert, B. D. and L. Reutter. Developing Resilience: How Women Maintain Their Health in Northern Geographically Isolated Settings." *Qualitative Health Research* 15.1 (2005): 49–65. Print.

Mehrabadi, A., et al. "The Cedar Project: A Comparison of HIV-Related Vulnerabilities amongst Young Aboriginal Women Surviving Drug Use and Sex Work in Two Canadian Cities." *International Journal of Drug Policy* (2007): 1-10. *Research Gate*. Web. 20 Apr. 2016.

Metropolitan Action Committee on Violence against Women and Children (METRAC). "Sexual Assault Fact Sheet." *METRAC Action on Violence*, n.d. Web. 20 Apr. 2016.

Priest, Lisa. *Conspiracy of Silence*. Toronto: McClelland and Stewart, 1989. Print.

Shapiro, E. R. "Family Bereavement and Cultural Diversity: A Social Developmental Perspective." *Family Process* 35.3 (1996): 317–322. Print.

Sinclair, Judge C. M. Foreword. *Black Eyes All of the Time*. Eds. Anna McGillivray and Brenda Comaskey. Toronto: University of Toronto Press, 1999. ix-x. Print.

Smith, D. *The Seventh Fire: The struggle for Aboriginal government*. Toronto: Key Porter Books, 1993. Print.

Statistic Canada. "Aboriginal Identity." *Statistics Canada*. Government of Canada, 2015. Web. 20 Apr. 2016.

Statistics Canada. *Women in Canada: A Gender-Based Statistical Report 5th ed. Statistics Canada*. Government of Canada, July, 2011. Web. 20 Apr. 2016.

Thompson, M. P. and P. J. Vardaman. "The Role of Religion in Coping with the Loss of a Family Member to Homicide." *Journal for the Scientific Study of Religion* 36.1 (1997): 36-50. Print

Van Kirk, S. *Many Tender Ties: Women in Fur-Trade Society, 1670–1870*. Winnipeg: Watson & Dwyer Publishing Ltd, 1980. Print.

"Women in First Nations Politics." *CBC News*, 22 Nov. 2005. Web. 20 Apr. 2016.

II.

THE ONGOING ERASURE OF INDIGENOUS WOMEN

5.
The Unmournable Body of Cindy Gladue

On Corporeal Integrity and Grievability

CAROLINE FIDAN TYLER DOENMEZ

THE CANADIAN JUSTICE SYSTEM is one of the institutional frameworks in which Indigenous women frequently struggle to be afforded adequate protection and representation. One of the most egregious recent examples of this was the case of Cindy Gladue, a thirty-six-year-old Cree woman and mother of three teenage girls. On March 18, 2015, a nearly all male and entirely non-Native jury acquitted white trucker Bradley Barton for her murder. Gladue, a sex worker, had gone to a hotel in Edmonton, Alberta, with Barton on June 22, 2011. The next morning Barton "discovered" her in the bathtub, submerged in her own blood ("Bradley Barton Found Not Guilty"). The medical examiner at the trial testified that she had died from massive blood loss due to a four-inch wound in her vagina, caused by a sharp object. However, Barton's lawyer stated that his client "didn't mean to harm Gladue, and that the wound was caused accidentally by ... rough sex" (Johnston and Lilwall). Despite admitting to causing the laceration that resulted in Gladue's death, the jury found Barton not guilty of first-degree murder and chose not to convict him of the lesser offence of manslaughter. Barton walked free. Many aspects of the trial undermined the unambiguous and startling brutality that Gladue was subjected to and further violated her bodily integrity, including the unprecedented use of her preserved vagina as an exhibit in the courtroom. What logics were at work that could explain the court's decision to exonerate Barton, and to condone the continued mutilation of her body? What makes it possible to portray Gladue as someone who consented to this violence?

UNMOURNABLE BODIES, UNGRIEVABLE LIVES

Following the Charlie Hebdo killings in Paris in early January 2015, Teju Cole wrote a piece titled "Unmournable Bodies." The chapter contrasts the outrage that the Western world exhibits over (white) deaths caused by Muslim extremists with the apathy it displays towards other instances of extreme violence, such as the killings of Palestinian children in Gaza or the recent massacres in the Central African Republic. He writes about the "consensus on mournable bodies," a concept that speaks to Judith Butler's 2004 book, *Precarious Life: The Powers of Mourning and Violence*. In it, she writes: "The question that preoccupies me in the light of recent global violence is, Who counts as human? Whose lives count as lives? And, finally, What *makes for a grievable life*?" (20) Later, she asks:

> What, then, is the relation between violence and those lives considered as "unreal"? Does violence effect that unreality? Does violence take place on the condition of that unreality? If violence is done against those who are unreal, then, from the perspective of violence, it fails to injure or negate those lives since those lives are already negated. (33)

I wish to extend Cole's and Butler's thinking on "unmournable bodies" and "ungrievable-unreal lives" to the crisis of the missing and murdered Indigenous women and girls in Canada. Despite the sheer quantity and brutality of these crimes against Indigenous women, various state institutions have responded with overwhelming indifference. This indifference is sporadically interrupted by either fleeting empathy (Simpson) or active antagonism, including the dismissal of this crisis as simply an issue of "crime." This stance blatantly disrespects the concern, the outrage, and the important data of Indigenous leaders, victims' families, and organizations. The obstinate passivity of the political and legal institutions, I will argue, is tied to colonial conceptions of Indigenous women and girls' lives as inevitably degenerate and disposable, which is rationalized by the projection of criminality onto their bodies. Moreover, this "unmournability" can be viewed through Lisa

Stevenson's formulation of a Canadian state that simultaneously disavows and anticipates Indigenous death.

AWAITING INDIGENOUS DEATH

Stevenson's book *Life Beside Itself: Imagining Care in the Canadian Arctic,* examines regimes of care imposed on the Inuit in Nunavut by the Canadian state. First, she looks at the state's attempt to curb the tuberculosis epidemic of the 1950s and 1960s, and then juxtaposes it with contemporary suicide-prevention campaigns. In looking at what she calls the "psychic life of biopolitics" (28) she notes the way in which the expectation of death is folded into these ostensibly benevolent projects, wherein "caregivers exhort Inuit to live while simultaneously expecting them to die" (7). She also includes a fruitful discussion of what it means for the state to "have" a dead Indian, to collect it as a statistic, while being indifferent to the individual whom that statistic represents. Although the state of Canada does not, exactly, "exhort" Indigenous women to live, it certainly *postures* as being invested in their survival, as testament to the state's "caring." However, the Harper government's intransigent refusal to co-operate with calls for an inquiry signals its apathy. Moreover, the federal government's efforts to ameliorate the problem concentrate more power and money in the hands of state actors, such as the police forces, while cutting funds to the Native Women's Association of Canada (NWAC) and other Indigenous organizations. By refusing to collaborate with Indigenous peoples on this issue *on their own terms* and take their suggestions seriously, the state ultimately fails to engage with the crisis in a meaningful or productive way. As Stevenson writes, this creates "a simultaneous expectancy—the sense in which we, as bureaucrats and citizens of a bureaucratic regime, are awaiting the deaths we are indifferently trying to prevent" ("The Psychic Life of Biopolitics" 593). This awaiting and indifference depend on the historical and ongoing criminalization of Indigenous female bodies, which casts them as belonging to spaces of ineluctable violence that erases the state's role in producing their vulnerability. In this way, the state is always waiting for more Indigenous women to disappear, not only to add to its database and numbers but also to keep capturing them within an imagined space of turpitude and frailty, seized then in death as a statistic. Indigenous women and girls are always on the brink of death for a state that requires their disappearance to legitimize its ongoing acts of dispossession and the evasion of their own history—a history that structures the very problem that they supposedly become.

A BRIEF HISTORY OF THE CRIMINALIZATION OF INDIGENOUS WOMEN

One of the gendered processes of the settler colonial project in Canada has been the attempt of the federal government to undercut the power and status of Indigenous women. One of the most prominent legislative initiatives in this regard was the *Indian Act* of 1876. This act made Indigenous men property owners and heads of households, which legally erased the Indigenous status of any woman who married a white man. The *Indian Act* defines "Indians" as: "*First.* Any male person of Indian blood reputed to belong to a particular band; *Secondly.* Any child of such person; *Thirdly.* Any woman who is or was lawfully married to such person" (Canada, "An Act to Amend"). This bill disenfranchised thousands of Indigenous women and severed their connections to their communities, cultures, and lands, rendering them acutely isolated and vulnerable if they had married non-status or non-Native men. The loss of membership within Indigenous, reserve communities extended then to their children. This assimilationist policy, meant to reduce the number of Indigenous peoples, left the women who "married out" entirely dependent on their husbands; they were geographically cast out of their communities *by law*, often resulting in crises when they faced abusive relationships or divorce. The result of this legislation, as Jabobs and Williams argue "was a major disruption of traditional kinship systems, matrilineal descent patterns, and matrilocal, post-marital residency patterns. Furthermore, it embodied and imposed the principle that Indian women and their children, like European women and their children, would be subject to their fathers and husbands."

Although this law was amended with Bill C-31 in the case of *Lovelace vs. Canada* in 1985, this state policy has continued to affect Indigenous communities as they grapple with questions of membership, identity, land, and relations. The imposed androcentric nature of the law undermined, if not obliterated, women's autonomy and traditional roles and left many of them on the margins of society. This is a critical example of how the Canadian legal system has functioned to erase Indigenous women, whose political and life-giving power has historically threatened the settler colonial project.

Media coverage has often played a potent role in contributing to the perception of the inherent criminality of the Indigenous female body while rendering structural violence opaque. According to Sherene Razack, this expectation can be dated back centuries: "Newspaper records of the nineteenth century indicate that there was a conflation of Aboriginal woman and prostitute and an accompanying belief that when they encountered violence, Aboriginal women simply got what they deserved. Police seldom intervened, even when the victims' cries could be clearly heard" (130). More recently, as Jennifer England writes, Indigenous women have been rendered either invisible when they suffer violence or hyper-visible as criminals in media reports, where implicit links are made between their indigeneity and their "deviant" behaviour (England 315). Yasmin Jiwani and Mary Lynn Young examine this same hyper-visibility of missing and murdered Indigenous women in Vancouver's Downtown Eastside in the plethora of toxic media reports that paint them as morally dubious individuals. One example of this was the coverage of the murder of April Roech, who was discursively associated with "every" missing woman: "She had much in common with the women on that list. She was battling a drug problem as were others. She was known to work as a prostitute, as were they" (896). Jiwani goes on to describe the ideological function of this tone: "the coverage conforms to these societal constructions, invoking and re-inscribing popular stereotypes of these women as being hypersexual, thereby minimizing the reality of the violence done to their bodies ... such stereotypes reinforce middle-class notions of propriety and hegemonic femininity" (896). The media projects degeneracy outwards and onto the Indigenous populations, cementing a sense of distance from such violence and their lack of involvement in generating it. Despite these instances of hyper-visibility, Indigenous women are more frequently rendered invisible in the numerous instances when their cases do not make the news. For example, the "Highway of Tears"—a stretch of road in British Columbia where approximately forty Indigenous women and girls have gone missing—did not garner sustained attention from the police or media until the disappearance of a white woman, Nicole Hoar, in 2002 (Human Rights Watch 37).

Indigenous women are frequently criminalized in their interactions with police and legally disappeared into prisons. Despite making up 3 percent of the female population of Canada, they constitute 34 percent of women in federal correctional facilities ("Aboriginal Women One Third"). This trend is growing progressively dire: between 2002 and 2012, the number of Indigenous women in prison increased by 97 percent, according to a study by the Department of Justice (Rennie). The 1991 Aboriginal Justice Inquiry concludes that the overrepresentation of Indigenous peoples in the criminal justice system has deep historical and social roots; it also emphasizes systemic discrimination at all levels as a contributing factor to the disproportionate incarceration rates. A 2013 Human Rights Watch report expands on the deeply internalized discriminatory practices against Indigenous women and girls in British Columbia by police forces. The report found, for example, that Indigenous women who are intoxicated and lack transportation home are often incarcerated, whereas white women in the same position are likely to be driven home by police (47). Moreover, even when Indigenous families went to police officers for help locating missing loved ones, they often reported experiencing bias and dismissal. One former police officer, referring to the Highway of Tears, was quoted saying: "The native girls on the highway—I was up there. If they're natives, nobody gives a shit" (37). Indigenous sex workers who report being assaulted are often transmuted from victims into criminals, when police view them as the subject of an investigation (Sayers, "Statement"). The "assumption of criminality" has also been extensively documented in Wally Oppal's report on the missing and murdered women in Vancouver's Downtown Eastside, in which he lambasts the conduct of the local police officers, noting their tendency to blame victims, and concludes that "the initiation and conduct of the missing and murdered women investigations were a blatant failure" due to "gross systemic inadequacies and repeated patterns of error" (3). He underscores the role of "systemic bias, particularly in the form of negative stereotyping" (58) in these cases. These examples exhibit deeply entrenched patterns of discrimination and subsequent criminalization of Indigenous women.

Having established this abbreviated overview of the ways in which the media, the justice system, and the law have disappeared Indigenous women over time, I now want to consider how these colonial logics of Indigenous, female bodies played out in Gladue's trial, and how, to quote Sherene Razack, there was such "small a chance ... of [her] entering the court's and Canadian society's consciousness as a person" (96).

THE WHITE MALE PREROGATIVE TO SEX

Many elements of the trial brought into stark relief the ways in which Gladue's killer was afforded more humanity and empathy than she was, despite his many inconsistencies and dubious claims. Firstly, Barton maintained that the fatal wound inside of Gladue's vagina was caused from "rough *consensual* sex" (Johnston and Lilwall, emphasis added). However, toxicology reports showed that Gladue's blood alcohol content was four times over the legal driving limit, making it impossible for her to consent (Brake). Moreover, Barton lied about his connection to Gladue: in his 911 call, he reported an "unknown woman" ("Bradley Barton Found Not Guilty") dead in his bathtub, although video footage from the hotel showed Gladue and Barton entering and exiting his hotel room the day of and the day before her murder. He also claimed in court that Gladue had "told him she was menstruating" (Dimanno) when he first made her bleed by forcing his fist into her vagina. The jury was not told about the violent pornography on Barton's laptop, which provincial court Judge Ferne LeRevered labeled "disturbing pornography" showing "extreme penetration and torture" (Cormier, "Crown Seeks"). This information was never brought to the trial, as the judge ruled it had been obtained illegally. Despite substantial evidence of Barton's mendacity and perturbing proclivity for sadistic pornography, the proceedings of the trial afforded him the benefit of the doubt and reinscribed the right of the white male to "rough sex," even when that sex was so violent it came at the cost of life. This ranking of white male pleasure above the very existence of the Indigenous woman unequivocally casts Gladue's body as unworthy of life itself and then as ungrievable.

THE SANCTITY OF THE COLONIAL CONTRACT

Sherene Razack's groundbreaking piece "Gendered Racial Violence and Spatialized Justice: The Murder of Pamela George," provides haunting parallels with Gladue's story. Razack's work explores the brutal killing of Pamela George—a twenty-eight-year-old Sauteaux mother of three from the Sakimay Indian Reserve—who had moved to Regina and began working in the sex trade after struggling financially. On April 18, 1995, after duplicitously luring her into their truck, two college-aged white men sexually assaulted and beat her to death. Despite their later claims in court that they had simply been drunk, one of George's killers, Alex Ternowetsky, had reportedly told a friend that "she deserved it. She was an Indian" (Roberts). Razack analyzes how the violence that George was subjected to was essentially unaccounted for in her trial: it was recast as an inevitable outcome of her race and the geographical space that she occupied as someone off her reserve, vulnerabilized into "dirty" spaces of transactional, unclean, and unsafe sex work. In both cases, the idea of the contract as inherent to sex work was vital to diminishing the violence enacted on her body. Razack writes:

> The naturalization of violence is sustained by the legal idea of contract.... Because she consented to provide sexual services, the violence became more permissible. The moment of the violence is contained within the moment of the contract and there can be no history or context, for example, the constraints on her choice and the historical conditions under which the bargain was made. (144)

Myths about autonomy and individual choice cast victims, such as George and Gladue, as willing participants in the violence that robs them of their own lives. Since sex workers engage in an exchange of services for money, they are then seen to be responsible for what happens to them next. Razack summarizes: "Prostitutes are considered in law to have consented to whatever violence is visited upon them" (126). In the Gladue case, great emphasis was placed on the consensual nature of the sexual torture that resulted in her death, although, as previously stated, records showed that the alcohol content in her blood level would have made it impossible for her to consent. In response to this, Barton's defense argued that Gladue was a heavy drinker (Kaye), again assigning blame to the victim for the violence that was inflicted on her. Moreover, Justice Robert Graesser told the jury that Gladue's consent on the first night that she and Barton had sexual relations "could be used to support a finding of honest but mistaken belief in consent" on the second night (Cormier, "Crown Seeks"). Razack states in relation to George that "While George was to be judged for engaging in prostitution, the men were not to be judged for having purchased her services. Put more plainly, her activity was a crime which carried the risks of violence, while theirs was a contract" (152). Settler male violence becomes legitimized through the rationality of the contract and the legal system's subsequent deference to this concept. Critiquing the Gladue case, scholars and activists Sarah Hunt and Naomi Sayers argue in a piece for *The Globe and Mail* that

> The criminalization of prostitution conspired to make the victim's sex work experience the origin of the violence she faced instead of placing fault in the violent actions of the assailant. If the defence concedes that Mr. Barton committed the acts that contributed to Cindy's death, the fact that money changed hands does not magically nullify the act. An acquittal should not have been an option. (2)

The weight placed on the theoretical neutrality and autonomy of the contract shifts the criminal nature of the event onto the sex worker. This manoeuvre diminishes her suffering and personhood and exculpates the perpetrator, which undermines the grievability of Gladue's life.

"SEX WORK IS NOT A DEATH SENTENCE"

Crucial to the proceedings of the trials of Pamela George and Cindy Gladue are the spatialized logics that imagine sex workers and Indigenous peoples as already belonging to a space of violence and criminality. As Razack argues in relation to George, a common perception of the death of an Indigenous sex worker amounts to "an Aboriginal woman got a little more than she bargained for" (127). This bias was reproduced in the legal process, perhaps most starkly illustrated in the infamous moment from George's trial when the judge instructed jurors that they should take into account that George was "indeed a prostitute" (Razack 152). Similarly, at Barton's trial, his defense lawyer stated: "And by the way, she's a prostitute. She's there for a good time" (Carlson). I want to argue that this commentary represents a strategy through which the lives of Indigenous, female sex workers are cast, in Butler's terminology, as "unreal." As Butler posits: "If violence is done against those who are unreal ... it fails to injure or negate those lives since those lives are already negated" (33). In this way, the legal system—with its long history of disappearing Indigenous women and its ongoing pattern of allowing killers to act with impunity—continues to indifferently anticipate deaths of Indigenous women and negate their lives.

DEHUMANIZATION IN DEATH

Gladue was sexually violated twice: once by Barton and a second time by the Crown. As part of their case, Crown lawyers presented her preserved vagina in the courtroom, which is believed to be the first time in Canadian history that a human body part was submitted as an exhibit (Barrera). Neither Barton's defense team nor Justice Graesser could find a precedent for this decision (Cormier, Personal correspondence). Standard procedure is to use post-mortem photos, with police officers and coroners producing testimony to authenticate the images. However, acting Chief Medical Examiner Graeme Dowling stated that the removal of Gladue's body parts during autopsy was "rare and disturbing, but necessary for proper examination" (Cormier "'This will be

Upsetting'"). Dowling testified that Gladue's wound was caused by a sharp object, such as a knife or a broken piece of glass; the display of Gladue's vagina was ostensibly meant to convince jurors of this theory. Dowling elaborated: "The photographs, to me as a pathologist, don't portray the nature of this injury as accurately as the physical specimen itself.... We tried to do the best we could with photographs, but they don't tell the whole story. They are a bit dark" (Cormier, "'This was Demeaning'"). During his testimony, Dowling snapped on rubber gloves and moved Gladue's tissue around on a projector for jurors to view the wound. This bodily intrusion—conducted on a dismembered vagina with an audience of a mostly male and entirely non-Indigenous jury—is unnervingly macabre. It compelled the jury to engage in a raced and gendered act of voyeurism, as they inspected her most intimate body part. Crown Prosecutor Carole Godfrey supported the admittance of the tissue, stating: "This can be done in absolute good taste, almost like a biology class" (Cormier, "'This was Demeaning'"). The equation of Cindy's body with that of a dissected specimen in a science class gives voice to a deep colonial conception of Indigenous bodies as subhuman. Moreover, Godfrey's comment was directed towards the jury, addressing a concern that *they* might be disturbed by the proceedings, but was not directed towards Gladue's family members or other Indigenous spectators. In other words, Godfrey's justification for the use of the body tissue did not make room for the possibility of Indigenous distress or opposition. Despite the Prosecutors' various attempts at rationalizing their decision, the fact remains that Barton killed Cindy Gladue by cutting through the inside of her vagina. The Crown then replicated this violence by cutting her vagina *out* of her.

The dismemberment and parading of Indigenous body parts is not unprecedented in North American history. However, most documented cases are located in times of early settlement and war between First Nations and European settlers. When British pilgrims killed the Pokanoket King Philip in Rhode Island in 1676, for example, they cut off his head and hands to celebrate the destruction of his physical and national body: "He was quartered and hung up upon four trees.... After which, his head was sent to Plymouth, and exposed upon a gibbet for twenty years; and his hand to Boston, where it was exhibited in savage triumph" (Apess 48). Ned Blackhawk opens his seminal text *Violence Over Land: Indians and Empire in the early American West* with the image of a young woman stringing together a necklace of severed Indigenous ears, which the Spaniards have commissioned as a show of their strength. In the Sand Creek massacre of 1864, American troops cut the vaginas out of Native women they had slaughtered—"Squaws snatches were cut out for trophies," testified Captain Silas Soule (Horwitz 50)—and worn, along with cut-off breasts, on their hats. These examples all took place against a backdrop of explicit tension and animosity between settlers and Indigenous peoples over dispossession and defense of land. However, the violence committed against Cindy Gladue took place in a supposedly post-racial and post-conflict context. If the dismemberment of the Indigenous body can be understood as a display of the dissymmetry of power between the state and its subjects (Foucault 49), Gladue's treatment is a contemporary manifestation of this often disavowed and disguised colonial insistence on maintaining absolute dominance over Indigenous bodies.

There is also something to be said for the desecration in breaking apart Gladue's physical wholeness. Her body is cremated, yet part of her has remained in the custody of the Crown. The severance of her physical site of reproduction constitutes an act of unmaking the Indigenous woman. Christa Big Canoe, a First Nation lawyer and legal advocacy director at Aboriginal Legal Services of Toronto, notes: "Privacy interests do not end at death and there is nothing more private than the intimate body parts of a woman." Big Canoe goes on to highlight the fact that this act also ignores Indigenous perspectives and traditions surrounding death: "It appears that the court did not contemplate Cindy›s dignity, death rites, or any Indigenous perspective on caring for the dead.... Like others, I hope that Cindy can be made whole and she receives proper ceremonial death rites." This shows the way that bodies are treated as ungrievable, in that they are subjected to violence even in death, and denied the traditional mourning rites of their family or community. Moreover, Stevenson's formulation of a government that "has a dead Indian" is visible here. Gladue's body was taken by the state and was handled in a manner that denied her female indigeneity and reaffirmed the state's total sovereignty over her physical remains.

THE PSYCHIC LIFE OF THE VERDICT AND SENDING CINDY HOME

Gladue's murder and her subsequent brutalization in death require settler societies to interrogate our conceptions of, as Butler puts it, "who counts as human" and "whose lives count as lives" in settler colonial contexts. When the Canadian courts allow men to torture and kill Indigenous women with impunity, the logics that underwrite the violence are recognized as living, breathing, colonial expectations of Indigenous elimination that have inscribed, all around us, a "consensus on mournable bodies" that paint Indigenous peoples as subhuman and undeserving of justice. This case requires us to think beyond the boundaries between racialized and gendered bodies and spaces, and the ways our social, legal, and political systems are complicit in the disappearances of hundreds of Indigenous women and girls.

The treatment of Gladue's body by the court calls into question the professed neutrality of the relationship between Canadian institutions and Indigenous peoples. When the court atomizes her body in such a way and replicates a historically military act of triumph, an act meant to terrorize Indigenous populations into docility and subservience to the state, we are forced to ask whether the genocidal logics of conquest have, in fact, been extinguished. Despite the Crown's professed scientific rationale for using her tissue in the courtroom, I want to refer to Stevenson's discussion in *Life Beside Itself* of how a certain state-mandated act may have "a psychic life all its own" that constitutes "more than the fact of its occurrence" (73) in order to suggest that the impact of the Court's decision has similarly engendered or reiterated a felt knowledge (Million 56) among Indigenous women and their communities. The Crown's willingness to mutilate and display a part of Gladue's body reminded Indigenous women everywhere of their status in the eyes of the state as subsumed in criminality and the expectation of death. As Indigenous scholars and activists Sarah Hunt and Naomi Sayers succinctly summarize: "There is no justice for Indigenous women" (2). And one of Gladue's close friends, Vanessa Day echoes such a sentiment: "It... seemed like she didn't matter. That spoke volumes to us as Aboriginal women" (Carlson). In reflecting on Gladue's case, it is clear that the state not only failed to uphold its obligation to punish Barton but engaged in an act of bodily dismemberment that perpetuated, not prevented, violence against Indigenous women.

I want to close this chapter by recognizing the ways that Cindy Gladue was reclaimed by Indigenous communities in the days following the case's conclusion. There were protests and marches from St. John's to Vancouver, with participants holding signs that read: "It's not OK to murder us," "Protect our Women," "Cindy is Loved & Valued," and "Cindy Matters" (Jancelewicz). Various scholars and activists ardently affirmed the grievability of her life, while calling out the appalling failure of the state to deliver justice to her and her family. Gladue's life and body were desecrated by Bradley Barton and then by the Court, but Indigenous peoples everywhere refused to accept this verdict and its symbolic overtones. Their displays of love for Gladue sent her on her journey with restored dignity and humanity. Naomi Sayers, Indigenous feminist and sex worker activist, wrote: "Our bodies are not terra nullius. Our bodies are not empty. They belong to us. They belong to this land. Cindy is on her way home. The ancestors will keep her warm and safe now. And her body always belonged to this land" (Sayers, "Our Bodies").

WORKS CITED

"Aboriginal Women One Third of All Female Prisoners: Report." *CBC News North*, Dec. 2013. Web. 15 Aug. 2015.

Apess, William. *Eulogy on King Philip: as Pronounced at the Odeon, in Federal Street, Boston*. Boston: Self-Published, 1836. Print.

Barrera, Jorge. "Defence in Cindy Gladue Case Used For-Hire U.S. Pathologist Who Questions Validity of Shaken-Baby Syndrome." *APTN National News*, 1 Apr. 2015. Web. 3 April 2015.

Big Canoe, Christa. "Cindy Gladue Suffered Her Last Indignity at Murder Trial." *CBC News Aboriginal*, 2 Apr. 2015. Web. 4 Apr. 2015.

Blackhawk, Ned. *Violence Over the Land: Indians and Empires in the Early American West*. Cambridge, Mass.: Harvard University Press, 2006. Print.

"Bradley Barton Found Not Guilty in Death of Cindy Gladue." *CBC News*, 18 Mar. 2015. Web. 24 Mar. 2015.

Butler, Judith. *Precarious Life: The Powers of Mourning and Violence*. New York: Verso, 2004. Print.

Canada. Indigenous and Northern Affairs Canada. "An Act to Amend and Consolidate the Laws Respecting Indians." *Indigenous and Northern Affairs Canada*. Government of Canada, n.d. Web. 3 June 2015.

Carlson, Kathryn Blaze. "Aboriginal Groups Listed on Action Plan Say They Were Not Consulted." *The Globe and Mail*, 16 Feb. 2015. Web. 16 Feb. 2015.

Casper, Monica J. "Highway of Tears: A Review." *The Feminist Wire*, 7 May 2015. Web. 3 June 2015.

Cole, Teju. "Unmournable Bodies." *The New Yorker*. Condé Nest, 9 Jan. 2015. Web. 11 Jan 2015.

Cormier, Ryan. Personal correspondence. 15 April 2015.

Cormier, Ryan. "This Will Be Upsetting': Edmonton Jurors Examine Woman's Body Part in Rare Legal Testimony." The *Edmonton Journal,* 27 Feb. 2015. Web. 2 Apr. 2015.

Cormier, Ryan. "'This Was Demeaning': Body Part as Evidence in Cindy Gladue Murder Trial Comes under Fire." *nationalpost.com*. The National Post, 30 Mar. 2015. Web. 10 Apr. 2015.

Cormier, Ryan. "Crown Seeks New Trial in Cindy Gladue Murder Case after Bradley Barton Acquitted." *The National Post*, 2 Apr. 2015. Web. 15 May 2015.

England, Jennifer. "Disciplining Subjectivity and Space: Representation, Film and Its Material Effects." *Antipode* 36. 2 (2004): 295-321. Web. 4 April 2015.

Foucault, Michel. *Discipline and Punish: The Birth of the Prison*. New York: Vintage Books, 1977. Print.

Horwitz, Tony. "Massacre at Sand Creek." *Smithsonian* 45.8 (December 2014): 50. Web. 3 Apr. 2015.

Hunt, Sarah, and Naomi Sayers. "Cindy Gladue Case Sends Chilling Message to Indigenous Women." *The Globe and Mail,* 25 Mar. 2015. Web. 26 Mar. 2015.

Jacobs, Beverley, and Andrea Williams. "Legacy of Residential Schools: Missing and Murdered Aboriginal Women." *Speaking My Truth*. Aboriginal Healing Foundation, n.d. Web. 28 Aug. 2015.

Jancelewicz, Chris. "Cindy Gladue Case: Rallies Seek Justice for Slain Aboriginal Woman." *Huffington Post*, 2 Apr. 2015. Web. 15 May 2015.

Jiwani, Yasmin, and Mary Lynn Young. "Missing and Murdered Women: Reproducing Marginality in News Discourse." *Canadian Journal of Communication* 31.4 (2006): 895-917. Print.

Johnston, Janice, and Scott Lilwall. "Bradley Barton Trial in Killing of Cindy Gladue Enters Jury Deliberations." *CBC News*, 17 Mar. 2015. Web. 2 Apr. 2015.

Kaye, Julie. "Opinion: Justice for Cindy Gladue Demands an Appeal of Recent Verdict." *The Edmonton Journal*, 26 Mar. 2015. Web. 5 May 2015.

Million, Dian. *Therapeutic Nations: Healing in an Age of Indigenous Human Rights*. Tucson: University of Arizona Press, 2013. Print.

Native Women's Association of Canada (NWAC). "Aboriginal Women and the Legal Justice System in Canada: An Issue Paper." NWAC, June 2007. Web. 24 Mar. 2015.

Oppal, Wally. "Forsaken: The Report of the Missing Women Commission Inquiry: Executive Summary." *British Columbia Ministry of Justice*. Government of British Columbia, 19 Nov. 2012. Web 19 April 2014.

Razack, Sherene. "Gendered Racial Violence and Spatialized Justice: The Murder of Pamela George." *Race, Space and the Law: Unmapping a White Settler Society*. Toronto: Between the Lines, 2002. Print.

Rennie, Steve. "Huge Increase in Number of Aboriginal Women in Canadian Prisons." *The Toronto Star*, 2 Dec. 2014. Web. 15 Aug. 2015.

Roberts, David. "Pair Guilty in Slaying of Regina Prostitute." *Walnet*. N.p., 21 Dec. 1996. Web. 10 Apr. 2015.

Rolston, Adriana. "Highway of Tears Revisited." *Ryerson Review of Journalism*. The Ryerson Review of Journalism, 1 June 2010. Web. 10 May 2015.

Sayers, Naomi. "Our Bodies Are Not Terra Nullius." *Kwe Today*,

19 Mar. 2015. Web. 22 Mar. 2015.

Simpson, Audra. "The Chief's Two Bodies: Theresa Spence and the Gender of Settler Sovereignty." Presentation at Unsettling Conversations, Unmaking Racisms and Colonialisms: 14th Annual Critical Race and Anticolonial Studies Conference. University of Alberta and Athabasca University. 17-19 Oct. 2014. Web. 1 Nov. 2014.

Stevenson, Lisa. "The Psychic Life of Biopolitics: Survival, Co-operation and Inuit Community." *American Ethnologist* 39.3 (2012): 592-613. Print.

Stevenson, Lisa. *Life Beside Itself: Imagining Care in the Canadian Arctic.* Oakland: University of California Press, 2014. Print.

"Tears Flowed as Families of Missing, Murdered Forced to Select Roundtable Delegates." *APTN National News*, 27 Feb. 2015. Web. 28 Feb. 2015.

Human Rights Watch (HRW). "Those Who Take Us Away: Abusive Policing and Failures in Protection of Indigenous Women and Girls in Northern British Columbia, Canada." HRW, 13 Feb. 2013. Web. 1 May 2015.

6.
Analyzing Erasures and Resistance Involving Indigenous Women in New Brunswick, Canada

JOSEPHINE L. SAVARESE

'WHAT [ARE] OUR CHILDREN going to be left with?' asked Mi'kmaq land defender Annie Clair in an interview at a fundraiser at the K'jipuktuk (Halifax) based Mi'kmaw Native Friendship Centre in the spring of 2015 (Arsenault).[1] The silent auction was held to raise money for a trial regarding Clair's involvement in an anti-shale gas protest in 2013 near the small community of Rexton, New Brunswick. One of the protestor's actions was to set up an encampment to stop Texas-based Southwestern Energy Resources from shale gas exploration on unceded Mi'kmaq territory (Howe). Clair faced six charges, including several counts of obstruction of justice, resisting arrest, and assaulting a peace officer, which stemmed from incidents in September and October 2013. For Clair, the prosecution was disrespectful towards her First Nations heritage. She reasoned that the environmental protest was the "right thing" to do and urged supporters to 'keep fighting, no matter what' (Arsenault). The charges against Clair were dropped two years later in September of 2015 with no explanation (Choi).

Through analysis of what I label "erasures and resistance," I work to isolate factors that prohibit Maritime Indigenous women from realizing inclusion and citizenship, which, thereby, increases the likelihood of victimization. Alongside Annie Clair's story, I examine the conviction of Curtis Bonnell for sixteen-year-old Hilary Bonnell's murder in September 2009 near the Esgenoôpetitj (Burnt Church) First Nation in northeastern New Brunswick. Hilary disappeared on the Saturday morning of the Labour Day weekend after spending the prior evening celebrating the end of the summer holidays with her friends. She was last seen walking on the Micmac Road dressed in "a light jean skirt, a white top, a black sweater and flip flops" (*R. v. Bonnell*, NBQB 376, para 28). An adult relation, Curtis Bonnell, was arrested two months later. An offender with "a history of violence and particularly past sexual violence convictions," Curtis Bonnell was identified as a suspect early in the investigation (*R. v. Bonnell*, NBQB 376, para 29). He was accused of detaining Hilary against her will, sexually assaulting her and suffocating her on the lawn of the backyard of his home on the Esgenoôpetitj First Nation. While in custody, Curtis Bonnell admitted his crimes to police and to an Elder. Curtis disclosed he buried Hilary's body deep in the woods of the Acadian Peninsula near Tabusintac, New Brunswick, to avoid detection. On November 9, 2009, Mr. Bonnell led RCMP officers to the burial spot to exhume the body. In 2012, Curtis Bonnell was convicted of first degree murder by a jury. Justice Fred Ferguson of the New Brunswick Court of Queen's Bench acknowledged that Hilary was among 'a long list of aboriginal Canadian women' that had 'disappeared from our streets' (Bisset). Bonnell's appeal against his conviction was dismissed in January 2015 (*R. v. Bonnell*, NBCA 6).

This chapter scrutinizes these New Brunswick stories for insights on the varied factors that result in Indigenous women going missing. Although this study firmly denounces the murder of a young teenaged girl, it moves past concentrating on personal violence. Stopping individual violent offenders is necessary; however, I argue that a focus on individualized harm may mask systemic types of erasure that are equally problematic, including the suppression of women's voices on matters of policy, governance, land and human security, and self-determination. To illustrate this point, I use the Royal Canadian Mounted Police actions against shale gas protesters, including Annie Clair, as an illustration of victimization by the state (Howe). Using an interdisciplinary lens to scrutinize violence seems even more pressing following revelations of abuses by police of Indigenous women in Québec. In April 2016, Dawn Lavell-Harvard, president of the Native Women's Association of Canada, confirmed that sexual, physical, and institutional violence towards Indigenous women and girls has deep roots. In support of those who told their stories, Lavell-Harvard hoped that "shining light in these dark places" might "one day" result in Indigenous women seeing "justice" by revealing subjugated truths (NWAC, "Stands with Indigenous"). Her aim of galvanizing reform by revealing individual and state oppression also propels this publication.

By placing two seemingly dissimilar cases in conversation, I link the destruction of the land and the dramatic numbers of missing and murdered Indigenous women in Canada. Rauna Kuokkanen, a Toronto-based Indigenous scholar originally from Ohcejohka-Utsjoki, Sápmi (Finland), encourages scholars to identify these connections. In Kuokkanen's view, the solutions to "rampant violence against Indigenous women" are most likely to be found in "approaches that address sexual, physical and state violence together and simultaneously" ("Globalization" 223). Drawing from Kuokkanen's point, I suggest that political, social, and economic inequities are best theorized as forms of violence rather than only systemic factors driving violence. Promoting the capacity to "[see, understand and analyze] the gendered character and aspects of different forms of violence" is, for Kuokkanen, an essential role for researchers and advocates ("Globalization" 217).

In an upcoming section, the well-known case Lovelace v. Canada is cited to affirm the need to think beyond criminal law violations when considering disappearances. The case demonstrates the Canadian state's willingness to undermine Indigenous women's legal entitlements (Palmater, "Genocide" 27-54). The legislative response, Bill C-31 an *Act to Amend the Indian Act*, reinstated the status of women who married outside their communities. However, it also introduced the "second-generation cut-off" clause that prohibited reinstated mothers from conferring status to their children. Because Sandra Lovelace was a resident of New Brunswick, her fight for recognition particularly haunts the situations analyzed in this text. It foreshadowed the human rights challenges that resurfaced decades later in Annie Clair and Hilary Bonnell's struggles for a viable existence.

While amplifying victimization, I also investigate both women's agency, an underexplored topic in relation to violence against women. Specifically, I seek to establish that Annie Clair and Hilary Bonnell acted in keeping with what Michi Saagiig Nishnaabeg author and scholar Leanne Betasamosake Simpson labels "presencing" in *Dancing on Our Turtle's Back* (96). Presencing, for Simpson, involves renewing relationships between one's self and the land, even if it is largely occupied by settler societies. For example, Simpson describes a National Aboriginal Day when she joined dancers, artists, singers, drummers, community leaders, Elders, family and children parading through Nogojiwanong (Peterborough, Ontario) in "a quiet, collective act of resurgence" (11). She explains that "[spaces] of storied presencing" are created through the "movement of body and sound, testimony and witnessing, remembering, protest and insurrection" (96). Intrigued by Simpson's work, I investigate ways Annie's and Hilary's behaviour constituted micro and macro presencing.

SIGNIFICANCE

The Maritime examples show that the challenges posed by racialized, gendered, class-based, and colonial-inspired violence are national in scope, as Julie Kaye pointed out in a 2015 lecture "Mobilizing Collective Outrage from the West to the Atlantic: Canada's Violence Against Indigenous Women" held in Fredericton. Irrespective of Kaye's finding, there are few studies on disappearances in Atlantic Canada. The limited research may be partly due to lower numbers of reported homicides. In *Missing and Murdered Women: A National Operational Overview,* the Royal Canadian Mounted Police reports that five Indigenous women were intentionally killed between 1980 and 2012 in the province of New Brunswick, representing 4 percent of homicide victims (9). This percentage is considerably lower than in other regions, including the Prairies, where approximately 50 percent of homicide victims are Indigenous women (RCMP).

Though less dramatic, statistics from this province are disconcerting given that Indigenous people comprise around 2 percent of New Brunswick's population. Activists from Indigenous nations in the Atlantic have emphasized women's susceptibility in their calls for action. The 2014 homicide of Loretta Saunders, a graduate student and an Inuk woman from Newfoundland and Labrador living in Halifax, tragically reinforced the over-victimization. In response to the homicide, Cheryl Maloney, the president of the Nova Scotia Native Women's Association, demanded a national inquiry. She stated that "Every Aboriginal girl in this country is vulnerable," including Atlantic Indigenous women (CBC, "Loretta Saunders"). During an Atlantic tour of the REDress Project in the fall of 2015, Métis artist Jaime Black called for public awareness because of the silences around missing and murdered Indigenous women. At the REDress Project opening at St. Thomas University in Fredericton, Sharlene Paul—president of the Indigenous Women's Association of the Maliseet and Mi'kmaq territory and a member of the Tobique First Nation—pointed out that Aboriginal women across Canada are currently not valued (CBC, "Red Dresses Stark Reminder").

The fact that New Brunswick's Indigenous population is youthful means that future acts of violence are likely without swift remedial action. In the "Strategic Framework to End Violence against Wabanaki Women in New Brunswick" published in 2008, the New Brunswick Advisory Committee on Violence Against Women links this heightened vulnerability to colonization (1-34). Women from the collective Atlantic Indigenous nations were honoured community members and leaders in pre-contact societies.[2] After European contact, women's status was eroded, which severely affected Wabanaki men's treatment of women in their communities. According to the Advisory Committee report, these factors contribute greatly to contemporary Indigenous women's experience of violence. The Strategic Framework recognizes that violence against Indigenous women is a severe problem of long standing, which requires an immediate and effective response (6).

Given these findings, it is not surprising that Pam Palmater, originally from Ogpi'kanjik or the Eel River Bar First Nation in northern New Brunswick, calls for systemic reform. She urges all levels of government to grant sovereignty to the varied Indigenous nations and peoples (147-167). As a Mi'kmaw woman, she sought to be

> a contributing citizen of a strong, vibrant, inclusive Mi'kmaw Nation, which is self-determining and encour-

> ages participatory governance over our land and resources, international relations, and economies that are based on our traditional values and principles that have evolved to address modern situations. ("Matnm Tel-Mi'kmaw" 159, spelling taken from Palmater)

As a former resident of New Brunswick and a Mi'kmaq woman, Palmater's insights are particularly valuable to this study.

ANALYZING ERASURES AND REGIMES OF DISAPPEARANCE

In this section, I explain this study's dual focus on personal and state violence. I refer to other scholars who see research into violence against Indigenous women as important while also working to study other forms of social and political violence. Australian scholar Deborah Rose Bird and Canadian professor Dara Culhane underscore the importance of theorizing the multiple ways women become invisible, from physical disappearances to marginalization. Based on their reasoning, I assert that figuratively erasing Indigenous women by destabilizing their claims as citizens is an equally important topic in collections such as this one. Rose Bird, for example, defines erasure as follows: "Erasure ... covers a range of practices and intellectual strategies from massacre to denial to economic rationalism. Erasure is the process of removing or marginalizing the autonomous power and presence of the living systems (human and non-human) that are being colonized" (8). For Culhane, the term "regime of disappearance," coined by Goode and Maskovsky, helps to explain the colonial structures that have silenced Downtown Eastside women in Vancouver. It is defined as "a neo-liberal mode of governance that selectively marginalizes and/or erases categories of people through strategies of representation that include silences, blind spots, and displacements that have both material and symbolic effects" (595).

These definitions by Rose Bird and Culhane aid this scholarship because they define erasures and disappearances in broader terms beyond personal violence. They aim to theorize the larger structural and interpersonal contexts in which disappearances occur. The comprehensive term "regime of disappearance" positions both

Hilary Bonnell's death and the criminalization of Annie Clair as resulting from oppressive structural frameworks. The use of this term helps to position both outcomes as equally problematic examples of the misuse of power.

Writing in 1996, Deborah Rose Bird describes the diminished position of Indigenous women in relation to Indigenous land tenure. In "Land Rights and Deep Colonising: The Erasure of Women," she describes how women were excluded from hearings on land claims. Rose Bird attributes the overreliance on men's testimony to what she labels as "deep colonizing," whereby potentially de-colonializing policies benefit some at the expense of others (11).

In the Canadian context, the historic case of Sandra Lovelace, who was born on the Tobique First Nation in New Brunswick and described as "Maliseet Indian" in documents submitted to the United Nations, typifies the strategies of erasure that colonial states use to deny legal and political status to Canadian Indigenous women. In 1981, Sandra Lovelace argued that s. 12(1)(b) of the *Indian Act* was discriminatory in depriving Indigenous women of their legal status and corresponding entitlements when they married non-Indigenous people. Her claim was upheld by the United Nations Human Rights Commission. Though often celebrated as a victory for women's equality, the outcome of the case has been confusion and even bitterness for communities across Canada, including Atlantic Indigenous nations (Palmater, "Genocide"). The government's legislative response, Bill C-31, made the position of Indigenous communities even more precarious by narrowing future generations ability to claim status (Nicholas). Even when supposedly remedying past injustice, the Canadian settler state acted to the disadvantage of Indigenous women by failing to extend resources to communities that faced population growth. The new laws were written to ensure that the numbers of persons with legal status trickled off over time. Remedying legal misrecognition is an important, ongoing struggle that influences Indigenous women's present-day vulnerability to violence because it regularizes their precarious status (Eberts; Share).

In 2003, Dara Culhane brought attention to the Indigenous women who were missing from and murdered in one of Canada's most marginalized neighbourhoods. Culhane's work on women's invisibility in Downtown Eastside Vancouver remains influential in Canada (Baloy). Culhane rebukes the indifference to the murders of women from that neighbourhood and links the homicides to other forms of marginalization. Notably, Indigenous women of the Downtown Eastside were only recognized by the dominant society when demonized as drug users and sex workers, engaged in "risky" lifestyles.

In response, Indigenous women organized against state inaction regarding the widespread disappearances of women from the neighbourhood. For example, a flyer distributed at Downtown Eastside Women's Memorial March held on February 14, 2001 in Vancouver poignantly stated:

> WE STAND ON OUR MOTHER EARTH AND WE DEMAND RESPECT. WE ARE NOT THERE TO BE BEATEN, ABUSED, MURDERED, IGNORED. (Culhane 593; capitals in original)

As Culhane's article makes plain, murder was not the only way that women were made invisible. Through their protests, the women from the Downtown Eastside sought recognition for their demands.

INTERSECTIONS BETWEEN THE CASES

The two cases under review overlap in ways that are important to this study. It is relevant that Hilary Bonnell and Annie Clair shared a history and an identity as members of two Mi'kmaq nations, Elsipogtog and Esgenoôpetitj (Palmater, "Matnm Tel-Mi'kmawi" 149). The fates of the two women also intertwined in concrete ways, which I explore in this section. Symbolically, it is important that Annie Clair moved to Neguac, an Acadian community near Esgenoôpetitj First Nation in March, 2009, to live closer to family. When she reflected on the incident, Clair realized Curtis Bonnell would have driven past her home in Neguac on his way to the burial site (Clair "Human Stories). In a 2014 radio interview, Hilary's mother, Pam Fillier, reported that she had not slept in a bed since Hilary's death. She often slept in a chair, feeling as though she was waiting for her daughter. After Hilary's death, Pam Fillier recalled seeing mothers on television pleading for their child's return, thinking she would never face a similar situation. In conclusion, she stated: "Now, I am her" ("The Missing, The Mourned"). The interviewer was Annie Clair.

More theoretically, both situations demonstrate the centrality of land to Indigenous women's security. Vanessa Watts, a Mohawk, Anishnaabe, member of the Bear Clan and scholar, writes about ways the exploitation of the land fuels the mistreatment of women. In her 2013 publication, "Indigenous Place-Thought and Agency Amongst Humans and Non-Humans (First Woman and Sky Woman Go On a European World Tour!)," Vanessa Watts argues that disregard for Indigenous women and disrespect for Indigenous land are intertwined. Watts describes these violations as "essentially tied to one another" (31). Watts decries the fact that the "land is increasingly being excavated, re-designed, torn apart" (31). For Watts, the fact that vicious crusades are simultaneously waged against "land" as well as women who are cast as "non-human" is not surprising, given the settler dream of complete domination (31). Irrespective of the injuries inflicted on Indigenous territories, Watts stresses that connections to the land are inspirational in the struggle for justice. She states: "Only if the land decides to stop speaking to us will we enter the world of dislocation where agency is lost and our histories become provocative Indian lore in an on-going settler mistake" (33).

In the next section, I aim to show that Indigenous women and girls are caught by structures that normalize personal violence and authorize state harm, including environmental destruction in Indigenous territories. By closely investigating Hilary Bonnell's death and Annie Clair's criminalization, I identify how Indigenous women are made susceptible to disappearance through individual and state repression.

ANALYSIS OF THE CASE STUDIES

The two seemingly differing cases involving a murder conviction and the charges against a land defender are closely analyzed. They are treated as sources of complementary revelations on the varied regimes of power and knowledge that partially or even totally silence Indigenous women in Canada, albeit in ways that are contested and resisted. Annie Clair's near criminalization and Hilary Bonnell's untimely death are investigated to determine how Indigenous women are systematically undermined to achieve what Eve Tuck and K. Wane Yang label "settler futurity" (1-3) and what Laura Landertinger describes as an "orchestrated removal" (59-87). When critical sociologist Carmella Murdocca asserts that settler colonialism is founded on the "logic of dehumanization," she helps to reveal some of the ideological underpinnings that drive the disappearances interrogated in the next passages (220).

THE MURDER OF HILARY BONNELL

In 1999, Canadians learned about Esgenoôpetitj First Nation when the Supreme Court of Canada affirmed Mi'kmaq treaty rights in the case R v. Marshall, a decision that generated "racist public outrage" (McMillan, Young, and Peters 429). In 2002, filmmaker Alanis Obomsawin contextualized the events that transpired in Miramichi Bay in the National Film Board production "Is the Crown at War With Us?" A decade later, the homicide of a youthful Mi'kmaq girl, Hilary Bonnell, by her adult cousin, Curtis Bonnell, returned Esgenoôpetitj (Burnt Church) First Nation to the public eye. By giving prominence to Hilary's murder, I join with others who denounce the personal violence Indigenous women disproportionately experience. The Native Women's Association of Canada commemorates many missing and murdered women through projects such "Digital Life Stories." In one segment, Hilary's story is told by her mother and stepfather, Pam and Fred Fillier.

Through a review informed by qualitative critical discourse analysis (Park) of the reported judgements and select news stories, I closely investigate ways in which themes of racialized violence found in other Canadian cases materialize in an Atlantic Canadian example. Here, Bonnell's murder is scrutinized to reveal the racialized and gendered factors that have been connected to murders and disappearances in more prominent cases, such as the homicides by Robert Pickton against women in Vancouver's Downtown Eastside (Hugill; E. Craig). The offender, Curtis Bonnell, is one of the few violent offenders to have confessed to his crimes against one of the women profiled as a missing and murdered Indigenous woman. Excerpts from Curtis' statements to the police in the seven reported decisions and in news stories provide a rare opportunity to scrutinize the offender's thought processes.

Curtis Bonnell, then twenty-nine years old, became a suspect shortly after Hilary's disappearance on September 5, 2009. A known sexual offender, he was captured on a video surveillance camera at the convenience store that Hilary visited in the early morning of her disappearance. He left shortly after she did and intercepted her walking on MicMac Road. He confined her in his truck, transported her to his home, and sexually assaulted and murdered her. According to the Crown prosecutor, Bonnell was particularly enraged after a fight the previous day with his common law wife who departed with their infant son. He stated to police: 'Fuck! I was overboard! Started when [I] left and I was furious on everything!' (*R v Bonnell*, NBQB 395 para 71).

Elder David Gehue travelled to New Brunswick from Nova Scotia at Curtis's request. Gehue earned Curtis Bonnell's trust at a national gathering of spiritual Elders at Big Cove First Nation approximately ten years prior, when Gehue was a healer (*R v Bonnell*, NBQB 34, para 14). The Elder was successful in prompting a confession from Bonnell, which was recorded with a wiretap.

TRACING THE MARKERS OF GENDERED AND RACIALIZED INEQUITIES

Previous scholarship has brought attention to the multiple vulnerabilities of those who have gone missing and/or have been murdered. In "Person(s) of Interest and Missing Women: Legal Abandonment in the Downtown Eastside," Halifax based legal scholar Elaine Craig explains that the "endangered do not come from every walk of life" (3). Notably, she offers a correction: "To be more precise then, poor women and Aboriginal women are disappearing" (3). These women are overrepresented among those affected by "an undeniable epidemic of violence in Canada today" (3). When Elaine Craig positions systemic factors as causal regarding Canada's violence towards Indigenous women, she affirms earlier research findings (Hugill). Hilary Bonnell shared many of the gender, race, and class-based markers that position Indigenous women for violence. The circumstances of Hilary's death align with the common factors reported by the RCMP in 2014, including her vulnerability based on race, age, and even geographic location due to the remoteness of her place of death.

SEX WORKER DISCOURSES

One of the perhaps more surprising parallels between Hilary's murder and other cases is the way the offender attempted to connect her to sex work to justify his actions. In his confession, Curtis Bonnell claimed Hilary Bonnell flagged his truck down for a ride on the morning of September 5 while she was walking on MicMac Road. Curtis claimed Hilary agreed to have sex in exchange for one hundred dollars (*R v Bonnell*, NBQB 395, para 37). Curtis maintained that he had paid Hilary for sex on previous occasions (*R v Bonnell*, NBQB 395, para 74), and claimed he killed Hilary because she "freaked out" and began yelling, hitting, swearing at him when he withdrew the offer. When Hilary threatened to disclose his actions, he hit her and put his hand over her mouth to make her stop screaming (*R v Bonnell*, NBQB 395, para 38). His version of events lacks any credibility, yet it provides insight on Curtis' assessment of Hilary Bonnell. He seemed to equate Indigenous women, including Hilary, with sex workers who occupy a marginalized status in mainstream society in an attempt to justify his actions (E. Craig; Hugill). The dominant society's discourses around Indigenous sex workers' inhumanity are well entrenched in the consciousness of the white settler Canadian nation.

Sharene Razack's seminal work on the murder of Regina based sex worker Pamela George in 1995 by two white males is of note (91-130). Following Razack, it appears likely Curtis Bonnell believed that the sex worker identity he ascribed to Hilary minimized his culpability. He might also have thought that this racialized script would be believable in the white court system (Savarese). In his confession, he suggested to RCMP agents that he deserved more lenient treatment because of his "co-operation" with the investigation. Curtis Bonnell admitted to sexually assaulting Hilary in the backyard of his home—a space he treated as a domain beyond justice that is explicitly raced, classed and gendered allowing him to act without regard for Hilary (Razack 128).

In general, Curtis Bonnell appeared to view Indigenous bodies as always sexually available to him. In his confession to police, Curtis provided evidence that he was "looking for sex" on the Saturday morning before he met Hilary (*R v Bonnell*, NBQB 395 para. 59). Curtis' mindset seems consistent with the settler colonial presumption of sexual authority over Indigenous females that Razack tracks. Statements made in a December 1, 2009 interview with Cpl. Greg Lupson illustrate that Curtis Bonnell felt entitled to forcible sex. Curtis acknowledged he "had sex with [his] cousin, just like [his] other ones" in seeming reference to his past history of sexually preying on family members. He further admitted to "kissing [Hilary], and feeling her up, and getting on top of her" (CBC, "Bonnell Admits"). When Hilary fought back and cried out, Curtis Bonnell suffocated her in a real and symbolic act of silencing. The Crown explained Curtis' determination "to take 'No' from a 16-year-old" (Bisset).

Scholars point to the ways that sexual violence against Indigenous women is a product of ongoing colonial violence (Razack; E. Craig). The justice system diverts attention to individuals by failing to acknowledge historical oppressions. As a result, the system judges Indigenous peoples through individualized discourses that depict offenders as well as victims as worthless (Dylan, Regehr, and Alaggia). Given these findings of institutional apathy, it is tempting to characterize the prosecution and conviction of Curtis Bonnell as signs of greater responsiveness from law enforcement. The fact that an arrest and prosecution occurred within months may appear to honour Hilary's life beyond the indifference shown to previous homicides (Hugill). In fact, RCMP Inspector Roch Fortin stated at a news conference after Curtis Bonnell's arrest that RCMP members were 'literally working around the clock' after Hilary was reported missing ('It's a Little Bit of Justice for My Little Girl'). A more cautious reading of the prosecution is suggested by Hilary's family. During an interview with Annie Clair, Pam Fillier challenged RCMP statements. She reported that the RCMP was initially unresponsive. After taking her statement, Pam "didn't hear from them again." She was led to believe that Hilary's disappearance was unimportant to the authorities. Fillier spoke to the media to force the police to investigate more thoroughly. According to Fillier, the officers seemed to prefer 'just thinking [Hilary was] just another Indian girl getting drunk, out partying and didn't go home' (Clair, "Human Stories").

The reported judgments and news stories also perpetuate the concept of Indigenous degeneracy, which were central in both Razack's and E. Craig's analysis and also worried Pam Fillier. Though more pronounced in relation to Curtis, Hilary is also vilified on a careful reading, one modelled on Nick Chagnon's methodology, outlined in "Heinous Crime or Acceptable Violence? The Disparate Framing of Femicides in Hawai'i" (13-45). Following a qualitative review of news articles on homicides against women, Chagon discovered that the coverage tells "two stories—that of a social problem and that of acceptable violence" (39). The "acceptable violence frame" was used to make the crimes appear "somewhat routine, unproblematic, or inevitable" (38). In reports from the Bonnell trial, vestiges of the "acceptable violence" frame that Chagnon describes appear through veiled racialized discourses of inferiority and Indigenous moral vacuity. The continued repetition of the fact that Hilary and Curtis were first cousins is an example. A headline from a 2012 Canadian Broadcasting Corporation news story written during the trial states "Bonnell Admits He Killed Cousin Hilary after Sex." The article refers to the pair having sex thirteen times. The impression left with the reader is that Hilary possibly consented. The fact that Curtis Bonnell forcibly overcame and sexually assaulted a terrified Hilary was mentioned only once.

The reported judgements contain lengthy discussions about procedural matters, including *Charter* rights, the admissibility of evidence, and prior case law. In contrast, very few facts appear in the decisions about Hilary, apart from the more clinical description of her actions on the evening prior to her disappearance and on the morning of her murder. Oddly, Hilary disappears in the reports of her murder and in the trial that ensued. A story of legal "rescue" of an Indigenous victim might have surfaced in contrast to the "legal abandonment" that Craig makes plain in her careful study of the prosecution of Robert Pickton. This might have happened by acknowledging Hilary's worth and viability in contrast to the dismissive tone towards Pickton's victims. The opportunity for humanization, however, never materialized. The significance of her loss to her family and community is mostly subsumed by the more prominent account of incest between cousins turned violent. Though largely missing from the court rulings, Hilary's violent death shattered her family and community. Over five hundred people attended her funeral in November 2009 including Chiefs from Atlantic Canada and then Lieutenant Governor of New Brunswick Graydon Nicholas ("Hundreds Attend Funeral"). One of the few acknowledgements of Hilary's value appears in a description by her mother, as she said that Hilary was a "happy sixteen year old girl" at the time of her death (*R v Bonnell,* NBQB 376, para 25). When pressed on whether Hilary deserved this treatment, even Curtis tearfully acknowledged: "In my heart, as a sober man, no. As a sober man, no." He explained, "No person deserves that. Not one person" (*R v Bonnell,* NBQB 24 para 148).

The conviction of Curtis Bonnell shows that the incapacitation of dangerous predators is essential. Sole reliance on imprisonment is, however, limited as a long-term strategy for safety (E. Craig). It often derails systemic solutions by amplifying Indigenous "guilt" and re-inscribing colonial "innocence." When testifying at his trial for first degree murder, Curtis Bonnell seemed to acknowledge his own worthlessness in the eyes of the white settler state. He explained his decision to bury Hilary's body rather than going to the authorities to report what he claimed was an accidental death. Bonnell testified in a seemingly convincing way: 'I was just another lying Indian. I had just gotten out of jail. Who was going to believe me?' (*R v Bonnell,* NBCA 6, para 104).[3] This claim does not excuse his actions and could reflect Curtis' intelligence as well as his capacity for manipulation. At the same time, his statement also implies that he perceived himself as degenerate and racialized, which helped him to justify further violations against Hilary.

Pam Palmater's scholarship discusses some of the inequities faced by Atlantic Canadian Indigenous peoples that shaped Curtis's worldview by reinforcing gendered entitlements alongside racialized stigma ("Genocide"). The Bonnell prosecution is problematic in the way Hilary becomes largely invisible as a victim deserving of acknowledgement and justice (196). Following

Morgan Bassichis and Dean Spade's points in "Queer Politics and Anti-Blackness," I reason that Curtis Bonnell's prosecution may support the former Conservative government's view that racialized men are the most feared predators for Indigenous women, which ignores the state's complicity with violence. Razack's view that dominant institutions ignore "historical and contemporary relations of domination" is evident in the prosecution of Curtis Bonnell, in which his degeneracy was hyper-amplified (129). In his efforts to prompt a confession, Corporal Lupson emphasized the disdain of the white community as a reason why Curtis should confess to his crime. Corporal Lupson stated that "everybody ... you know the whites on the outside ... looking at the community [were saying] look at the turmoil" (*R v Bonnell,* NBQB 24 para 57). Corporal Lupson promised to defend Bonnell if he acknowledged his guilt and said he would praise Curtis' confession to the "whites" by stating that a "lesser man would not have done what he did" (para 57).

Other scholars have focused on the legacy of colonialism in the Atlantic region (Gould and Semple). David Bedford, a political theorist and Aboriginal politics specialist at the University of New Brunswick, laments that the Supreme Court of Canada's Marshall decision generated varied results for communities such as Esgenoôpetitj, namely that the "Maritime reserves are a little richer and have a few more jobs, but the wounds are no closer to being healed, traditions are no closer to being preserved, and communities are no closer to being united" (218).

Some applaud the conviction of Curtis Bonnell as a step towards safety, particularly for the women of Esgenoôpetitj and possibly for Bonnell's infant son. Yet, at the same time, it enabled the settler state to position itself as a saviour, who was able to secure a conviction. Although considerable funds were spent on the prosecution of Bonnell and his incarceration, it appears that no resources went into making the local community safer. Indeed, after Hilary's demise her family and friends unsuccessfully worked to raise money for a youth centre that they planned to name "Hilary's House" ("Building Hope"). For writer and scholar, Leanne Betasamosake Simpson, resources like the proposed Hilary's House, are crucial for safety. Self-esteem and strong identities, states Simpson, result from "living in ways that illuminate that identity and that propel [communities] towards *mino bimaadiziwin*, the good life" (*Dancing* 13).

REMAKING WHITE INNOCENCE IN THE CRIMINALIZATION OF ANNIE CLAIR

The arrest and indictment of Annie Clair, a Mi'kmaq land defender from Elsipogtog First Nation in 2013, is the second case study. It is a less typical one for a collection on missing and murdered Indigenous women. On October 17, 2013, Clair and thirty-nine others were arrested in an early morning RCMP raid of an encampment occupied by protestors involved in a blockade established against shale gas exploration (Howe; McLellan). Until the fall of 2015, Annie Clair faced six charges for her efforts as a land defender against shale gas exploration. Some of the charges were based on allegations that Clair had blocked a Southwestern Energy Resources Canada truck used for seismic testing. Shortly after Annie's arrest, on October 31, 2013, Amnesty International posted a notice of concern because of the anti-fracking protests by the Elsipogtog Mi'kmaq Nation in New Brunswick. Benjamin Craig, campaigner for the human rights of Indigenous peoples, stated: "Like so many disputes around the lands and resources of Indigenous peoples in Canada, this conflict could have been avoided by a rigorous commitment on the part of government to respect and uphold the rights of Indigenous peoples as set out in Canadian and international law." The matter was originally scheduled for a four day trial. On September 21, 2015, the Crown announced it was staying the charges (Choi). The charges were pending for a two year period, which was partly used to fundraise for the costly defence. The attempted prosecution demonstrates the state's willingness to criminalize resistance to further environmental degradation (Howe). Halifax-based lawyer Gordon Allen compared Annie to civil rights activists in the United States, who are currently recognized as "heroes or people raising awareness for something" (Choi). Annie Clair stated her resistance was not motivated by a desire for fame; she wanted to 'protect the water, the air and the land' (Devet).

Clair's treatment by the criminal justice system appears to show the potential for women to "go missing" through structural erasures involving human rights violations (Just Associates and Nobel Women's Initiative). Although Clair's charges were not prosecuted, her case illustrates the colonial state's willingness to criminalize activism directed towards resecuritization through the reclaiming of Indigenous land. In his study of 372 news articles, McLellan found that "While 'ethical' promises of opportunity resounded in articles that noted the welfare and economic disadvantage of the Elsipogtog community, this neglected and normalized an ongoing process of environmental racism, Indigenous oppression, and state sanctioned violence" (35). In *Debriefing Elsipogtog: The Anatomy of a Struggle,* independent journalist Miles Howe offers an insider's view of the dramatic events of the protest. Howe was embedded in the protest to the point of being arrested. He describes the ways that the state undermined the resistance by ignoring the rights and obligations enshrined in historic Peace and Friendship Treaties. In relation to the prosecution of Annie Clair and the militarized reaction to the protesters by police, McLellan echoes Howe's findings. McLellan argues that spectators could best evaluate the conflict if they realized that "resurgent Indigenous movements are working to provide Indigenous people with an opportunity to decolonize oppressive state-sanctioned violence, assimilative legal practices, a lack of legally binding consultation practices that grant autonomy and self-governance, and marginalized portrayal through mass media" (35). Mainstream news media framed the conflict as resulting from the criminality of the protesters, which obscured alternative understandings of the resistance. Alternative views that presented the protest in the context of an ongoing struggle for Indigenous rights appeared in the Aboriginal Multi-Media Society (AMMSA) and the New Brunswick Media Co-op.

The erasures experienced by Clair and others do not necessarily result in violence or death, although extensive violence against Indigenous women has historically occurred at standoffs and blockades. They mute the political dissent necessary to galvanize reforms towards decolonization, partly by channeling energy away from activism and towards fighting criminal charges.

SITUATING BODILY TERROR WITHIN THE LARGER REGIME OF STRUCTURAL RACIALIZED AND GENDERED VIOLENCE

In the preceding commentary, I queried how a close investigation of the near prosecution of Annie Clair could expand knowledge of the settler state's efforts to disappear or erase Indigenous women. Elaine Craig affirms the need to theorize the processes that deprive Indigenous women victims of violence of their "citizenship and humanity" (7). These "hegemonic structures" are deeply implicated, she states, when women's lives are lost because they work to "produce citizenship and preserve humanity" at the expense of others who are abandoned (7). To deepen this important conversation on missing Indigenous women, I used the insights of scholars (Kuokkanen; Palmater; Watts) to examine a case that does not involve a "classic" disappearance through a homicide or foul play. Bassichis and Spade urge scholars and advocates to locate the systemic structures that propel violence. They reject the view that violence is comprised of "individual acts that 'bad' people do to 'good' people who need protection and retribution from state protectors (law enforcement, policymakers, administrators)" (196). Instead, Bassichis and Spade argue that "situating bodily terror as an everyday aspect of a larger regime of structural racialized and gendered violence" is more accurate (196). It incorporates oppressive state violence, which often surfaces as criminalization (196). Their call for systemic reform also encourages solutions based on community building, through efforts such as Hilary's House, rather than crime control. Esgeoopetitj First Nation resident Jeannie Bartibogue appeared to think in comparable ways. She argues that Hilary Bonnell's death revealed the need for a 'hard look' at what was occurring at the community level. The fact that there were not 'many things happening for [the] youth' was, for Bartibogue, alarming ("Youth Centre Planned").

Here, I argue that the case studies are more accurately read for what they jointly reveal about system failure resulting from the everyday brutality that Indigenous women routinely experience. Read together, the two cases reveal some of the ways that the racialized boundaries of empire are sustained as a national project of exclusion and extermination. The case studies can be understood as part of a global phenomenon in which racialized bodies are targeted as threats to settler expansion. That these patterns emerge even in remote, seemingly pastoral contexts in rural New Brunswick, seems to show the depth of the globalized exclusions. The work of Melissa Wright helps theorize the disappearances of Canadian Indigenous women as a component of a global phenomenon that targets racialized bodies seen as threats to settler expansion. Though limited to two case studies, the forms of erasure in the cases show personal and collective victimization. The resulting disappearances reinforce logics and systems of intersecting exclusions, based on gender, race, sexuality, geography and nationhood through power and knowledge—making it likely that more women will experience similar erasures.

Given the interlocking oppressions, I argue that sovereignty for Atlantic Indigenous nations is fundamental to the well-being of Indigenous women. As Thomas-Muller stated: "One thing that is clear to me ... is that ... the answer always has and continues to be sovereignty over our land and our life" (qtd. in Landertinger 76).

TRACKING PRESENCING

Although the critical commentary in the preceding discussion achieves important aims, it is not the entire story that emerges from the cases. Through close scrutiny of the lived experiences of these two Maritime women who experienced violence, it is plain they resisted and, in the case of Annie, continue to resist. In the context of missing and murdered Indigenous women, it may seem extraordinary to discuss agency and resilience. For Eve Tuck (2009), the proliferation of "damage-centred research," which emphasies the problems faced by Indigenous communities, particularly women members, is part of the colonial violence women face (409-428).

I accept Tuck's concern by amplifying actions of agency to produce a record of both Hilary's and Annie's profound courage. A collection on missing and murdered Indigenous women is perhaps an unlikely place to take up Eve Tuck's call for strengths-based scholarship. Women's struggles to avoid disappearance have largely been absent in discussions of missing and murdered Indigenous women, given the pronounced power imbalances and horror the women experienced in the face of death. Culhane's focus on community residents engagement in "active resistance to these acts of erasure" is a powerful example of how more balance can be achieved (593). Culhane states that Indigenous women are fighting for "a claim for inclusion in the larger Aboriginal struggle for rights in place and to health, dignity, and justice" (594). The case studies reveal parallel ways that Annie and Hilary worked for recognition through protest and presencing.

Melissa Wright also examines the ways that women resist and contest political silences around femicide. She examines "Third World" women's challenges to the view that they are disposable, given their nominal value to capital. The innovative responses that she catalogues show that women labourers creatively counter global capitalism's perspective on their supposed limited worth. Writing in other contexts, a range of authors argue that even "bare life" or deep dehumanization can be and often is opposed in ways that are important if not always life preserving (Edkins and Pin-Fat). Regarding Indigenous women, Pam Palmater affirms their resiliency when she states: "Our Indigenous Nations have thrived for thousands of years, which means that we have the strength of history and the power of resistance on our side" ("Matnm Tel-Mi'kmawi" 149). Importantly, the women in both studies exemplify what Leanne Betasamosake Simpson calls "presencing." Indigenous women and girls order their lives to promote decolonization and to defy oppression. When embodied with presence, Simpson describes herself as "a bigger threat to the Canadian state and it's plans to build pipelines across my body, clear cut my forests, contaminant my lakes with toxic cottages and chemicals and make my body a site of continual sexualized violence" ("Anger, Resentment and Love"). Evidence that presencing can be threatening and, therefore, opposed appears in the cases under review. As noted, Annie Clair was charged with serious Criminal Code offences for her resistance to controversial shale gas exploration. Hilary's efforts to enjoy her community in safety were thwarted by a predator bent on violence.

The grief and horror experienced by families and loved ones confronting disappearances and state inaction are undeniable. Prior research has achieved the important task of exposing the degree of risk faced by Indigenous women. While acknowledging the sorrow and outrage, I show women's resistance to brutality through illustrations from both case studies. On this front, Annie Clair's advocacy for her community appears the better example of agency given her direct challenge to shale gas development (Howe). Important successes were realized, including a moratorium on hydraulic fracturing in December 2014 and the staying of the charges against Annie Clair in 2015. In press statements from the fall of 2015 when the charges were dropped, Clair made it clear that she was continuing to work against the erasures of Indigenous peoples and communities. The resistance by Elsipogtog land defenders in collaboration with environmental activists has reframed politics in New Brunswick. Following Anna J. Willow, it can be asserted that "a distinctive new way of being and relating within their ... homeland" has resulted from this resistance (271). Like the activism against clearcutting that "transformed" the northern Ontario nation of Kakipitatapitmok, the resistance at Elsipogbog reinforces New Brunswick's story as one of struggle. Paralleling the Grassy Narrows conflicts, New Brunswick activists were granted an opportunity "to comprehend, configure, and communicate their place in the world" through victories over the colonial state through the moratorium on shale gas development, however temporary this may prove (271).

Tracking Hilary's agency is, admittedly, a sadder task because Hilary's efforts did not save her life. Curtis disclosed Hilary was alive for only about fifteen minutes from the time he picked her up to the moment he suffocated her (CBC, "Bonnell Admits"). Through a close reading of the judgement and news reports, I suggest Hilary's opposition to domination is also apparent in her small, seemingly ordinary gestures. Examined carefully, her presencing strategies as a young Indigenous woman emerge from the reported cases (de Finney). In the *Under the Shadow of Empire, Indigenous Girls' Presencing as Decolonizing Force,* Sandrina de Finney emphasizes the importance of situating "Indigenous girls' everyday processes of resurgence and presencing as they take shape amid intersecting forms of traumatic violence that colonial states and societies produce" (9). The last time that Pam Fillier heard from her daughter was the early morning prior to her death (*R v*

Bonnell, NBQB 289 para 10). In what de Finney might recognize as a presencing strategy, Hilary called her mother at 3:00 a.m. in the morning to discuss their plan to go shopping the next day (8-26). During the trial, various witnesses confirmed that Hilary appeared happy about the plan. During the interview with Annie Clair, Fillier reported the conversation ended with the parties expressing love for each other. Hilary's last actions are significant because Fillier never heard from her only daughter again. Hilary's expression of affection for her mom can also be theorized with de Finney. That some of Hilary's last known expressions were of love might, in de Finney's view, complicate settler narratives of Indigenous girls existing in "ungrievable bodies" (borrowing Butler's term), which possess no "hope" or "capacity" as "victim bodies, disenfranchised bodies" (10).

It is also important to note that Hilary struggled against Curtis and attempted to resist his sexual violence. The text messages Hilary sent to her first cousin and close friend, Haylie Bonnell, on the evening before her disappearance were described as shifting from a "party atmosphere theme" to her final messages that " demonstrated that she was afraid of something or someone" (*R v Bonnell,* NBQB 376, para 6). Hilary's urgent calls went unanswered because her cousin's phone was dead. Specifically, Hilary forwarded four text messages to her cousin during the time she was confined by Curtis. They are reproduced here as they appeared in the 2015 appeal judgement (NBCA 6 para 67).

> 1) 07:25 a.m.: "OMG Haylie I wanna leave" (Oh my God, Haylie, I want to leave)
> 2) 07:40 a.m.: "where are yooou" (Where are you?)
> 3) 07:52 a.m.: "Plea8e answer me im scared" (Please answer me, I am scared.)
> 4) 08:20 a.m.: "OMF text me im scared" (Oh my fuck, text me, I am scared.)

Curtis Bonnell's argument that the messages should have been excluded by the lower courts was rejected by the New Brunswick Court of Appeal. Important from a presencing perspective, the text messages work against the characterization of Hilary's state as one of absolute victimization, even though Hilary's extreme fear is obvious. The capacity to fight back against a physically dominant predator was limited. These moments show Hilary's courageous efforts to counter the very real and terrifying violence that she encountered using the limited means available.

Even an abbreviated and incomplete source of information such as the New Brunswick court judgments show her strong, albeit thwarted, determination to survive. Elijah Adiv Edelman argues that resistance is possible even in the face of crushing marginalization. He states that, "Even within the barren death worlds and inside a seeming wasteland of corpses, fissures can be wrenched open through which vitality, and life, emerge" (187). Irrespective of the scale of their struggles, Annie's resistance and Hilary's actions appear brave given the powerful forces that they both confronted. The legacy of their resistance has the potential to benefit future generations.

This is particularly so because Annie Clair's and Hilary Bonnell's efforts take place within a context of Atlantic Indigenous resurgences. According to Prosper, McMillan, Davis, and Moffitt, Maritime Indigenous communities are returning to the practice of *Netukulimk*. As a result, traditional Mi'kmaq cultural and spiritual connections are a guiding resource for stewardship and self-governance (1-17). The Esgenoôpetitj First Nation seemed to act in accordance by demonstrating sadness and unification following Hilary's death, undermining the more typical narrative of Indigenous chaos. In December 2009, RCMP Inspector Roch Fortin, who was involved in the investigation, stated: "I have witnessed first-hand the way the community has come together—first to try to locate Hilary and then to say goodbye to her. The compassion and caring [displayed] for one another has been extraordinary" ("It's a Little Bit of Justice for My Little Girl"). I will cite a few other positive examples, among the many that are occurring in this region. The development of a comprehensive community-based Aboriginal criminal justice system in Elsipogtog, New Brunswick appears to be a success story, according to research by Don Clairmont. The Healing to Wellness Court (HWC), established in 2012, is the centre point of the restorative justice programming on Elsipogtog First Nation.

It is also of note that a Peace and Friendship Alliance, a coalition of Indigenous and non-Indigenous supporters, was formed in New Brunswick in March 2015. Indigenous members include several Wolastoq (Maliseet) bands, such as St. Mary's First Nation, Woodstock First Nation, Tobique First Nation, and Madawaska First Nation, along with Mi'kmaq representatives. Environmental groups, including the Council of Canadians and the Conservation Council of New Brunswick, have aligned with organic farmers and others in the struggle to protect the land, air and water "for all our relations and for future generations, and taking united action for a healthy planet" (Council of Canadians "Peace and Friendship Alliance"). The Peace and Friendship Alliance has held five well-attended meetings as of January 2016 (Council of Canadians, "Activists to Challenge"). Alma Brooks, an Elder and grandmother, explained at the most recent meeting that the Peace and Friendship Alliance was important because Atlantic territories were never ceded or surrendered by Indigenous nations (Council of Canadians "Peace and Friendship Alliance").

CONCLUSIONS

In this chapter, I have explored how the knowledge produced about missing and murdered Indigenous women can be expanded through a close examination of Atlantic Canadian studies. I attempt to build on the efforts by organizations, including the Native Women's Association of Canada, to ensure that the national scope of the tragedy is acknowledged. I also examine how our understanding might deepen if we were to make Indigenous women's diminished participation in social and political life a clearer focal point in collections on missing women. Central to this text is the argument that the research needs to theorize individual acts of violence against women as well as the broader social context and the wider institutions and culture that give rise to violent behaviour.

This study has firmly denounced the murder of a young, vibrant girl. At the same time, it has investigated the case beyond the personal violence often featured in prior scholarship. Moreover, the chapter has magnified the economic, legal, and political factors that positon Indigenous women for disproportionate violence. Land defender Annie Clair's criminalization and the murder of teenager Hilary Bonnell reveal a great deal about Canada's violence towards Indigenous women. By drawing from the lived experiences of two women who resisted or continue to resist violence in different circumstances and with differing results, I have argued that there are more who might be counted as "missing" and have outlined ways the disappearances were contested and even incomplete. By critically analyzing the case studies to undermine dominant claims, "resistant knowledges" have been produced, which Haritaworn, Kunstman and Posocco argue are necessary to "unmap" the "geopolitics of violence, abandonment, and death" (21).

In defense of her resistance to shale gas expansion, Clair affirms her responsibilities to future generations when she described the struggle as an effort 'for all the generations to come' (Devet). Clair's affirmation of the importance of acting on behalf of children and communities concludes this chapter. Her statement works against the erasures I sought to problematize by highlighting the colonial context in which silences emerge as well as the various ways Indigenous women manifest resistance by asserting presence.

ENDNOTES

[1]The paper uses varied spellings of Mi'kmaq depending on the source cited.

[2]New Brunswick is part of the original territory for three of the five nations that make up the Wabanaki Confederacy. The three nations are the Mi'kmaq, Wolastoqiyik, and Passamaquoddy.

[3]On other points, his testimony is clearly untruthful. On the stand, Curtis contradicted his confessions to the police and to Elder David Gehue stating he had no direct knowledge of how Hilary died.

CASES CITED

R v Bonnell 2011 NBQB 349 (CanLII)
R v Bonnell 2011 NBQB 376 (CanLII)
R v Bonnell 2012 NBQB 103 (CanLII)
R v Bonnell 2012 NBQB 309 (CanLII)

R v Bonnell 2012 NBQB 321 (CanLII)
R v Bonnell 2012 NBQB 395 (CanLII)
R v Bonnell 2015 NBCA 6 (CanLII)

WORKS CITED

Arsenault, Dan. "Supporters Hold Silent Auction for Activist Annie Clair." *The Chronicle Herald News*, 12 Apr. 2015. Web. 1 May 2015.

Bassichis, Morgan, and Dean Spade. "Queer Politics and Anti-Blackness." *Queer Necropolitics*. Eds. Jin Haritaworn, Adi Kuntsman, and Silvia Posocco. Abingdon/Oxon: Routledge, 2014. 191-210. Print.

Baloy, Natalie JK. "Spectacles and Spectres: Settler Colonial Spaces in Vancouver." *Settler Colonial Studies* (2015): 1-26. Web. November 1, 2015.

Bedford, David. "Emancipation as Oppression: The Marshall Decision and Self-Government." *Journal of Canadian Studies/Revue d'études canadiennes* 44.1 (2010): 206-220. Web. 1 Nov. 2015.

Bissett, Kevin. "Defence lawyer asks if crime was committed in Bonnell case." *CTV News Atlantic*, 1 Nov. 2012. Web. 1 May 2015.

Bissett, Kevin. "Mother of Slain Teen Hopes Bonnell Is Haunted by His Actions." *CTV News Atlantic*, 14 Nov. 2012. Web. 1 Nov. 2015.

"Building Hope in Esgenoôpetitj" *New Brunswick Media Co-op*. NB Media Co-op. 6 Apr. 2010. Web. 1 May 2015.

Canadian Broadcasting Corporation (CBC). "Bonnell Admits He Killed Cousin Hilary after Sex." *CBC News*, 9 Oct. 2012. Web. 1 Nov. 2015.

Canadian Broadcasting Corporation (CBC). "Loretta Saunders Homicide Sparks Call by Native Group for Public Inquiry, Inuk Student Was Studying Missing and Murdered Aboriginal Women." *CBC News*, 26 Feb. 2014. Web. 1 Nov. 2015.

Canadian Broadcasting Corporation (CBC). "Red Dresses Stark Reminder of Missing, Murdered Aboriginal Women, Artist Jaime Black's Moving REDress Project Comes to Fredericton." *CBC News*, 27 Oct. 27 2015. Web. 30 Oct. 2015.

Canadian Broadcasting Corporation (CBC). "Youth Centre Planned to Honour Hilary Bonnell." *CBC News*, 1 Feb. 2010. Web. 30 Oct. 2015.

Chagnon, Nicholas. "Heinous Crime or Acceptable Violence? The Disparate Framing of Femicides in Hawai'i." *Radical Criminology* 3 (2014): 13-45. Web. 1 Nov. 2015.

Clair, Annie Margaret. "Human Stories behind Canada's Tragic Epidemic of Missing and Murdered Aboriginal People." *The Coast*. Coast Publishing, n.d. Web. 1 Nov. 2015.

Clairmont, Don. "The Development of an Aboriginal Criminal Justice System: The Case of Elsipogtog." *UNBLJ* 64 (2013): 160 -186. HeinOnLine. Web. 11 Dec. 2015.

Choi, Jennifer. "Annie Clair, Anti-Shale Gas Protester Free, Charges Dropped, Annie Clair Says the Charges She Faced in Connection with Anti-Shale Gas Protests Send a Message." *CBC News*, 21 Sept. 2015. Web. 22 Sept. 2015.

Council of Canadians. "The Peace and Friendship Alliance—The Emergence of a Powerful Movement in New Brunswick and Indigenous Communities." *The Council of Canadians*. 26 Jan. 2016. Web. 11 Mar. 2016.

Council of Canadians, "Activists to Challenge Energy East during May 2016 Municipal Elections in New Brunswick." *The Council of Canadians*. 7 Dec. 2015. Web. 11 Dec. 2015.

Craig, Benjamin. "New Brunswick Anti-Fracking Protests." *Amnesty International*, 21 Oct. 2013. Web. 1 Nov. 2015.

Craig, Elaine. "Person(s) of Interest and Missing Women: Legal Abandonment in the Downtown Eastside." *McGill Law Journal* 60.1 (2014): 1-42. HeinOnline. Web. 1 Nov. 2015.

Culhane, Dara. "Their Spirits Live within Us: Aboriginal Women in Downtown Eastside Vancouver Emerging into Visibility." *The American Indian Quarterly* 27.2 (2003): 593-606. Web. 1 Nov. 2015.

De Finney, Sandrina. "Under the Shadow of Empire: Indigenous Girls' Presencing as Decolonizing Force." *Girlhood Studies* 7.1 (2014): 8-26. Print.

Devet, Robert. "Elsipogtog Land Defender Annie Clair Fights Legal Charges." *Halifax Media Co-op*. Halifax Media Co-op. 8 Apr. 2015. Web. 1 May 2015.

Dylan, Arielle, Cheryl Regehr, and Ramona Alaggia. "And Justice for All? Aboriginal Victims of Sexual Violence." *Violence against Women* 14.6 (2008): 678-696. Web. 11 Dec. 2015.

Eberts, Mary. "Knowing and Unknowing: Settler Reflections on Missing and Murdered Indigenous Women." *Saskatchewan Law Review* 77 (2014): 69. Web. November 1, 2015.

Edelman, Elijah Adiv. "'Walking while transgender': Necropolitical Regulations of Trans Feminine Bodies of Colour in the Nation's Capital." Eds. Jin Haritaworn, Adi Kuntsman, and Silvia Posocco. *Queer Necropolitics*. Abingdon/Oxon: Routledge, 2014. 172-190. Print.

Edkins, Jenny, and Véronique Pin-Fat. "Through the Wire: Relations of Power and Relations of Violence." *Millennium-Journal of International Studies* 34.1 (2005): 1-24. Web. 11 Dec. 2015.

Fillier, Pam. "The Missing, The Mourned—Missing and Murdered Aboriginal People in Canada: Segment 1: Annie Clair's Interview with Pam Fillier, Mother of Hilary Bonnell." Interview by Annie Clair. *The Coast*. Coast Publishing, n.d. Web. 1 Nov. 2015.

Gould, Gary P., and Alan J. Semple. *Our Land: The Maritimes: The Basis of the Indian Claim in the Maritime Provinces of Canada*. Fredericton, NB: Saint Annes Point Press, 1980. Print.

Haritaworn, Jin, Adi Kunstman, and Siivia Posocco. "Introduction." *Queer Necropolitics*. Eds. Jin Haritaworn, Adi Kunstman, and Siivia Posocco. Abingdon/Oxon: Routledge, 2014. 1-21. Print.

Howe, Miles. *Debriefing Elsipogtog: The Anatomy of a Struggle*. Halifax: Fernwood Publishing, 2015. Print.

Hugill, David. *Missing Women, Missing News: Covering Crisis in Vancouver's Downtown Eastside*. Halifax: Fernwood Publishing, 2015. Print.

"Hundreds Attend Funeral of N.B. Aboriginal Girl Who Went Missing Two Months Ago." *The Canadian Press*. The Canadian Press, 20 Nov. 2009. Web. 1 Nov. 2015.

"It's a Little Bit of Justice for My Little Girl." *The Canadian Press*. The Canadian Press, 10 Dec. 2009. Web. 1 Nov. 2015.

Just Associates and Nobel Women's Initiative. *From Survivors to Defenders: Women Confronting Violence in Mexico, Honduras & Guatemala*. Ottawa: Just Associates, 2012. Print.

Kaye, Julie. "Mobilizing Collective Outrage from the West to the Atlantic: Canada's Violence Against Indigenous Women." St. Thomas University, Fredericton, New Brunswick. 28 Oct. 2015. Lecture.

Kuokkanen, Rauna. "Globalization as Racialized, Sexualized Violence: The Case of Indigenous Women." *International Feminist Journal of Politics* 10.2 (2008): 216-233. Print.

Landertinger, Laura C. L. "Settler Colonialism and Carceral Control of Indigenous Mothers and their Children: Child Welfare and the Prison System." *Criminalized Mothers, Criminalizing Motherhood*. Eds. Joanne Minaker, and Bryan Hogeveen. Bradford, Ontario: Demeter, 2014. 59-87. Print.

McLellan, L. Hudson. *Contemporary Settler Colonialism: Media framing of Indigenous Collective Qction in Elsipogtog, Mi'kma'ki*. Diss. Dalhousie University. 2015. Web. 1 Nov. 2015.

McMillan, L., Janelle Young, and Molly Peters. "Commentary: The 'Idle No More' Movement in Eastern Canada." *Canadian Journal of Law and Society/Revue Canadienne Droit et Société* 28.3 (2013): 429-431. Web. 1 Nov. 2015.

Murdocca, Carmela. "Visual Legalities of Race and Reparations." *Canadian Journal of Law and Society/Revue Canadienne Droit et Société* 29.2 (2014): 219-234. Web. 11 Dec. 2015.

Native Women's Association of Canada (NWAC). "Digital Life Story of Hilary Bonnell." NWAC, 13 Aug. 2014 Web. 5 Apr. 2013.

Native Women's Association of Canada (NWAC). "NWAC Stands with Indigenous Women of Val D'Or; Encourages All Survivors of Police Violence to Continue Coming Forward." NWAC, 1 Apr. 2016 Web. 22 Apr. 2016.

New Brunswick Advisory Committee on Violence against Women "Strategic Framework to End Violence against Wabanaki Women in New Brunswick." New Brunswick: New Brunswick Advisory Committee on Violence against Women, 2008. Print.

Nicholas, Andrea Bear. "Colonialism and the Struggle for Liberation: The Experience of Maliseet Women." *UNBLJ* 43 (1994): 223. Web. 1 Nov. 2015.

Obomsawin, Alanis, dir. *Is the Crown at War with Us?* National Film Board of Canada, 2002. Film.

Palmater, Pamela D. "Stretched Beyond Human Limits: Death by Poverty in First Nations." *Canadian Review of Social Policy* 65/66 (2011): 112-149. Print.

Palmater, Pamela D. "Matnm Tel-Mi'kmawi: I'm Fighting for My Mi'kmaw Identity." *The Canadian Journal of Native Studies* 33.1 (2013): 147-159. Web. 1 Nov. 2015.

Palmater, Pamela. "Genocide, Indian Policy, and Legislated Elimination of Indians in Canada." *Aboriginal Policy Studies* 3.3 (2014): 27-54. Web. 1 Nov. 2015.

Park, Hijin Race. "Nation and Citizenship in 'Mothers Who Kill Their Children': The Case of Rie Fujii." *Criminalized Mothers, Criminalizing Motherhood*. Eds. Joanne Minaker and Bryan Hogeveen. Bradford, Ontario: Demeter, 2014. 164-183. Print.

Prosper, K., L. McMillan, A. A. Davis, and M. Moffitt. "Returning to Netukulimk: Mi'kmaq Cultural and Spiritual Connections with Resource Stewardship and Self-Governance." *The International Indigenous Policy Journal* 2.4 (2011): 1-17. Web. 21 May 2014.

Razack, Sherene H. "Gendered Racial Violence and Spatialized Justice: The Murder of Pamela George." *Canadian Journal of Law & Society* 15.2 (2000): 91-130. Web. 10 May 2013.

Rose, Deborah Bird. "Land Rights and Deep Colonising: The Erasure of Women." *Aboriginal Law Bulletin* 3.85 (1996): 6-13. Print.

Royal Canadian Mounted Police (RCMP). "Missing and Murdered Aboriginal Women: A National Operational Overview." RCMP, 27 May 2014. Web. 5 June 2014.

Savarese, Josephine L. "'Doing No Violence to the Sentence Imposed': Racialized Sex Worker Complainants, Racialized Offenders, and the Feminization of the Homo Sacer in Two Sexual Assault Cases." *Canadian Journal of Women and the Law* 22.2 (2010): 365-395. Web. 1 Nov. 2015.

Share, Zoe. "The Legacy of Canadian Colonialism: The Case of Violence against Aboriginal Women." *Politicus Journal* 1.1 (2014): 4-14. Web. 1 Nov. 2015.

Simpson, Leanne. *Dancing on Our Turtle's Back: Stories of Nishnaabeg Re-creation, Resurgence and a New Emergence*. Winnipeg: Arbeiter Ring Publishing, 2011. Print.

Simpson, Leanne Betasamosake, "Anger, Resentment and Love: Fuelling Resurgent Struggle." *Leanne Simpson*. n.p., 8 June. 2015. Web. 1 Nov. 20.

Tuck, Eve. "Suspending Damage: A Letter to Communities." *Harvard Educational Review* 79.3 (2009): 409-428. Web. 2 Oct. 2015.

Watts, Vanessa. "Indigenous Place-Thought and Agency Amongst Humans and Non-Humans (First Woman and Sky Woman Go On a European World Tour!)." *Decolonization: Indigeneity Education & Society* 2.1 (2013): 20-34. Print.

Willow, Anna J. "Conceiving Kakipitatapitmok: The Political Landscape of Anishinaabe Anticlearcutting Activism." *American Anthropologist* 113.2 (2011): 262-276. Web. 1 Nov. 2015.

Wright, Melissa W. *Disposable Women and Other Myths of Global Capitalism*. New York: Routledge, 2006. Print.

7.

The Duty of the Canadian Media in Relation to the Violence against Native Women

Lessons Drawn from the Case of Ciudad Juárez

ISELA PÉREZ-TORRES

IN THE STRUGGLE UNDERTAKEN by the mothers of Indigenous victims of violence and by Canadian civil organizations for their right to justice, and in order to bring to an end the crimes committed against Native women, the media have a heavy responsibility, one which has ethical, social and historical dimensions. The reasons for these cases' lack of attention, which has resulted in impunity as well as in the continuation of the problem, should be addressed in the Canadian press in a way that is more than merely informative. The media, and journalists in general, should be actively involved in seeking a solution to the problem, which implies recognizing and assuming its moral and professional obligation to abstain from a discriminatory discourse that reinforces violence and lack of civic solidarity.

The violence against Native women in Canada and the activism undertaken by their families have some parallels with the case of Ciudad Juárez, México, where women on the lowest end of the social scale have been subject to discrimination and violence for more than two decades, with impunity. This panorama of violence on the American-Mexican border is played out within the structure of a patriarchal state, and the victims are largely women living in conditions of poverty and exploitation. The circumstances of their lives are conditioned by a political and economic system that considers them disposable (Wright 27-28). It is system that originates in both the First and Third Worlds[1] because of the presence of factories from México, the United States, Europe, and Asia.

The violence persists in spite of numerous recommendations from international bodies, including the sentence pronounced in 2009 by the Interamerican Court of Human Rights (CoIDH) against the state of México for failing to protect the lives of these women and for violating their human rights by not guaranteeing their right to the appropriate legal procedures and justice.[2] The families of the victims have been constant in their struggle, as have the international bodies, but despite this, the violence continues with impunity.

It is worth asking what has happened in México and in line with the objectives of this chapter, what responsibility can be attributed to the media for the lack of attention given to the problem and potential solutions. Among other factors—which are not the subject of this paper but are still important—the role that the media has assumed has been crucial in ensuring the impunity of the offenders and public indifference. Most media have ignored the calls of the victims' families for greater attention to these cases, a function that they are obliged to fulfil in the face of such a serious social problem as violence against women. On the contrary, the media, with few exceptions, has hostilely acted against those who demand justice which is the same stance as taken by the political and entrepreneurial elite (Orquiz). The discourse of discrimination and contempt directed towards the victims and the struggle of their families—as expressed by public officials who have even gone so far as to blame the murdered women for supposedly provoking their aggressors—has increasingly become a campaign reproduced by the majority of the local media.

The Canadian media should realize that by disseminating a message that either subtly or directly discredits and criminalizes the women who are fighting to bring to an end the disappearances and murders, such as those have taken place in Ciudad Juárez, they only reinforce impunity and weaken any possibility of citizen support being given to the surviving families. In this chapter, I will present some of the challenges that the Canadian media and journalists should accept in relation to this problem. I take as my reference the description of events and the attitudes adopted by the media and some journalists in Ciudad Juárez, which may have contributed to the both continued violence and impunity.

THE DISCOURSE OF POWER AND DISCRIMINATION

The violence directed towards certain women in Juárez is related, among other things, to a problem of exclusion that makes their lives vulnerable. This circumstance has been tolerated and even encouraged by central state power, and the reiteration of a discourse with an ideologically discriminatory content has been a determining factor for this violence against women. On this part of the Mexican border, discrimination is based not only on ethnic origin or the color of the women's skin but also on other features of their lives and environment. These women are impoverished; they have had no opportunity to study or have abandoned their studies because of the necessity to work. They live in marginalized areas on the edge of the city where high levels of destitution and delinquency are recorded (Monárrez 29-31). But what does discrimination have to do with journalists and the media? Discrimination and racism are the products of a domino system that reproduces and perpetuates itself through the social behavior of dominant groups or elites and through the establishment of relationships based on the abuse of power (Van Dijk 192-193). In the case of the women, this discrimination is exacerbated because it is also a cultural problem related to gender, which has historically made women and their lives more vulnerable.

One of the ways of breeding discrimination is through public discourse. Both media and journalists are an important link in the preservation of this discriminatory ideology. This is, in principle, one of the most tangible flaws of the media coverage in that area of the Mexican border, where women and men are not portrayed in the same way. For this reason, with some exceptions,[3] the way in which society is presented with cases of disappearances and murders of women frequently flows from a discourse that is sexist or contemptuous towards the victims of violence, and comes from the very authorities responsible for seeking justice for these women. It is true that over a period of more than two decades, the Mexican government has adopted some measures, and some specialized institutions have been created in order to follow up on the problem, but it remains patently obvious, because of the reigning impunity and the continuing occurrence of incidents, that these measures have been ineffective.[4] Moreover, the meagre measures themselves came about as a result of the struggle and persistent demands of the victims' families and the intervention of international organizations. They were not the result of genuine political determination on the part of the Mexican governing elite.

The power of the state and of the economic and political elites has exercised significant control on the information dealing with violence towards women. The dissemination or the concealment of information, at least by the most powerful media, is a mechanism that sustains the system of dominance and can influence or manipulate the way people think and act in order to justify impunity. This media control does not only take place in Ciudad Juárez but also internationally. A possible explanation for this is provided by Teun van Dijk in his book *Discourse and Power*, in which he states that the elites who hold power cannot ignore the media because it is the key to the control of public discourse. "Power is related to control and control of the discourse implies privileged access to its production and, therefore, to its contents" (Dijk 12-13).

Press conferences, official bulletins or communications, and the timing and way in which they are given, are always, or almost always, slanted towards the interests of the group in power, whether that is the state or any other elite. The intention is to maintain control, and as a result, these groups in power define not only what is permitted and what is not, but also what is permitted to be perceived as real and what is not; what every action or movement, in this case of women, should mean for the rest of society. But worse still, there is an implied warning as to what would happen to those who join forces with any movement in favor of women. This situation confirms what Michel Foucault (178) points out about truth—that it is bound together with the system of power that produces and maintains it, and to the consequences that it can be expected to produce.

This strategy to maintain control over the public discourse is reinforced every day by the selective publication of opinions or silences. If, in a private context, the relations of power and domination to which these women are subject are an example of the cultural and political conditions with which they have to deal every day, the media not only reproduces but also appropriates this ideology and reinforces it. The publication of information about the problem of violence against women reproduces the ideology about women and their role in public life, which is a cultural construct. The struggle of the victims' mothers raises the question of a change in the whole structure of the state and that implies dismantling the system of domination that the victims have to face. It also makes clear that the media must undergo significant transformation.

The editorial line that the media maintains, with respect to the activism of the victims' mothers, reflects the patriarchal culture that predominates in this northern region of México. In the round-up of local news, the number of items or the space dedicated to the subject of violence against women is largely limited to the sensational details of each finding but leaves out the analysis of the problem and does not usually address or follow up the irregularities committed by the authorities in each case. On this last matter, the *Report by the International Experts Commission of the United Nations Office on Drugs and Crime on its Mission to Ciudad Juárez*, Chihuahua, Mexico, produced in November 2003, also refers to the information coverage given to the cases of murdered women (ONUDD 49). The report points out the lack of any kind of technical training program for reporters[5] as well as the incentives for the state itself to promote this lack of training.

With respect to the way in which coverage is given to these cases, it is not just a question of the media and journalists focusing on recording an incident but rather being aware of the fact that from the mass of incidents that occur each day, violence against women may occupy a prime space on account of its seriousness or it may not be esteemed important. It is precisely on this point of the space assigned and the focus given to the information where the media and journalists can slip into complicity or have the gratifying satisfaction of contributing towards the solution of the problem. The focus of a news item may be part of the discourse of the dominating elite and, therefore, may be a conditioning factor for civic action.

"IT IS THE WOMEN WHO ARE GUILTY. THE WOMEN ARE THE ENEMIES"

The tenacious control of information exercised by the dominant elites in Ciudad Juárez is such that an official discourse has blamed the victims for the very crimes that they have suffered. They have been accused of leading a "double life" and, thus, provoking their own murderers. In some cases, in which the victims were minors, the responsibility was laid on their families for not protecting them. An example of this is the case of Cynthia Rocío, ten years of age, who was murdered in February 1997. Francisco Barrio Terrazas, the then governor of the state of Chihuahua, and his representative in Ciudad Juárez, never had time to give an interview to the family of the child when she was found to be missing. Nevertheless, once her murdered body was discovered, the ex-governor declared that Cynthia had been uncared for because she had tooth decay and was suffering from calcium deficiency. The reaction from the media was similar. When the family sought its support in order to ask for the cooperation of the public in the search for the child, the media's reply was again similar: "In *El Diario de Juárez* [newspaper] they told me that once or twice they regarded it as a social service, but afterwards we would have to pay"— pay for the publication a "missing" notice to ask for the public for help in searching for the girl. "Only when the body was found did they [the media] show any interest in Cynthia and her plight. Of course, then, there were lots of photos and it began to be lucrative for the newspaper, which filled its pages with the news" (R. Pérez, "Crímenes De Mujeres").

Another disturbing aspect of this problem is that the concern of public officials, entrepreneurs, and pro-government journalists was focused not on the seriousness of the crimes but on the international disrepute brought to the city by the publication of these murders and their impunity. The mothers were accused of "tarnishing the city's image" and of "benefitting financially from the crimes committed against their daughters." The media pronounced the same judgement on activists and journalists who denounced the impunity or who wrote about these cases and the infringements of human rights carried out by the authorities responsible for the investigations. These communication companies added their weight to the public indictment and denounced the mothers of the victims, activists, and journalists for supposedly having benefitted from the violence. But at the same time, there was clearly a contradiction on the part of some media outlets, since they publicly expressed their concern for these cases, ignoring the presumed sham and the financial gain of the families of the victims.[6] But they also published articles about the damages that this group of women supposedly caused to the most powerful entrepreneurs in Ciudad Juárez, who make a living from the exploitation and the labor of a large sector of female workers on their factories (Monárrez 49-51).

In some of the publications, there are paragraphs such as the following: "[the women's movement] has created and exaggerated an unreal image of the climate of delinquency that exists here, which has deterred national and foreign investors and, as a consequence, damaged the economic development" of Ciudad Juárez (Guerrero and Minjares). In this text, published in a local newspaper in 2004, it is stated, on behalf of public officials and businessmen, that femicide is a myth, and that those who denounce the impunity are only profiting from the grief caused by the murders. But in this instance, the significance of "myth" was taken in the sense of a lie, an invention. Thus, the discourse of power is used as a manipulative mechanism whose main aim is to attenuate the severity of this social problem.

An interesting fact about the campaign waged against women fighting the violence in Ciudad Juárez is that some women were chosen to write reports that echoed the official discourse. How do such things happen? How can it be that women themselves contribute to the weakening of the movement of other women? It is important to take into consideration that most media outlets have formed alliances with patriarchal groups with the very people who claim that the image of the city is worth more than the lives of women. So, the message and the messengers in this case are not the result of coincidence. The message scores a double hit on the movement for women for justice because it discredits them but at the same time it is women who are promoting it and who subscribe to it. How can anyone doubt the message if women are themselves the messengers? This fact presents women once again with very important questions: they are up against a whole power structure that excludes women, especially a certain group of women, and considers them inferior, usable, and disposable. Kate Millet states that the patriarchal system has been so astute that it has been able to set women against women, "as a result of the subtle but constant pronouncement of their inferiority which, ultimately, they accept as a fact" (121).

Some journalists have published reports in which they have just reproduced the official version on the issue. As for example, the *Journalism Auditing*, a report about the *kidnapping* and violence against young women in *Juárez* on 2003 elaborated by local journalists. It reproduced the official facts and figures from cases (Otero and Montañez). Oscar Máynez, chief at the Criminology Department at Chihuhaua State Attorney General's Office between 2000 and 2002, has said after this brief's presentation that the auditing was created with edited data because even cases managed by his department were not included (R. Pérez "Presentan Auditoría Editada").

In the same vein, there are many articles in which the issue of violence against women was underestimated as reflected on the front page of *El Diario [newspaper]* on March 2004, as the following quote illustrates: "Women are not the only victims of murder, as the manipulated numbers from the last eleven years report. Men have also been murdered and executed for more than a decade as statistics show" ("Contra la Violencia" *El Diario*). However, this publisher was referring to the crimes against drug dealers, another serious problem at the Mexican border.

This situation has brought a lot of attention considering that the number of kidnappings and murders of women have always been a controversial topic. The reason why is because the amount of cases reported by Mexican Justice authorities has been called into question by civil organizations and academic researchers. Another example is the April 2009 edition of a Mexican digital magazine that does not comment on these discussions but does explain in one of the first paragraphs of the article that "Not all the murderers were men. In the list there are nine women" (J. Pérez). Although the fact is important, the way in which the information is presented—emphasizing that not all the murderers are men—is tendentious, as if these nine cases made a huge difference in contrast with the number of murders committed by men. The number of crimes amounted to 1,432 committed by men in the period between 1993 and 2012,[7] according to information gathered by Julia Monárrez Fragoso, an investigator at the *Colegio de la Frontera*. According to the organization *Red Mesa de Mujeres de Ciudad Juárez,* at the beginning of 2013, around two hundred kidnappings[8] of women had been registered and more than 140 female bodies, murder victims, had not yet been identified by the forensic service of Ciudad Juárez (R. Pérez, "Ni el Tiempo"). Among all the femicides that have been registered, there is no point of comparison between those committed by men and those committed by women, although both are worthy of condemnation. It is true that both cases are forms of violence, but although they result in a crime, they are not carried out with the same aggravating circumstances. The victims of femicide committed by men have suffered kidnapping, torture, sexual violence, and murder. Those crimes committed by women do not involve, for example, torture and sexual violence.

Millet has made the following observation about the treatment given by the media to information related to offences committed by women: "When a woman is accused of some violation of the law she usually attracts a level of public attention totally out of proportion to the real nature of her acts" (121-122). Even more so when in cases of femicide, they are compared with crimes committed by men, as seen in the previous example.

Perhaps after these publications some honest journalists feared that they would be blacklisted for having tarnishing the image of the city or for disseminating information that was classified as false,[9] at least according to the discourse of the groups of power, including the media entrepreneurs. Or they may simply have abstained from reporting on the subject. This is a triumph for power because when the media and journalists participate in the control of public discourse, they also become part of the controlled or dominated group.

ISOLATION AS A STRATEGY

In her reflection on *The Origins of Totalitarianism*, Hannah Arendt points out that human beings who are isolated are powerless. "Isolation is the dead-end that men are forced into when the political sphere of their lives has been destroyed" (380). As a necessary condition for control, the reflection of Arendt about isolation may help to understand what has happened in Ciudad Juárez. By isolating women and their movement, the political elite and some media are denying them the recognition that they have the capacity to contribute something new to society, to add something of their own experience. Women have also been abandoned by people in general and the consequence of that is the body of citizens denies itself the possibility of receiving what they need in to avoid more violence and impunity. This isolation has also weakened the victims' families, which have been formed and disbanded continually in Ciudad Juárez,[10] resulting in a lack of continuity in their fight and their pursuit of empowerment.

Clearly the intention of the media in their coverage of the struggle of the victims' mothers has been precisely to nullify their sense of belonging to society and their awareness of being citizens with rights. The situation is aggravated by the fact that the support that should come from civil organizations has been weakened, and their efforts have largely been directed towards the political sphere to bring about changes in the structure of the state, prevent violence, and correct the system of justice. But the humanitarian aspect of their work has been of a limited scope.[11] An equation that combines discredit through the discourse against the families and the victims on the one hand, and lack of citizen solidarity on the other, has a high cost for the organization of the mothers of the missing and murdered women.

The story about the forced exile in 2010 of Marisela Ortiz Rivera, the director of the organization *Nuestras Hijas de Regreso a Casa*, is a case in point. There has been no follow-up of her situation in the media, or of the other activists, and her struggle continues to be shrouded in silence on the part of most of the local media. The case of the murder in 2010 of Marisela Escobedo, the mother of Rubí, who was murdered by her husband in 2009, is another item of news that is only interesting to the media, when the hint of scandal may attract greater attention. The crime was committed outside the Chihuahua government building, where Marisela was carrying out a demonstration to demand the arrest of her daughter's murderer. But she was alone, without the supporting voices of some of the stronger human rights organizations. These voices were not heard until after Marisela had been murdered.

Another case is that of Josefina Reyes, the mother of two murdered girls, who became an activist for justice and was murdered herself in 2009. Her whole family had to flee the country in 2011 following the crimes committed against three of their family members for persisting in their demand for justice. Since the crimes and the exile of the whole family, none of the media has followed up on their situation or on the supposed investigation that the Mexican authorities promised to carry out against members of the Mexican army, whom the family had identified as being responsible for the crimes.

In this context, space dedicated to finding solutions to problems or to bringing attention to the most vulnerable is not precisely what the women's movements find in media publications. Media outlets have taken too long to understand the social movements and the struggle of women. In some cases, some exposure has been given to the movements, but this has been on the initiative of certain journalists, both men and women, not because there exists an editorial policy that attaches importance to them.

The way in which this subject has been treated by most of the media will attract the attention of anyone looking for the causes of the ongoing problem and the lack of citizen solidarity. Nevertheless, the roots of these issues go much deeper still and include other cultural and political factors. But perhaps everything that has been described in this chapter can be better understood if it is seen as one shortcoming, which is neither material nor intellectual but a human shortcoming. I am referring to the kind of poverty that suppresses the capacity to be conscious of others; the poverty that makes us forget that we are people first and professionals second. If we are unable to be conscious of others as people who are part of our world, seeing them as part of our existence, then we will not recognize the moment when we are needed as journalists.

The Canadian media outlets have a great opportunity before them to make a difference. They can work to dignify the victims and their families and contribute to the correction of the injustices and inequalities from which the victims are suffering. They can put a brake on and eliminate political decisions and actions that do not guarantee the safety of Indigenous women and that have violated their rights. Journalists have the human and professional responsibility to cover and give appropriate follow-up to all these cases of violence and to the struggle of their families. They must distance themselves from patriarchal and racist ideologies, from the discourse of the elite and their economic interests, and take as an example the great lesson that the families of the Indigenous victims of violence are giving right now to Canadian society as a whole: the value of their daughters and of Indigenous life.

ENDNOTES

[1]She is a Mexican journalist, originally from Ciudad Juárez, who now lives in asylum in Spain. All translations were done by the author.

[2]The ICHR resolved to give the sentence to Mexico for the violation of human rights in 2009 on account of the case known as "Campo Algodonero. González y otras," which refers to crimes committed against three of a group of eight young girls, whose tortured bodies were found in an area that had previously been used for the cultivation of cotton. The murders would have taken place between November 6 and 7, 2001.

[3]Some journalists have taken a personal interest in the problem and have tried in their work to respect the human rights of the families concerned and the victims, but they have faced censoring, moral harassment, and threats.

[4]The following are two emblematic examples of this situation: in 2003, the Office of the Special Prosecutor for Crimes of Violence against Women was created. Its task was to analyse the records of the crimes and determine which of the public officials leading the investigations were responsible for negligence and omission. None of the officials were sanctioned because the statute of limitation on the crimes had expired. In the same year, the Special Commission for the Prevention of Crimes against Women was also created, but the problem continued, and the prosecutor was transferred to the capital city, with the same role but at a national level, no longer

just for Ciudad Juárez.
[5]The report of the Commission of Experts of the UN was drawn up after carrying out an analysis of the records of the cases of violence against women in Ciudad Juárez.
[6]Starting in 2004, the media in Ciudad Juárez intensified the "financial gain" campaign as well as in the days leading up to the oral proceedings when the families of the victims appeared before the Interamerican Court of Human Rights in April 2009.
[7]I am grateful to Dr. Julia Monárrez for providing me with this information from her data base.
[8]In an interview that I carried out in 2013 with Cecilia Espinoza, a member of the *Red Mesa de Mujeres*, she clarified that the number of disappearances may be higher, since it has been difficult to achieve transparency in the handling of the information about the cases. I am grateful to Cecilia Espinoza for supplying me with cases involving the disappearances of women recorded by the organization.
[9]While I was working for the newspaper 'Norte' (1999–2005), some male journalists openly refused to cover the subject, while others were not given the assignment on a daily basis in spite of their interest in these cases. It was considered that the subject of violence against women was a women's problem and as such should be covered principally by women.
[10]The following are some of the groups that have been formed by families and friends of the missing and murdered women, both in Ciudad Juárez and in Chihuahua, the state capital: *Voces sin Eco, Nuestras Hijas de Regreso a Casa, Justicia para Nuestras Hijas, Familiares y Amigos de Mujeres Desaparecidas y Asesinadas, Madres de Mujeres Desaparecidas y Asesinadas, among others.*
[11]Some of the activists have reported having received threats, and this situation has also weakened the attempts to strengthen the mothers of the victims.

WORKS CITED

Arendt, Hannah. *Los Orígenes Del Totalitarismo* [*The Origins of Totalitarianism*]. Trans. Guillermo Solana. España: Santillana, 1998. Print.

Espinosa, Cecilia, Personal interview, 25 Sept. 2014.

Corte Interamericana de Derechos Humanos (CoIDH). Sentencia *Caso Campo Algodonero. González y Otras Contra México* [*Judgment Cotton Field Case. González and Others Against* México]. Santiago: Corte Interamericana de Derechos Humanos Santiago de Chile, 2009. Print.

"Contra la Violencia, Soluciones de Fondo" [Against Violence, Deep Solutions]. Editorial. *El Diario* 13 March 2004, Ciudad Juárez ed.: 1A. Print.

Foucault, Michel. *Microfísica Del Poder* [*Mirophysics of Power*]. Trans and Eds. Julia Varela and Fernando Alvarez-Uría. Segunda ed. España: Las Ediciones de la Piqueta, 1979. Print.

Guerrero, Cecilia, and Gabriela Minjares. "Hacen Mito y Lucro De Los Feminicidios" ["Myth and Profit with Femicides"]. *El Diario* 22 July 2004: 1A. Print.

Millet, Kate. Política Sexual. México [Sexual Politics]: Aguilar, 1995. Print.

Monárrez, Julia. *Peritaje Sobre Feminicidio Sexual Sistémico En Ciudad Juárez. González y Otras Contra México. Campo Algodonero* [*Expert Opinion on Sistemic Sexual Femicides in Juarez City. González and Others Against México. Cotton Field*]. Santiago, Chile: Corte Interamericana de Derechos Humanos. Caso 12498, 2009. Print.

Orquiz, Martin. "Basta De Denigrar a Juárez: Sectores" ["Enough to Denigrate Juárez: Sectors"]. *Diario,* 22 Apr. 2004. Web. 18 June 2013.

Otero, Calderón A., and Elías Montañez. *Homicidios De Mujeres: Auditoría Periodística: Enero 1993-Julio 2003* [*Homicides against Women: Journalistic Audit. January 1993-July 2003*]. Ciudad Juárez, Chihuahua, México: Instituto Chihuahuense de la Mujer. July 2003. Print.

Organización de las Naciones Unidas contra la Droga y el Delito (ONUDD), Informe de la Comisión de Expertos Internacionales de las Naciones Unidas sobre la Misión en Ciudad Juárez, Chihuahua, México, [*Report by the International Experts Commission of the United Nations Office on Drugs and Crime on its Mission to Ciudad Juárez*] 2003. Print

Pérez Espino, J. "Homicidios de Mujeres: nombres, rostros y móvil de los asesinos" ["Crimes against Women: Names, Faces and

Motive of the Murderers"]. *Al Margen*, 24 Apr. 2009. Web. 18 June. 2013.

Pérez Torres, Rosa I. "Crímenes De Mujeres." ["Crimes against Women"]. *Norte de Ciudad Juárez* 15 Mar. 2001: 5B. Print.

Pérez Torres, Rosa I. "Ni el Tiempo ni la Condena Frenan los Asesinatos en Ciudad Juárez" ["Neither Time Nor Condemnation Curb the Murders in Juárez City"]. *Zoom News*, 2013. Web. 18 June 2013.

Pérez Torres, Rosa I "Presentan Auditoría Editada" ["Journalistic Audit Is Presented"]. *Norte de Ciudad Juárez* 19 July 2003: 1A. Print.

Van Dijk, Teun Adrianus. *Discurso y Poder* [*Discourse and Power*]. Trans. Alicira Bixio. Primera ed. España: Gedisa, 2009. Print.

Wright, Melissa. *Disposable Woman and Other Myths of Global Capitalism*. New York: Routledge, 2006. Print.

III.
EDUCATION, AWARENESS AND ACTION

8.
Transnational Advocacy for the Missing and Murdered Indigenous Women

ROSEMARY NAGY

IN THE LAST DECADE, seven United Nations human rights treaty committees, the UN Special Rapporteur on the Rights of Indigenous Peoples, the United Nations Human Rights Council, and the Inter-American Commission on Human Rights have all expressed significant concern about disproportionate levels of violence against Indigenous women and girls in Canada and the lack of progress in combatting it (Amnesty International, *A Summary of Amnesty International's Concerns*). In addition, prominent human rights NGOs, such as Human Rights Watch and Amnesty International, have written damning reports on missing and murdered Indigenous women (MMIW) in Canada. Many of these advocates have called for a national public inquiry, a recommendation repeated most recently by the United Nations Human Rights Committee during its review of Canada in July 2015. The former Conservative government under Prime Minister Stephen Harper steadfastly refused to establish a national inquiry. However, the new Liberal government, under Prime Minister Justin Trudeau, has (at time of going to press) completed pre-inquiry consultations, and he plans to launch a national inquiry in the near future.

Thus, with the new government, there is much hope that there will be greater compliance, policy and attitude changes.[1] Transnational pressure arguably helped bring about this shift. Moreover, continued transnational advocacy will be required, including in the form of constructive dialogue, to promote and ensure the implementation of the rights of Indigenous women. This chapter addresses the nature and impact of transnational advocacy. I examine how Canada has responded to transnational advocacy for Indigenous rights in the past by looking at two examples: *Lovelace v. Canada* (1984) and Canada's belated endorsement of the United Nations Declaration on the Rights of Indigenous People in 2010. I examine changing conceptions of self-determination vis-à-vis Indigenous women's rights over the different examples. Despite the state-centric framework of international law, I argue that transnational advocacy for the MMIW can be read as an expression of Indigenous self-determination and one, moreover, that centres on Indigenous women's human rights.

TRANSNATIONAL ADVOCACY

Transnational advocacy refers to organized networks of actors from groups such as international and domestic non-governmental organizations (NGOs), local social movements, regional and intergovernmental organizations (IGOs), churches, unions, media, foundations, and/or parts of the parliamentary or executive branches of government (Keck and Sikkink). These groups operate voluntarily, on the basis of shared principles, and with the frequent exchange of information and services. They promote norm implementation, monitor state compliance with human rights and other international legal obligations, frame issues, and bring norms, ideas, and discourses into policy debates. As Margaret Keck and Kathryn Sikkink write, "Activists in networks try not only to influence policy outcomes, but to transform the terms and nature of the debate" (2).

Transnational advocacy networks are likely to form when domestic channels for resolving conflict are blocked, hampered, or ineffective due to repression or lack of responsiveness (12). Keck and Sikkink argue that a "boomerang pattern" of influence develops when domestic NGOs bypass their state and seek international allies to bring pressure from the outside and amplify domestic demands (13). Sikkink, elsewhere, further proposes that "insider-outsider coalitions" occur when neither domestic nor international pathways are entirely blocked: domestic activists concentrate their efforts at home but "will keep international activism as a complementary and compensatory option" (165). Transnational activists primarily exert pressure on states through "naming and shaming," monitoring and persuading, although stronger tools, such as sanctions and prosecution, are also possible through intergovernmental organizations.

Once states become party to an international human rights treaty, they are committed, at least on paper, to fulfilling their obligations to promote and protect the enshrined rights through law and policy within their own borders. Following Risse and Sikkink's "spiral model" of norm socialization, once a state has signed onto an international human rights treaty—even as a tactical concession in the face of transnational pressure—there is reduced space for strategic manoeuver because the state can no longer deny the legitimacy of that norm. What was at first instrumental adaptation starts to change as states become "entrapped in their own rhetoric" and communication with critics begins to take the form of argumentation and dialogue rather than denial (Risse and Sikkink 28). As human rights norms become institutionalized in domestic law and take root in societal discourse, transnational pressure remains important for ensuring compliant state behaviour (35). Even if state behaviour does not yet conform to the norms, those norms gain prescriptive status with constitutive effects (Risse and Sikkink 8). In short, the principled ideas behind human rights norms help to constitute identities to which states aspire, that is, as members in good standing in the international community. Accordingly, the presence of domestic-international linkages also helps to explain the longer-term dynamics of domestic change as norms become habitualized and implemented as a matter of course.

The spiral model has five stages—repression, denial, tactical concessions, prescriptive status, and rule-consistent behaviour—and though arguably causal, it is not necessarily a linear or inevitable process (Shor). However, it is useful for understanding Canada's position on the MMIW as being in transition from prescriptive status to rule-consistent behaviour with respect to the rights of Indigenous women. The MMIW have been on the international radar since at least 2004, when Amnesty International's first *Stolen Sisters* report was released. The Human Rights Committee, which monitors the International Covenant on Civil and Political Rights, raised concern about policing failures in 2006. In 2008, the

Committee for the Elimination of Discrimination against Women (CEDAW) recommended the development of a national action plan and an examination of reasons for the failure to investigate cases of missing or murdered women (6). In 2012, the Committee on the Elimination of Racial Discrimination and the Committee on the Rights of the Child expressed grave concern about disproportionate levels of violence against Indigenous women and girls and the lack of progress in combatting it. That same year, the Committee against Torture also recommended enhanced efforts to respond to violence against Indigenous women.

During Canada's universal periodic review before the Human Rights Council[2] in 2013, at least twenty-four countries expressed concern about the MMIW, with nine pressing for the development of a national action plan and/or the establishment of a national inquiry (Amnesty International, *A Summary of Amnesty International's Concerns*). James Anaya, former special rapporteur on the rights of Indigenous peoples, recommended after his 2013 country visit that Canada undertake a "comprehensive, nationwide inquiry." He also reported that the Conservative government efforts—which included budgeting twenty-five million dollars over the next five years for community safety plans, victim services, and healing and risk-reduction strategies—have not abated "continuing calls for greater and more effective action" (11). Similar concerns were reiterated during the 2015 review of Canada at the Human Rights Committee, which called for a national inquiry, a review of all relevant legislation, the investigation, prosecution and punishment of perpetrators, as well as the provision of reparation to victims and addressing root causes of violence to Indigenous women and girls (para. 9).

The various committee reports are the result of reporting mechanisms embedded in the treaties in which states self-report, and civil society organizations may submit alternative or "shadow reports." In the case of the MMIW, these organizations have included Amnesty International Canada, the Canadian Feminist Alliance for International Action (FAFIA), Human Rights Watch, the Native Women's Association of Canada (NWAC), the British Columbia CEDAW group, the Six Nations Traditional Women's Fire Council, Assembly of First Nations, First Nations Summit, the Indigenous

Bar Association, the Canadian Federation of University Women, and the National Council of Women Canada.

Other international-domestic linkages are apparent in the 2012 joint request by NWAC, FAFIA and the Miami University Law Clinic to the Inter-American Commission on Human Rights (IACHR) to hold thematic briefings on the disappearance and murder of Indigenous women and girls in the province of British Columbia. The IACHR followed up with a country visit in 2013 and a 126-page report in 2015. Stressing the importance of a "comprehensive holistic approach" (para. 306), the IACHR recommendations included a national level action plan or national inquiry, better data collection, police training, and due diligence supports to victims and their families.

Similarly, the CEDAW country visit in 2013 was in response to complaints from NWAC and FAFIA of grave and systematic violations of human rights. There were nine additional letters of support asking CEDAW to conduct an inquiry from various legal, Indigenous, and community organizations, as well as letters from five members of Parliament and the opposition caucus of the British Columbia legislature (CEDAW, *Report of the Inquiry* paras. 8-9). The CEDAW committee found Canada to be in grave breach of Convention articles concerning due diligence, equal legal protection, the elimination of discrimination by state and non-state actors, and the implementation of measures to ensure the full development and advancement of women (paras. 201-212).

Under Prime Minister Harper, Canada accepted thirty-four of the thirty-eight recommendations. But it did not accept the call for a national inquiry or national action plan. It also did not accept the finding that Canada is in grave violation of Indigenous women's rights under the Convention because, in part, the committee "has not accorded sufficient weight to a number of significant and crucial actions" already taken (CEDAW, *Observations of the Government of Canada* para. 6, 11). In contrast, the Trudeau government has now met with six UN experts (from the CEDAW committee, the IACHR, and several special rapporteurs) in order to discuss essential elements of a national inquiry (Canadian Newswire). Following the spiral model, this suggests a promising shift toward dialogue and the institutionalization of norms.

STATE COMPLIANCE

Compliance with international treaties can refer not only to adhering to the substance of rules and norms but also to following procedural obligations and the "spirit of the treaty" (Jacobson and Weiss qtd. in LeBlanc, Huibregtse, and Meister 790). Although Canada has a strong international human rights record, particularly for the ratification of instruments and active participation at the UN, its current record is "less exemplary when it comes to complying with the findings and recommendations that come out of international reviews" (Amnesty International, *Matching International Commitments* 6). Amnesty International argues that UN review bodies now often focus on the inadequacies of Canada's process for implementing recommendations as a "serious, substantive human rights concern" itself (Amnesty International, *Matching International Commitments* 9).

Looking to past examples, insider-outsider pressure regarding Indigenous issues has made some difference. When Sandra Lovelace won her case before the Human Rights Committee (HRC) in 1981 regarding sex discrimination in the *Indian Act,* Canada subsequently removed the "marrying out" clause in 1984 with Bill C-31. Lovelace was part of a Maliseet group of women who sought to improve local living conditions for women and children in their reserve community of Tobique, New Brunswick. They soon came to realize that being non-status Indians—a legal status they had lost when they "married out" to "non-status" men—was at the root of their poor and abusive living conditions (Silman).

As part of their protest, the Tobique women decided to amplify their demands through transnational advocacy, creating a "boomerang pattern" to increase pressure against hampered domestic channels, which included opposition from Indigenous male leadership and a 1974 Supreme Court decision that upheld the marrying out clause (*Lavell v. Canada*). Since domestic legal channels had been exhausted, the Tobique women were able to use the complaints procedure under the Covenant on Civil and Political Rights. Upon *Lovelace's* acceptance of admissibility, Canada communicated that it intended to amend the Indian Act in light of what it recognized as serious difficulties. However, it did not admit to discrimination in Lovelace's case, and it insisted that the Indian Act was in agreement with the Covenant (Bayefski 247-248). In contrast, the HRC found that because Lovelace had married a non-Indian, the *Indian Act* violated her right to enjoyment of cultural life (para. 166).

Amendments were finally legislated four years later, in 1985, under Bill C-31. A.F. Bayefski argues that government stalling and delays in changing the legislation "evidence[d] insufficient regard for Canada's international obligations" (264). At the same time, the complexity of argument across First Nations communities in the context of constitutional change necessitated time-consuming consultations and negotiation (Hamill; Barker). Overall, there is little doubt that the government was greatly embarrassed by the ruling. Furthermore, by this time, Canada was also preparing to ratify CEDAW and wanted to be seen as a good member of the international community (Silman 188). Amendments, thus, occurred partly in response to *Lovelace* and partly to bring the *Indian Act* in line with the equality provisions of the Charter of Rights and Freedoms, which had come into force in 1985.

Another example of transnational advocacy resulting in change is Canada's belated endorsement of the United Nations Declaration for the Rights of Indigenous Peoples. When the UN General Assembly adopted the Declaration in 2007, Canada, the United States, Australia, and New Zealand were the only nations to vote against it. Although the negative vote was widely decried both at home and abroad, the Canadian government insisted that it had "principled and well-publicized concerns" with the Declaration and its adoption process (qtd. in Joffe 71). The government's substantive concerns included "provisions dealing with lands, territories and resources; free, prior and informed consent when used as a veto; self-government without recognition of the importance of negotiations; intellectual property; military issues; and the need to achieve an appropriate balance between the rights and obligations of Indigenous peoples, member States and third parties" (Canada, Aboriginal Affairs and Northern Development).

Nevertheless, in the face of an international barrage of criticism and repeated calls at home to sign the Declaration—especially in light of the prime minister's 2008 residential schools apology—the

Canadian government finally endorsed the Declaration on November 12, 2010. The endorsement occurred with little fanfare, only a press release on its website, which stressed that the Declaration is a legally non-binding aspirational document and not part of customary international law. The government maintained its concerns over issues of land, resources, and free, informed and prior consent and stated that the Declaration would be interpreted in a manner "fully consistent with Canada's Constitution and laws" (qtd. in Lightfoot 113).

Anishinaabe scholar Sheryl Lightfoot argues that Canada engaged in "selective endorsement" of the Declaration, meaning that it "under-committed" to the international norms by "[writing] down the content of the norms themselves so that they would align with ... current policies and practices thus assuring compliance without any intent of further implementation" (102). Yet, this "under-commitment" can be interpreted as aligning with the third stage of the spiral model: tactical concessions. Already, the space for denial of the norms enshrined in the Declaration is shrinking: the Truth and Reconciliation Commission has pointed to the Declaration as a framework for reconciliation; the federal election campaigns of the New Democratic Party, the Liberal Party and the Green Party all included a commitment to uphold and implement the Declaration (APTN News); alongside the new federal government's promise of implementation, recently elected Alberta premier Rachel Notley has also promised to implement the Declaration and make it law in that province (Morin).

The examples of *Lovelace* and the Declaration demonstrate that transnational pressure regarding the rights of Indigenous peoples can have some effect, albeit limited. Readers familiar with gender discrimination in the Indian Act will point out that the 1985 amendments simply delayed loss of status due to marrying out by one generation (the so-called second generation cut-off). However, this was probably the best outcome that women were going to get under the circumstances at that time, largely because of intra-Indigenous gender politics, as I discuss further below. Furthermore, the *Lovelace* decision provided encouragement to Indigenous women's political struggle and opened space for continued activism and dialogue (McIvor 115). Thus, from 1987 to 2009, Sharon McIvor's challenge to the "second generational cut-off" in Bill C-31 wound its way to the British Columbia Court of Appeal, which granted her a partial remedy. Dissatisfied with the decision and having exhausted all domestic legal routes,[3] McIvor has since petitioned the United Nations Human Rights Committee to claim denial of the right to an effective remedy for discrimination under Articles 26 (equality before the law) and 27 (right to enjoy cultural life).

In 2011, Canada responded very strongly against the complaint by touting the 2010 Gender Equity in Indian Registration Act (Bill C-3) as an effective remedy.[4] The Committee decision on the admissibility of the complaint is pending. In the meantime, however, during Canada's sixth review in July 2015, the Human Rights Committee raised gender discrimination in the Indian Act as an issue. Canada replied that Bill C-3 was an incremental step in the right direction and "no one sees it as anywhere near being concluded" (qtd. in Palmater). This seems to contradict its earlier submissions and, as Mi'kmaq professor and activist Palmela Palmater argues, this is "not a good faith application of either domestic or international law obligations in relation to gender equality."

But, perhaps, there is still some hopeful movement here in terms of advocacy and compliance. First, going to the UN is valued as a legal and political strategy insofar as Sharon McIvor has followed in the footsteps of Sandra Lovelace almost thirty years later. Second, the government's quick response to McIvor's complaint, in contrast to delayed responses for Lovelace, shows a shift in attitude. However negative Canada's response, it arguably reflects a desire to be seen as complying with international obligations and progressing in the Indigenous-Canada relationship. This desire hints at an aspirational identity that may, over time, compel leaders to more fully acknowledge and act on the gendered implications of colonization. Indeed, the conversation about gender discrimination in the *Indian Act* during the 2015 HRC review suggests that Canada now tacitly recognizes that more needs to be done and that it has less wiggle room. This is not to be naïve but rather to anticipate how "slowly but surely, governments become entrapped in their own rhetoric and the logic of arguing takes over" (Risse 28). Whether this actually occurs remains to be seen.

SELF-DETERMINATION AND GENDER-BASED VIOLENCE

Given electoral promises from all opposition parties to hold a national inquiry as well as significant support for a national inquiry within civil society, it appears that international reports and reviews are adding powerful fuel to the domestic fire. Transnational advocacy on the MMIW has served to highlight the gravity of the issue and to impugn Canada's international human rights reputation. Not coincidentally, advocacy regarding the Declaration and gender discrimination in the Indian Act is also profoundly connected to the missing and murdered women. The Native Women's Association of Canada identifies loss of Indian status, alongside other colonial structures of oppression, as a causal factor in Indigenous women's vulnerability to violence (*What Their Stories Tell Us*). The UN Working Group on Combatting Violence against Indigenous Women and Girls notes that gender-based violence should "not be addressed in isolation from the range of rights recognized for Indigenous peoples in general" (para. 17).

These rights are enumerated in the Declaration, most especially Article 22, which calls for states to take measures "in conjunction with Indigenous peoples, to ensure that Indigenous women and children enjoy the full protection and guarantees against all forms of violence and discrimination." The challenge, however, as Anishinaabe activist and scholar Hayden King argues, is that the voluntary nature of the Declaration "ultimately reduces the relationship to status quo ante—indigenous peoples struggling to convince Canada to recognize rights." This produces a form of negotiation that "entrenches and reinforces state authority over Indigenous peoples by requiring the latter [to] seek validation and permitting the former to offer modification of any potential rights." The implication here is that Indigenous autonomy or self-determination is profoundly undermined, and this is due to the very nature of international law, which tacitly recognizes the legitimacy of the state. Furthermore, as Anthony Anghie demonstrates, international law historically included "the aberrant Indian within a universal order [which was] then a basis for sanctioning and transforming the Indian" (744).

Yet *contra* contemporary arguments that Indigenous NGO participation in UN structures amounts to an "illusion of inclusion" (Corntassel), the development of Indigenous rights may be seen as the "extraordinary" and "transformative" result of the successful navigation by advocacy groups of "international organisations, forums and transnational networks" (Sargent 139). Furthermore, complaints procedures and reviews can serve to call the legitimacy of the state into question. When Indigenous activists take rights-based claims outside the state through international action, this becomes "the very exercise of autonomy and self-determination" (Kuokkanen 245; Barker 129). Participation in international lawmaking and in decision making regarding matters that affect Indigenous peoples is a procedural right to self-determination as outlined in articles 18 and 19 of the Declaration (Charters 234). And when the rights-based advocacy process is undertaken in accordance with Indigenous legal traditions and values, this may represent a "de-eurocentricised" expression of self-determination (Charters 237).

Historically, however, Indigenous women's rights and Indigenous self-determination have been at odds with one another. Indigenous women seeking their rights "have been repeatedly accused of being disloyal to their communities" and of introducing alien concepts as a result of being corrupted by "Western feminists" (Kuokkanen 236). When the Tobique women occupied the local band office and Sandra Lovelace brought her case to the United Nations, the women were castigated and threatened by some community members (Silman). The tellingly named National Indian Brotherhood (now Assembly of First Nations) fought long and hard against their cause, as they believed that gender should be subordinate to sovereignty and that Indigenous women were "putting their own selfish, personal interests before those of the collective" (Barker, 150). Moreover, male Indigenous leadership assumed that entrenched rights to self-government would take care of women's concerns. Despite repeated arguments by Indigenous women that showed otherwise, male Indigenous leader interpreted their stance as anti-sovereignty (Barker 150).

Moving ahead thirty years, Sami scholar Rauna Kuokkanen argues that Indigenous discourses of self-determination have expanded beyond state-centric notions of independent statehood and non-interference (243), the latter of which prevailed in the National Indian Brotherhood's stance on gender discrimination. Self-determination now appears as "an internationally recognized right that belongs to all peoples, not only to nation-states" (Kuokkanen 243). Balancing the individual and collective in the context of violence against women, Kuokkanen argues that "[i]f women are not surviving as individuals in their communities due to physical or structural violence, collective survival as a people is also inevitably called into question" (248). This is a relational argument that "recognizes the interdependence and interconnectedness of individuals, groups, and, as emphasized by non-Indigenous peoples, the human and non-human worlds" (248). Kuokkanen's approach is a far cry from the rational self-interest of the atomistic liberal individual. Furthermore, positioning gender equality and Indigenous self-determination as mutually constitutive enables us to get at the intersectional nature of violence against Indigenous women and to locate gender-specific (sexual) violence within racialized structures of oppression and colonialism.

CONCLUSION

An intersectional approach is precisely the approach taken in analyses of the missing and murdered Indigenous women, such as NWAC's Sisters in Spirit project. Furthermore, this research is conducted in accordance with Indigenous methodologies, which arguably gives expression to a "de-eurocentricised" sense of self-determination. Indigenous and women's rights groups, NWAC and FAFIA in particular, have successfully built insider-outsider coalitions that have resulted in sustained pressure on Canada over the last seven years to better respond to the missing and murdered women. Although Canada's response to this compliance pressure generally appears to be slow, obstructive, and largely rhetorical, the brief analysis of past examples suggests that this is the nature of the beast. Although this is not an especially heartwarming conclusion, neither is it altogether pessimistic. The spiral model may move slowly, but it is moving. Moreover, by going outside the state in voicing complaints, transnational advocacy has assailed Canada's international reputation, mobilized and fueled public concern, and provided expression to alternate visions of Indigenous women's equality and self-determination. Thus, transnational advocacy can be an important tool for advancing both.

ENDNOTES

[1]Historically, however, both the Conservatives and the Liberals have a shameful record when it comes to the treatment of Aboriginal peoples. Thus, while I am currently buoyed with hope, the proof is in the (Liberal) pudding. It, therefore, makes sense, from a long-term perspective, to speak mainly in terms of Canada rather than specific governing parties.

[2]The Human Rights Council is a political body of the United Nations General Assembly comprised of state representatives. In contrast, treaty bodies, such as the Human Rights Committee, are comprised of experts who work as independent individuals.

[3]The Supreme Court of Canada declined to hear McIvor's appeal. No reason was given.

[4]Bill C-3 was legislated in response to the BC Court of Appeal decision in *McIvor v. Canada*. For a critical explanation of Bill C-3, see Shelagh Day's post on *rabble.ca*.

WORKS CITED

Amnesty International. *Matching International Commitments with National Action: A Human Rights Agenda for Canada*. Canada: Amnesty International Canada, 2012. Print.

Amnesty International. *Violence Against Indigenous Women and Girls in Canada: A Summary of Amnesty International's Concerns and Call to Action*: Submission to the Special Parliamentary Committee on Violence Against Indigenous Women (IWFA). Ottawa: Amnesty International, 2014. Print.

Anghie, Antony. "The Evolution of International Law: Colonial and Postcolonial Realities." *Third World Quarterly* 27.5 (Special Issue) (2006): 739-753. Print.

Aboriginal Peoples Television Network (APTN). "What the Four Federal Parties Have Promised Indigenous Voters So Far." *APTN*

National News, 18 Aug. 2015. Web. 18 Aug. 2015.

Barker, Joanne. "Gender, Sovereignty, and the Discourse of Rights in Native Women's Activism." *Meridians: Feminism, Race, Transnationalism* 7.1 (2006): 127-161. Print.

Bayefski, A.F. "The Human Rights Committee and the Case of Sandra Lovelace." *Canadian Yearbook of International Law* 20 (1982): 244-266. Print.

Canada. Indigenous and Northern Affairs Canada. *Indigenous and Northern Affairs Canada.* "Canada's Endorsement of the Universal Declaration of the Rights of Indigenous Peoples, Frequently Asked Questions." Government of Canada, n.d. Web. 25 Feb. 2014.

Canadian Newswire. "Missing and murdered Indigenous Women and Girls: International human Rights Experts Meet Canadian Government Officials." CNW *News Releases.* N.p., 1 Feb. 2016. Web. 16 Apr. 2016.

Committee for the Elimination of Discrimination against Women (CEDAW). *Concluding Observations of the Committee on the Elimination of Discrimination against Women: Canada.* New York: United Nations, 2008. Print.

Committee for the Elimination of Discrimination against Women (CEDAW). *Observations of the Government of Canada on the Report of the Inquiry Concerning Canada of the Committee on the Elimination of Discrimination against Women under Article 8 of the Optional Protocol to the Convention on the Elimination of All Forms of Discrimination against Women.* New York: United Nations, 2015. Print.

Committee for the Elimination of Discrimination against Women (CEDAW). *Report of the Inquiry concerning Canada of the Committee of the Elimination of Discrimination against Women under article 8 of the Optional Protocol to the Convention on the Elimination of All Forms of Discrimination against Women.* New York: United Nations, 2015. Print.

Charters, Claire. "A Self-Determination Approach to Justifying Indigenous Peoples' Participation in International Law and Policy Making." *International Journal on Minority & Group Rights* 17.2 (2010): 215-240. Print.

Corntassel, Jeff. "Towards a New Partnership? Indigenous Political

Mobilization and Co-optation During the First UN Indigenous Decade (1995-2004)." *Human Rights Quarterly* 29.1 (2007): 137-66. Print.

Day, Shelagh. "Because 153 Years of Sex Discrimination Is Enough." *Rabble.* N.p., 21 Dec. 2010. Web. 16 Apr. 2016.

Hamill, Sarah E. "McIvor v Canada and the 2010 Amendments to the Indian Act: A Half- Hearted Remedy to Historical Injustice." *Constitutional Forum* 19.2 (2011): 75-84. Print.

Human Rights Committee. "Concluding Observations on the Sixth Periodic Report of Canada." New York: United Nations, 2015. Print.

Inter-American Commission on Human Rights (IACHR). *Missing and Murdered Women in British Columbia, Canada.* Washington, DC, IACHR, 2014. Print.

Joffe, Paul. "Canada's Opposition to the UN Declaration: Legitimate Concerns or Ideological Bias?" *Realizing the UN Declaration on the Rights of Indigenous Peoples: Triumph, Hope, and Action.* Eds. Jackie Hartley, Paul Joffe, and Jennifer Preston. Saskatoon: Purich Press Limited, 2010. 70-95. Print.

Keck, Margaret E, and Kathryn Sikkink. *Activists Beyond Borders: Advocacy Networks in International Politics.* Ithaca, NY: Cornell University Press, 1998. Print.

King, Hayden. "When the UN probes Canada's First Nations Tragedy, Don't Expect Results." *The Globe and Mail,* 10 Oct. 2013. Web. 9 Oct. 2015.

Kuokkanen, Rauna. "Self-Determination and Indigenous Women's Rights at the Intersection of International Human Rights." *Human Rights Quarterly* 34.1 (2012): 225-50. Print.

LeBlanc, Lawrence J., Ada Huibregtse, and Timothy Meister. "Compliance with the Reporting Requirements of Human Rights Conventions." *International Journal of Human Rights* 14.5 (2010): 789-807. Print.

Lightfoot, Sheryl R. "Selective Endorsement without Intent to Implement: Indigenous Rights and the Anglosphere." *The International Journal of Human Rights* 16.1 (2012): 100-122. Print.

Lovelace v. Canada, Communication No. 24/1977: Canada 30/07/81, UN Doc. CCPR/C/13/D/24/1977 at para. 166.

McIvor, Sharon Donna. "Aboriginal Women Unmasked: Using

Equality Litigation to Advance Women's Rights." *Canadian Journal of Women & the Law* 16.1 (2004): 106-136. Print.

Morin, Brandi. "New Premier Tells Alberta's Indigenous peoples: 'I Am Looking Forward to Consulting with You and Learning from You.'" *APTN News*, 7 May 2015. Web. 7 May. 2015.

Native Women's Association of Canada (NWAC). *What Their Stories Tell Us: Research findings from the Sisters in Spirit Initiative.* Ohsweken, ON: Native Women's Association of Canada, 2010. Print.

Palmater, Pamela. "Canada's Testimony at the UN Human Rights Committee Needs Correcting." *Rabble*. N.p.,13 July 2015. Web. 13 July 2015.

Risse, Thomas. "Constructivism and International Institutions: Toward Conversations across Paradigms." *Political Science as Discipline: Reconsidering Power, Choice and the State at Century's End.* Eds. Ira Katznelson and Helen Milner. New York: Norton, 2002. 597-623. Print.

Risse, Thomas, and Kathryn Sikkink. "The Socialization of International Human Rights Norms into Domestic Practices: Introduction." *The Power of Human Rights: International Norms and Domestic Change.* Eds. Thomas Risse, Stephen C. Ropp, and Kathryn Sikkink. Cambridge: Cambridge University Press, 1999. 1-38. Print.

Sargent, Sarah. "Transnational Networks and United Nations Human Rights Structural Change: The Future of Indigenous and Minority Rights." *The International Journal of Human Rights* 16.1 (2012): 123-51. Print.

Shor, Eran. "Conflict, Terrorism, and the Socialization of Human Rights Norms: The Spiral Model Revisited." *Social Problems* 55.1 (2008): 117-38. Print.

Sikkink, Kathryn. "Patterns of Dynamic Multilevel Governance and the Insider –Outsider Coalition." *Transnational Protest and Global Activism: People, Passions and Power.* Eds. Donatella Della Porta and Sidney Tarrow. Lanham, ML: Rowan and Littlefield, 2005. 151-174. Print.

Silman, Janet. *Enough is Enough: Aboriginal Women Speak Out.* Toronto: Canadian Scholars' Press and Women's Press, 1992. Print.

United Nations (UN). *Report of the Special Rapporteur on the Rights of Indigenous Peoples, James Anaya*. New York: United Nations, 2014. Print.

United Nations Permanent Forum on Indigenous Issues. *Combating Violence Against Indigenous Women and Girls: Article 22 of the United Nations Declaration on the Rights of Indigenous Peoples*: Report of the International Expert Group Meeting. New York: United Nations, 2012. E/C.19/2012/6. Print.

9. How the Lens of the Global Locates Canada's Missing and Murdered Indigenous Women

Pedagogical Methods, Lessons, and Hope from the Classroom

BRENDA ANDERSON

AS A NON-INDIGENOUS PERSON who has directly benefitted from the colonization of prairie soil into white settler farmland, I am confronted with the question of what roles and responsibilities I now have in my privileged position as a white feminist academic choosing to be a witness to the past and an ally for the future. The issue of missing and murdered Indigenous women (MMIW) was the catalyst for turning my questions into action. The repeated horror of listening to news stories and reading posters on pharmacy windows asking, "Have you seen... Please call ..." led me to ask Indigenous women—Elders, activists, mothers and daughters—what key lessons a non-Indigenous ally needs to learn about *standing alongside*, and how those with social privilege *can make space for things to happen.*

This chapter is a practical reflection on my experiences since 2008 of teaching a university course on MMIW with an emphasis on Indigenous and feminist methodologies and pedagogies. I write in the spirit of the Truth and Reconciliation process, which has challenged all Canadians to locate themselves in the narrative of colonialism in order to commit to the full acknowledgement of our joint history, no matter how painful, as a means of beginning reconciliation. I write mainly for those who may wish to teach in this area, as I move back and forth between theoretical questions and personal observations from the classroom. I challenge readers, as I challenge students, to consider whether Canada needs to name our historic and current treatment of Indigenous women as *femicide*, as has been done in countries, such as Guatemala and

Mexico, in order to acknowledge not only the violence but the complicit acceptance of this phenomenon within our social and legal fabric.

Three ethical questions guide my teaching: what are effective steps that can be taught to non-Indigenous allies to facilitate movement through the inevitable but immobilizing "white guilt" to a more productive and accountable position of witnessing or standing alongside; how do we teach about trauma without further traumatizing or, put another way, how do we equip our future activists with concrete tools for self-care to prepare them to address violence against Indigenous women; what theoretical feminist and Indigenous methodologies work well in bringing Indigenous and non-Indigenous students together in community engaged research. These themes are reflected throughout this chapter as I discuss content and pedagogy. I conclude by offering a sample syllabus for a third year women's and gender Studies course on MMIW: A Global Perspective.

The course is designed to teach students about the history of colonialism in Canada and its effects on all Canadians in general, but Indigenous Canadians in particular, and Indigenous women and girls specifically. A theoretical emphasis on the intersections of racism, sexism, capitalism, and neo-liberalism, among many other layers of oppression, demands that we all, at some point in the class, recognize our own personal location in the oppression or experiences of oppression. The majority of students are females from white settler backgrounds, along with a number of self-identified Indigenous and Métis students, and one or two from more recent immigrant backgrounds. We usually number about thirty students, which is ideal for table-talk exercises designed to blend analysis with personal debriefing opportunities.

FROM THE LOCAL TO THE GLOBAL AND BACK AGAIN

The course is modelled after the goals and principles that guided a 2008 conference held in Regina on missing and murdered Indigenous women: to create a forum for all voices to be heard from the variety of areas that address this issue; to formulate a global analysis of colonialist gender violence from which to recognize patterns that occur in Canada; and to care for the whole person in this painful recognition that the problem goes far further and deeper than the individual acts of a few men. Those principles are brought to the classroom with the conference proceedings, *Torn from our Midst: Voices of Grief, Healing and Action from the Missing and Murdered Indigenous Women's Conference, 2008* (Anderson, Kubik, and Hampton). To move forward, we cannot afford to single out any one group in Canada to scapegoat (e.g., police, media, government), lest it mollify our own complicity in a colonialist country. In fact, perspectives from all areas are needed in order to grasp the full complexity of how a colonialist and sexist nation was created originally and is perpetuated currently. The global nature of colonialist violence against Indigenous women and the subsequent resistance movements clarifies what happens in our own backyard and offers paths forward on redressing the problems.

We begin the semester by locating the history of Indigenous women within Canada's pioneering history through showing their relationship to white settlers. We discuss the Pocahontas-squaw motif described by Janice Acoose to illustrate how and why the fantastical Native is framed in our national imagination as either the noble, exotic savage to be conquered or the beast of burden to be despised or pitied (49). We move to current media representations of Indigenous women, particularly the stories of victimized women, and pay attention to the language used and the assumptions made. These representations are juxtaposed with personal stories shared by family members who visit the classroom. Journalists also talk with us, and one in particular recounts how her representation of the issue has changed as she became more aware of Canadian history and of the stories from families. Journalism students accept the challenge to change the narrative when they enter the workforce. Resisting the historic pattern of blaming the victim is possible when white settler language and assumptions become recognizable, and students see the opportunities that they have to shape the national narrative of MMIW.

Although I begin the course with Canadian history, I frame violence against Indigenous women in the global context, examining Mexico, Guatemala and Australia. Moving outside our own frame of reference illustrates that colonialism survives off violence against brown-skinned women in these countries, for even though each country has its own unique history, the violence is replicated in similar ways. For instance, the effects of neo-liberal trade agreements connect misogyny with economics. Activists in Mexico and Canada witness the decline of local artisan's sales, particularly detrimental to Indigenous women, when multinational companies are allowed to become monopolies (Erno 57). They attest to the governmental and military violence perpetrated in Mexican towns such as San Salvador Attenco where attempts to remove Indigenous people from their land in preparation for free trade plans including premeditated kidnapping and raping women (Perez). Pastor Kim Erno's analysis of the effects of neo-liberal economics on Indigenous women pinpoints their vulnerability for "exclusion, exploitation, expulsion, (and finally) extermination" (60). Students are asked to locate if, and where, these stages occur for Canadian Indigenous women.

Mexican gender roles were shaped by the conflict between the Spanish and Catholic conquerors, by the manifest destiny of American frontierism (M. Anderson 22), and by the Mexican revolutionaries. Continuing today as the hegemonic masculine ideal, the *caudillo* ("military strong man") became "rooted in the family" as the independent breadwinner in contrast to the idealised feminine of domestic production (Healy 5). When neo-liberal economics no longer supports traditional livelihoods and instead favours employing young, easily coerced women as workers in sweatshops (Portillo), traditional machismo roles are displaced and increased domestic violence makes women vulnerable at home as well as at work (Healy 154). Women's deaths in the *maquiladoras* (commonly referred to as sweatshops) in northern frontier cities, such as Ciudad Juarez, have been linked to the lethal blend of frustrated misogyny, neoliberal economics, political corruption, and drug cartels (Bowden).

Recent works on Canadian Indigenous masculinities, such as Sam McKegney's *MASCULINIDIANS: Conversations about Indigenous Manhood*, mark a similar pattern for Indigenous men. The class discusses displacement of traditional male roles from an economic as well as social and spiritual perspective. The systemic exclusion, exploitation, expulsion and extermination of Indigenous People through Canada's reserve system, residential "schools,"[1] the Sixties Scoop, increased foster care and incarceration, and the resulting rise in gangs, exploitative forms of the sex trade and sex trafficking reads like a global manual on colonialism.

Being able to identify the global patterns of dislocation and alienation from traditional social values encourages students to hear our own context differently. Bringing police officers from the missing persons unit to discuss local cases and hearing about the lack of necessary resources and support for family members allow students to see how individuals often struggle within the systems purportedly designed to provide assistance. In contrast, government policymakers from the Saskatchewan Provincial Partnership on Missing Persons have shown what is possible when things are done differently, when all voices are present at the table (Pottruff). Speakers from local activist groups, such as Sisters in Spirit or Amnesty International, ensure students hear firsthand how systems of governance replicate the oppression against First Peoples generally and Indigenous women specifically. In one three-hour class, students see a PowerPoint presentation with the faces of Saskatchewan Indigenous women who have gone missing or been murdered, listen to police and provincial government responses, and write names of those who have most recently been taken onto an Amnesty banner. It becomes not just a question of the need for correct information and education, but shows students the measure of power, or lack of power, for those who work within government. The students begin to ask what challenges they will face when they find themselves working in police, judicial, or social work capacities.

The familiar pattern of British colonialism in Australia mirrors the historic violence against Indigenous women in Canada. The racist notion of "breeding out" Indigenous blood inspired the creation of the half-caste system in Australia. It is a jolting reminder of the intentions and consequences of Canada's Indian Act and Bill C-31, particularly in its implications for Indigenous women who experience the double burden of sexist and racist ideologies (Bourassa 75). We examine the Australian half-caste "school" system through the film *Rabbit Proof Fence* because it opens up space to speak about the potential of re-traumatizing people when their stories are told by outsiders (Noyce). Is it helpful, harmful, or both, to recount stories of girls being torn away from their mother's and auntie's arms to be driven away to the "school," when the actors themselves experienced that very trauma when they were girls? Is it okay for a white male director, no matter how sympathetic, to direct Indigenous girls to "get in touch with the pain" of trying to return to their families when they may suffer from intergenerational trauma?

In the Canadian context, the film *The Healing Circle* describes Canada's residential "schools," and the complicity of the churches in carrying out the government's program of cultural genocide. This film was created by the Anglican Church of Canada as one of their earlier reconciliation projects. It portrays the history of the "schools" and their lasting effects on people, many of whom attempted to erase the memories with drugs and alcohol. We discuss intergenerational trauma and connect today's increased domestic violence within Indigenous communities to the unaddressed trauma of the residential "school" system. At the same time, we note that the perceptions among non-Indigenous violent offenders that Indigenous people are disposable and their absence socially negligible. The intentionality behind the deliberate destruction of the family unit is stark, and we are no longer allowed to think of the present as an unfortunate and unintended consequence of past practices.

What students find most disturbing about the film, perhaps, are comments made by the teachers. Although most of the teachers in the film express considerable confusion over why they felt it was the right thing to do at the time, some say it was, and would still be, an appropriate response to "the Indian problem." Naturally, this raises the youthful ire of the classroom. However, it is not as simple as blaming people from the past. Anglican priest Cheryl Toth speaks to this response. She calmly notes to the class,

> While I understand you being upset at those types of comments, as am I, I'd like to suggest that many of us in this room, compelled to be here because of our sense of justice and wanting to make this a better world, might in fact have been amongst those who taught and worked in

> the residential schools. The sad and frightening fact is that many of those *well-intentioned* people genuinely felt they were helping those children.

This is met with silence because the next logical question is, "what am I doing right now that I think is helpful that might be looked at decades from now with similar horror?" Perhaps this is the strongest message to non-Indigenous students: the best role of an ally is to learn to stand alongside the efforts of those who have experienced the abuse and to listen to what they need.

The compelling notion of deep healing helps move students forward in this narrative. To describe this notion, I first contrast it to the concept of deep colonizing, as the covert "practices ... embedded in the institutions that are meant to reverse processes of colonisation" (Rose 1), which Deborah Bird Rose raises in the Australian context of land claims procedures. She describes Indigenous peoples' gendered relationships to the land and how deep colonizing continues to erase Indigenous women when this relationship is ignored in modern land claims court challenges (3). Differentiated sacred spaces traditionally demand women's voices be present at the negotiating table, yet court practice has been to exclude them (4), which neglects the knowledge to be gained from understanding which spaces, with their associated rituals, are, indeed, sacred to Indigenous women. Deep colonizing is the erasure of women's presence in sacred rituals and court systems alike. The questions students can pose in the Canadian context are what form does deep colonizing take in Canadian legal treaty contestations and environmental challenges? And what does the absence or presence of women at our highest courts say about our national views on Indigenous women?

In contrast, deep healing becomes a form of active witnessing associated with everything from sacred rituals to legal procedures. Family members of the missing and murdered, Elders, and Indigenous leaders require intentional, deep listening from the rest of Canada. How do students imagine deep healing could happen in Canada's court systems during trials relating to missing and murdered women? How will deep colonizing be replaced by deep healing in the Canadian context?

With this wealth of global and national stories interwoven throughout the semester, we arrive at a point where the class debates whether the term "femicide" fits our national context. My colleague, Leonzo Barreno, originally from Guatemala, describes that country's struggle with drug cartels and female "mules" who disappear along the drug routes to North America. He shows how activists in Guatemala and in Mexico define femicide in terms of not only enculturated violence against Indigenous women and girls but also the nation's complicity in its denial of any systemic problem (Barreno 71). A national inquiry in Canada—particularly when led by family members and the findings and recommendations of Sisters in Spirit researchers and backed by deep healing within legislative practices and policies cross the country—can redress Canada's femicide. Acknowledging its existence is the first step.

Weaving the local and global contexts together throughout the semester allows students to recognize patterns, reorganize their perspectives and priorities, learn about global efforts to end violence against Indigenous women, and commit to effective decolonizing and deep healing in Canada. That commitment is crucial for their own well being.

ACCOUNTABILITY AND BELONGING IN A CLASSROOM COMMUNITY

Locating ourselves in this issue is a constant thread. I relate my story of growing up in a farming community that did not acknowledge its white privilege. Racism was assumed, rarely challenged. In its best light, this at least affords me an awareness of what white guilt and tears are all about and how, as the late Elder Ken Goodwill advised me, they are neither required nor wanted. I learned that my heritage as the grandchild of a white Scottish settler from Prince Edward Island gives me certain insights into the task of reconciliation. I can tell where other's white privilege turns to white guilt. The class discusses those terms, and how neither can be the permanent abode of an ally. When we learn about a history that has been withheld from us, despite twelve years of grade school and university classes, and learn of its direct consequences in every Canadian life, we will feel rage and tears. Tempered, that realization becomes motivational. Untempered, it can lead to dissociation, as evidenced in rhetorical questions like, "how could *they* have done that to other human beings?" Carol Schick and Verna St. Davis note the essential task of pressing students to realize the *they* is *them*, today, now (57). Just as men need to stand alongside feminists, non-Indigenous allies need to move from the historical to the present and from the "tsk tsk" to a personal awareness of, and accountability for, their own white privilege. That transforms pity into deep healing.

White guilt is often accompanied by its fellow traveller, trauma. The potential for triggering students who themselves have suffered from abuse is real. I am not a psychologist, nor should a professor assume a counselling role. What I can provide is a number of ways to become aware of our own trauma. I tell the students I am concerned about the effects that studying trauma has on our classroom community, including myself. I bring in a psychologist to talk about the symptoms of, and responses to, post-traumatic stress disorder. I ask students to carefully consider whether this class is suitable for them given their own experiences. It is not uncommon to have students in the class who have had a family member stolen from them. Students are asked to talk about what they already do in terms of self-care. What are the simple habits we do but usually forget at the peak of semester deadlines? When do we know that we need a break from the topic? We share our simple stories and ways, discuss the efficacies of friendship, support groups, spending time in nature, and, if necessary, speaking with counsellors available at the university. Students are required to continue to assess their own capacity to respond to trauma as part of their journal reflections.

I have to be comfortable with how *making space for things to happen* means relinquishing control. I don't know what the guest speakers are going to say or how the students will respond. Students tell me that they go home to "have a good cry." Sometimes what they hear is upsetting because they don't agree with the speaker—what a wonderful opportunity to analyze the problems! It makes a difference to the students to point out that the fact they are in this class means they are already contributing towards the reconciliation process.

The notions of accountability and belonging within the classroom are often new constructs for students. One transformative learning tool is the interactive "blanket exercise." This was developed by KAIROS to involve people in reenacting the history and effects of colonialism on First Peoples, and can be led by anyone who is comfortable working with groups and with sensitive material. My college has partnered with the Canadian Roots Exchange Program to form a reconciliation team of young adult leaders (the requirement is that the team be comprised of Indigenous and non-Indigenous youth). The effect of the students sitting on blankets, only to be moved or removed from this Turtle Island of blankets as the history is recounted, including a narrative on MMIW, is profound, and when followed by a talking circle, brings the learning to a very personal accountability. The movement of the body engages and commits the whole person to the story. As one student noted to me, it made her feel physically connected to Canada's history.

This can be a painful experience for Indigenous participants. One student told me that, although his family was affected by the residential "schools," he had been kept largely in the dark about the stories. This was the first time he had "felt" the history. Although it is a sobering class, it shows what educational decolonization looks like. Acknowledging the past moves the nation forward, so the blanket exercise creates witnesses who are now accountable to the decolonizing process. A relationship is established between the past and the present, not to mention the participants.

Recognizing the intersections of sexism and racism for Indigenous women is heavy work. Feminist and Indigenous practices both emphasise that the personal is political. Feminist principles of individual rights mixed with social accountability and theoretical understandings of the intersections of oppression and privilege echo traditional Indigenous practices, such as the talking circle and the teaching of balancing out personal rights with social accountabilities. What has been particularly appreciated by students is my adaptation of Kim Anderson's work from *Life Stages and Native Women: Memory, Teachings, and Story Medicine*. Anderson uses the teachings from Elders to counsel inner city youth about how the four stages in life—birth, childhood, adult, and elder—bring membership and ownership to the whole community. In each stage, a balance is struck between personal accountability and the reciprocal knowledge that one belongs to a caring community. As babies bring joy, they require safety and nurturance. As youth bring energy and new questions, they require teachings and guidance. As the middle-aged provide material wealth, they require their children to be guided and sustained by Elders. Elders bring their time and knowledge; they require care and respect. Feminist? Indigenous? The labels matter not, but the teaching means a blending of the individualist and the collectivist with the aim of a healthy community. This portrayal of the ideal community is offered not to romanticize and locate Indigenous teachings in the past, nor is it to be understood as essentialist or normative. It is offered as non-gendered guiding principles that identify needs and gifts throughout our life journeys. Balancing notions of individual rights with accountability and social duty underscores what powerful decisions students can make in their lives.

An Indigenous feminist approach that redresses issues of violence against Indigenous women is found in Lina Sunseri's book *Being Again of One Mind: Oneida Women and the Struggle for Decolonization*. Laying the personal stories of women—mothers, daughters, Elders, activists—alongside the history of the Haudenosaunee nation, the book illustrates how Oneida women have negotiated the meanings of traditional womanhood as the drummers of the nation (16) and by "mothering a nation" (126), with the feminist commitment to non-essentialist gender roles. This understanding is not linked to reproduction but to all who "sustain the community and (support) women's achievement of self-empowerment" (131). The process of students evaluating methods of decolonization situated in women's self-empowerment speaks directly to redressing the vulnerability of Indigenous women and girls in Canada. Who are our nation's drummers and mothers?

CONCLUSION

This is the most difficult course that I teach. The reconciliation process that academics can engage in—*must* engage in—makes us all vulnerable, as a nation, as a community, as an individual.

But vulnerable to what? To painful and often unresolved stories, certainly, but also vulnerable to change. A national inquiry on MMIW, the gifts from the Truth and Reconciliation Commission, the growing leadership from within Indigenous women's circles, means the nation's deep healing work can begin. There is hope. The students who of their own initiative bring the REDress Project to campus, who hold awareness nights on MMIW, who faithfully attend the Sisters in Spirit annual vigils, and who demonstrate, ring bells, say "Not One More! Ni Una Mas!" show that each and every one of us has an integral part to play in countering our nation's legacy of femicide and ending its perpetuation. This is no fairy tale with a guaranteed happy ending, but we are capable of unwinding ourselves from the colonial project, and we are capable of weaving a new future. The evidence is already before us in the writing of this book.

The author is using quotation marks around school as a form of literary decolonization to raise the question of whether this term should continue to be used, given the overall lack of education received by children. For more information on adult's experiences in trying to obtain jobs with their diploma, see Topahedewin: The Gladys Cook Story.

WORKS CITED

Acoose, Janice. *Iskwewak-Kah' Ki Yaw Ni Wahkomakanak: Neither Indian Princesses Nor Easy Squaws*. Toronto: Women's Press, 1995. Print.

Anderson, A. Brenda, Wendee Kubik, and Mary Rucklos Hampton, eds. *Torn from Midst: Voices of Grief, Healing and Action from the Missing Indigenous Women Conference, 2008*. Regina: Canadian Plains Research Centre, 2010. Print.

Anderson, Kim. *Life Stages and Native Women: Memory, Teachings, and Story Medicine*. Manitoba: University of Manitoba Press, 2011. Print.

Anderson, Mark Cronlund. *Cowboy Imperialism and Hollywood Film*. New York: Peter Lang Publishing, Inc., 2007. Print.

Anglican Church of Canada. *The Healing Circle*. Toronto: The

Anglican Book Centre, 1995. Film.

Barreno, Leonzo. "From Genocide to Femicide: An Ongoing History of Terror, Hate, and Apathy." *Torn from Midst: Voices of Grief, Healing and Action from the Missing Indigenous Women Conference, 2008*. Eds. A. Brenda Anderson, Wendee Kubik, and Mary Rucklos Hampton. Regina: CPRC, 2010. 69-74. Print.

Bourassa, Carrie. "The Construction of Aboriginal Identity: A Healing Journey." *Torn from Midst: Voices of Grief, Healing and Action from the Missing Indigenous Women Conference, 2008*. Eds. A. Brenda Anderson, Wendee Kubik, and Mary Rucklos Hampton. Regina: CPRC, 2010. 75-85. Print.

Bowden, Charles. *Juarez: The Laboratory of Our Future*. Hong Kong: Aperture Foundation, Inc. Everbest Printing Company Ltd., 1998. Print.

Chakarova, Mimi, dir. *The Price of Sex*. Women Make Movies, 2011. Film.

Erno, Kim. "Political Realities: The Effect of Globalization on Indigenous Women." *Torn from Midst: Voices of Grief, Healing and Action from the Missing Indigenous Women Conference, 2008*. Eds. A. Brenda Anderson, Wendee Kubik, and Mary Rucklos Hampton. Regina: CPRC, 2010. 57-68. Print.

Healy, Teresa. *Gendered Struggles against Globalization in Mexico*. Burlington: Ashgate Publishing Ltd., 2008. Print.

McKegney, Sam. *MASCULINDIANS: Conversations about Indigenous Manhood*. Manitoba: University of Manitoba Press, 2014. Print.

Noyce, Phillip, dir. *Rabbit-Proof Fence*. Miramax Movies, 2002. Film.

Perez, Marta, public presentation on dvd in *Torn from Midst: Voices of Grief, Healing and Action from the Missing Indigenous Women Conference, 2008*. Eds. A. Brenda Anderson, Wendee Kubik, and Mary Rucklos Hampton. Regina: CPRC, 2010. Film.

Portillo, Lourdes, dir. *Senorita Extraviada*. Women Make Movies, 2001. Film.

Pottruff, Betty Ann. "Presentation of the Provincial Partnership Committee on Missing Persons." *Torn from Midst: Voices of Grief, Healing and Action from the Missing Indigenous Women Conference, 2008*. Eds. A. Brenda Anderson, Wendee Kubik, and

Mary Rucklos Hampton Regina: CPRC, 2010. 104-109. Print.
Ralston, Meredith, dir. *Hope in Heaven*. Halifax: CIDA & Ralston Productions, 2005. Film.
Rose, Deborah Bird. "Land Rights and Deep Colonising: The Erasure of Women." *Aboriginal Law* Bulletin 69 3.85 (1996): n.pag. 6. Web. 15 Dec. 2015.
Schick, Carol and Verna St. Davis. "Critical Autobiography in Integrative Anti-Racist Pedagogy."*Gendered Intersections: An Introduction to Women's & Gender Studies*. Eds. C. Lesley Biggs et al. 2nd ed. Halifax: Fernwood Publishing, 2011. 57-61. Print.
Sunseri, Lina. *Being Again of One Mind: Oneida Women and the Struggle for Decolonization*. Vancouver: University of British Columbia Press. 2011. Print.
Barry, Lisa, and Jim Boyles, dirs. *Topahdewin: The Gladys Cook Story*. Anglican Church of Canada, 2006. DVD.

Women's Studies 390AF

Missing Indigenous Women: A Global Perspective

Syllabus for Winter, 2015

****

Texts:

Acoose, Janice. *Iskwewak–kah'ki yaw ni wahkomakanak: Neither Indian princesses nor easy squaws.* Women's Press, Toronto

Anderson, A. Brenda, Wendee Kubik & Mary Rucklos Hampton, eds., *Torn from our Midst: Voices of Grief, Healing and Action.* CPRC, 2010.

Green, Joyce, ed., *Making Space for Aboriginal Feminism,* Fernwood Press, 2007.

Green, Joyce, ed., *Indivisible: Indigenous Human Rights.* Fernwood Press, 2014.

****

Course Definition & Goals:

Why are Indigenous women around the world more likely to "go missing" than non-Indigenous women? What does "sexualized racism" mean and how is it perpetuated through cultural scripts, institutions and systems? This class will examine the systems that intersect and perpetuate racism and sexism in colonized countries, specifically, Canada, Australia, Mexico and Guatemala. The social and economic effects of globalization on women will be studied, including the issue of sex trafficking abroad and in Canada. Expertise and voices from community activists will be integrated into this class, as will the first-hand stories of family members of missing women.

CLASS SCHEDULE

Jan.6: Introduction, Framework, Thematic and Theoretical Questions: Epistemic Violence within Colonialism, Sexualized Racism...
Film: "Pride and Prejudice: The Road to Human Rights and Multiculturalism in British Columbia"

Jan.13: Canada: Conflicting and Intertwining Canadian Narratives
Canadian Roots Exchange Presentation Readings: Green, Indivisible: pgs. 1-34
UR Courses: "Histories of Colonization, Generations of Hurt"

Jan. 20: Family Stories & Re/Presentations of the Stories
Films: "Finding Dawn," "Maria Campbell"
Lecture: Self-Care, Vicarious Trauma and Compassion Fatigue: How To (Can We?) Study Trauma Without Becoming Traumatized
Native Women's Association of Canada, Sisters in Spirit
Speaker:
Readings:
Acoose – whole book
Anderson, pgs 1-16, 32-56

Jan.27: Canada: Policing, Government and Activism
Guest Speakers: Gordon Barnes (Amnesty International), Betty Ann Pottruff
(Sask. Department of Justice), _____ (Regina Police Services, Missing Persons Division)
Film: "Morningstar Mercredi, Woman-Warrior"
Readings:
UR Courses: "Stolen Sisters, Amnesty International Report Summary"
Anderson, pgs. 75-109, 185-187

Due: Annotated Internet Bibliography – 15%

Feb. 3: Canada: The Legacy of Residential Schools and the Healing Process for All
Film: "The Healing Circle"

Guest Speaker: Mary Jesse and Jenna Tickell
Readings:
UR Courses: "One More Step: Living in Right Relationship"
Anderson, pgs.19-24,208-218 (and see Appendix A in book)
Green, Making Space, 14-71, 140-159

Feb. 10: Canada: Media – Tropes and Hopes
Guest Speaker: tba
Readings:
Anderson, pgs. 133-181
Green, Making Space, pgs. 124-139, 199-215, 221-232
First Hand in of Reflective Journal – 10%

Feb. 17: Study Week – No Class

Feb. 24: Mexico: Historical Context of Colonialism, Globalization and Machismo
Film: "Senorita Extraviada"
Readings: Luther Library OR Internet Book: Introduction to "Border Identifications: Narratives on Religion, Gender and Class on the U.S.-Mexico Border"
Anderson, pgs. 27-33, 57-68,113-116
Due: Research Paper Outline, Thesis Statement and Bibliography – 10%

Mar. 3: Mexico: Grassroots Resistance and Activism
Film: "Marta Perez – San Salvador Attenco"
Readings:
Luther Library: from yellow journal "Representations of Murdered and Missing Women," pgs. 26-37, 48-51
Anderson, pgs. 182-184,188-207
Guatemala: Guest Speaker Leonzo Barreno
Anderson, pgs. 69-74
Luther Library: Buried Secrets – Truth and Human Rights in Guatemala (optional)

Mar. 10: Australia: Colonialism, Residential Schools & The Missing Generations

Readings:
UR Courses: "We're Women We Fight for Freedom"and Reference Statistics
E-Book on Voyager, or at Luther Library: *Home Bodies: Geographies of Self, Place and Space.* Ed. Wendy Schisssel. Calgary: University of Calgary Press, 2006. In this book, read Pedersen, J. Maria. "Oppression and Indigenous Women – Past, Present, and Future, An Australian Kimberley Aboriginal Perspective," pgs. 15-26

Table-Talk Article Discussions

Mar. 17: Australia
Film: "Rabbit-Proof Fence"
Readings:
Green, Indivisible, pgs. 43-59

Table-Talk Article Discussions

Mar. 24: Sex-Trafficking Abroad (Philippines) and in Canada
Film: "Hope in Heaven"
Readings:
Anderson, pgs. 117-130, 221-243,
Green, Making Space, Chapters 7 & 14

Mar. 31:Resistance Movements
Readings:
UR Courses: Voices of Resistance,
Green, Indivisible, pgs. ____

Apr. 7: Theoretical Patterns
Second Hand-In of Reflective Journal – 10%
Research Papers Due
NO FINAL EXAM
No Assigned Readings

10.
Honouring "Our Sisters in Spirit"

An Interview with Film Director Nick Printup

JENNIFER BRANT AND NICK PRINTUP

When it comes to the issue of missing and murdered Indigenous women and girls, I am unfortunately connected to nine victims through my family, my friends, and my communities. I come from a family that consists of four sisters, and we were raised primarily by our single parent mother. In having this issue directly affect so many people around me I realize that the probability of my mother or one of my sisters becoming a victim is quite possible. To be connected to so many victims I take issue with the prime minister of Canada [Stephen Harper] stating that this crisis facing Indigenous women today is not to be viewed as some kind of sociological phenomenon but rather individual crimes that need to be treated as such.

NICK PRINTUP IS ONONDAGA BEAVER CLAN from Six Nations of the Grand River and also has family ties to Kitigan Zibi Anishinabeg First Nation through his father. These words shared by Nick in his documentary *Our Sisters in Spirit* express an all too familiar reality that we share as Indigenous peoples. The issue of missing and murdered Indigenous women not only hits home but is felt deep within our spirits as we collectively grieve for the women who are ripped from the hearts of our families and communities.

This chapter serves as a textured discussion that weaves together an interview with Nick, a review of his documentary *Our Sisters in Spirit*, along with the momentum this film project has engendered in terms of awareness, action, and support. This work expresses the deep love that we share for our women, as the backbone of Indigenous families and communities. It is a testament to their lives, their stories, and their spirits. The very act of putting this documentary together expresses the essence of "Forever Loved," as the film is interwoven with the stories of families, academics, and politicians, who are all working to put an end to the racialized and sexualized violence of Indigenous women and girls in Canada.

The film has not been publicly released yet, but Nick and his team have held several film screenings in various communities. I attended the first screening at Niagara College in November 2015. As I watched the documentary, I could feel the strength of spirit in the room as we collectively shared in this grief to honour our women and their stories. One of the women, Helyna Riveria, whose story was shared in the film, was a childhood friend to many of us in the audience. As a young girl, she lived only a few doors from my childhood home, and we attended programs together at the Fort Erie Native Friendship Centre. She is remembered for her beautiful and energetic smile. She was also a graceful jingle dress dancer who brought joy to all who watched her dance. Her children now carry the gift that she has passed down as they bring light to our community socials with their laughter and dance. Her story is one that is felt deep within our home community. The issue of missing and murdered Indigenous women and girls in Canada is one that affects all Indigenous women and families across Turtle Island, as we mourn together in the losses of a loved one, a friend, or a community member. The stories also bring strength and healing. All of these emotions are beautifully expressed in the film. After the screening, Nick and the film crew offered a Q and A to allow community members to ask any questions that they may have. It was powerful to listen to the stories of the entire crew and learn about the lessons that they learned during their experiences in putting the film together and travelling to First Nations communities. With Nick being the only Indigenous student, it was evident that this was a life-changing and eye-opening experience for the entire crew. I interviewed Nick on February 19, 2016, at Niagara College to find out more about the film.

THE FILM PROJECT

It is remarkable that as an Indigenous man, and college student, Nick has stepped forward to speak out about the issue through a student-led project and class assignment for the Niagara College Broadcasting and Film program. His film began as one of three projects selected out of twenty-three class pitches. He noted that less than half the class knew about the issue or that it was happening in Canada, and those that did know did not understand the severity. A big part of this assignment involved educating his class, faculty members, and college staff. The final product serves as a wonderful teaching tool to be used in post-secondary classrooms to continue promoting education and awareness. Beyond classrooms, it is a film that all Canadians should see to understand the root causes of this violence and to bring healing and reconciliation to a nation that continues to suffer a deep, dark, and ongoing colonial trauma. Indigenous and non-Indigenous peoples are all part of this reality and must, therefore, work together to be part of the solution.

When I asked Nick to share a bit about the background of the film, he talked about his personal connection to the issue, being connected to nine victims, and the understanding that he had to do more to bring awareness to this issue. He noted this is "an issue that's directly affecting so many loved ones around me." When he was tasked with coming up with a contemporary issue for his scriptwriting class, bringing awareness to missing and murdered Indigenous women in Canada was at the forefront. However, as he expressed, "I was hesitant in taking on this project at first because of all the emotion behind it. It is something that's affecting all of us in every possible way: emotionally, spiritually, physically." Nick knew that if he took on this issue for the film project, it would be immense, and he wasn't sure where he would begin or how to go about it. He talked about the sense of responsibility that he felt along with the need to serve the issue justice. He noted the difficulty in achieving this as a student without the resources or the time to pull together the kind of film that he felt was needed. He was worried about letting the community down. The students had only four months to plan it out and four months to film. He said, "it was a daunting task to even just say, I want to do it." Despite his initial hesitancy, he presented the idea to two of his class friends, who urged him to go forward with it. His friends encouraged him to pitch the idea to the class, and when he did, Nick gained the support of the entire group. It was hard for him to pitch the topic because it was so close to him. "It was the first time I was speaking about it, especially with people I had been in the program with for three years, who had never seen that side of me before. It got really emotional for me." The support of his friends, who encouraged him to put the idea forward, became a driving force in bringing the project to fruition. He is thankful for the support of the entire class who encouraged him to move forward on this issue. During a time when the former prime minister of Canada declared that the issue of missing and murdered Indigenous women was not very high on Canada's radar, it is heartening that this issue mattered to a class of non-Indigenous students who were open to learning more and getting involved.

As Nick pointed out, he has been actively involved in taking a stance and speaking out on this issue for ten years, but bringing it to his film class opened a new direction for dialogue: "I've participated in vigils and marches. I was at the first Sisters in Spirit vigil in 2006 in Ottawa. In hearing those stories, it becomes a very scary reality. I always wonder how can I do more ... and I think it's really great that I was able to turn my education into a tool to help my communities and my people. That's what this project allowed me to do." In turning his education into a tool to help his community, Nick has educated so many of his non-Indigenous peers and educators on the issue of missing and murdered Indigenous women and girls. We both agreed that education is a powerful tool that can promote awareness and inspire change.

I asked Nick about the reaction of his faculty, staff, and fellow students on the topic. He noted that many of them were just starting to learn about the issue: they had only heard something about it in the news or read something about it on social media. Although he acknowledged that different media sources are bringing awareness to the issue, it is still often overlooked. His peers who had heard something about the issue were often unsure of how to engage in and dialogue about it. We talked about the difference between reading about the issue in the news or online and having an informed understanding of it. Nick stated, "I've seen it on the news and the news doesn't do it justice." We talked about the need for empathy and compassion. From the interview, the screening, and the open conversation with the film crew, it is evident that this project has filled that need by creating a space for empathy and compassion.

The push for a national public inquiry has predominantly come from Indigenous women, but as we work to restore the balance within our communities and the reverence for Indigenous women, it is important that Indigenous men are walking alongside the women. As Nick made clear, "we need to all be working together. It doesn't need to be one or the other, women leading this or men leading, we need to take each other's hand and get through this together." Through Nick's work, and the work of John Fox, who is featured in the film, as well as the work of Lester Green, representing the Rotiskenrakehte Six Nations Men's Fire, Indigenous men are taking a strong stance and an effective role in the campaign for justice. Not only has Nick served as a role model for other Indigenous men, but he has also educated his non-Indigenous peers and faculty on the issue and pulled together supporters from around the world.

Nick talked about the importance of his cultural upbringing and noted that unlike many Indigenous youth of his generation today, he grew up with a strong cultural foundation and is deeply immersed in both the Haudenosaunee Longhouse and Anishnaabe Midewin Lodge. His culture plays a paramount role in how he conducts himself, as he draws strength from the cultural roots on both sides of his family. On his father's side he belongs to the Midewin Lodge Eastern Doorway and through his mother's side, the Sourprings Longhouse:

> Growing up and knowing who I was and having that sense of identity—it is rare for Indigenous youth to have that strong cultural upbringing, to have both sides of family so different but being exposed to both cultures. I have both of my [traditional] names—one in the Midewin Lodge and one in the Longhouse. I always knew I was Onondaga Beaver Clan through my mother. The high respect of women in

> the Midewin culture, like the Haudenosaunee who are a matrilineal people, was instilled in me from a young age. Having that respect and loyalty to women and being raised with sisters. [I knew] my role was to protect them.

These foundational teachings are what brought him to interview Chief Arnie General, Onondaga, Beaver Clan and Wendy Hill, Cayuga, Bear Clan from Six Nations of the Grand River, Haudenosaunee Territory for the documentary. The following teachings are shared in the film:

> If you stop and realize what the women are actually here for it's not for exploitation, not like the way it is today in society. Killing these women, raping them ... what kind of mentality and humanity is that ... when the role of the women is the most precious thing on earth. (Arnie General)

> It's through the women that our future generations get carried on. The woman is the backbone; the strength of the family—we sustain life, we give life. (Wendy Hill)

Arnie General and Wendy Hill also discuss the importance of understanding the traditional teachings on the roles and responsibilities of men and women. As Nick mentioned, however, there are many Indigenous youth who do not have a strong cultural grounding today. This can only be understood by looking back. As Nick articulated, "to begin to understand the severity of the tragedy facing Indigenous women today, you must first understand the history." In the documentary, Arnie and Wendy talk about the effect colonization has had on cultural teachings, drawing attention to the *Indian Act* and the residential school system. Wendy points out that although the *Indian Act* attempted to disrupt Indigenous social and family structures, a matrilineal way of life was maintained. She continues by drawing attention to how residential schools have disrupted healthy families and created a lot of hurt that is now passed down through the generations. She notes that "when young women left those schools they were lost."

The need to acknowledge the role of Canada's dark history of colonization in order to understand the violence against Indigenous women and girls in Canada is expressed by Beverly Jacobs, who is also featured in the film. As the former president of the Native Women's Association of Canada, Beverly Jacobs was asked to make a statement on June 11, 2008, in response to Canada's apology to residential school survivors. Featured in the film are the following words from her statement delivered in the House of Commons and later published in *First Voices: An Aboriginal Women's Reader*:

> The women that we represent have a statement. It's about the respect of Aboriginal women in this country. Prior to the residential school system, prior to colonization, the women in our communities were very well respected and honoured for the role that they have in our communities. Women are the life givers, being the caretakers of the spirit that we bring into this world, Our Mother Earth. We were given these responsibilities by the Creator to bring that spirit into this physical world and to love, take care of and nurture our children.
>
> The government's and churches' genocidal policies of the residential schools caused much harm to that respect for women and to the way women were honoured in our communities. There were ceremonies for young men and young women that taught them how to respect themselves and one another. These ceremonies were stolen from them for generations. (Jacobs 12)

Beverly Jacobs draws attention to the strength and resilience of the grandmothers in our communities, who held onto traditions so that younger generations would have access to them today. As Nick expressed, many youth have not had the opportunity to grow up with their cultural knowledge, but we see these traditions being revitalized today.

Opportunities for revitalization must be part of that reconciliation process, but like Beverly Jacobs, many Indigenous peoples are still waiting for the action a true apology entails. As Beverly states in the film, "when somebody is abusive and they're apologizing to you and they beat the crap out of you at the same time—that's not an apology—it has to be genuine there has to be action." The lack of action, and the failure of Canada to acknowledge the pervasive and ongoing abuses of Indigenous women and girls in this country was captured in the film through images of news headings, families stories, and the frustration of the interviewees urging the government of Canada to do something.

As an example, the film begins by offering statistics that underscore the extent of the crisis in Canada: "In 2014 the Royal Canadian Mounted Police released a report indicating that from 1980 to 2012, 1,181 Indigenous women and girls had either been missing or been murdered. This would be equivalent to over 20,000 non-Indigenous women and girls. Indigenous women and girls make up 4 percent of the female population, but they account for 16 percent of all female homicides." By drawing attention to the numbers, the film calls on viewers to grasp the severity of the issue and reflect on how the country might have responded if the women had not been Indigenous.

THE DEPTHS OF THE HIDDEN CRISIS

Our communities are small, which amplifies the effect of the crisis. As Nick articulated, "when I say that I am connected to nine victims, that's the reality for many Indigenous people, it's not just one but having multiple incidents or victims of violence in your life. And we're just talking about women here, this is an issue for men in our communities as well." This reality prompted Nick to raise the question, "Is being connected to so many missing and murdered girls considered normal? Is this the life experience of every Canadian because it certainly is for First Nations people and communities?" These powerful and provocative questions brought the film crew to Carleton University, where they interviewed five Indigenous students whom they had never met before. The students were asked, "How many know of someone who is missing or has been murdered?" All five knew someone.

Despite the appalling numbers and numerous pushes for a national response, the issue has largely remained a hidden crisis unknown to many non-Indigenous people. This is reflected in the title of Dr. MaryAnne Pearce's dissertation "An Awkward Silence: Missing and Murdered Vulnerable Women and the Canadian Justice System." Pearce, who was interviewed for the film, welcomed the film crew into her home and invited the students to stay for dinner while she shared her work in pulling together a database to document the horrific numbers. Her research was instrumental in helping the RCMP with their statistics and the release of their report "Missing and Murdered Aboriginal Women: A National Operational Overview." The RCMP had contacted her right after her dissertation became public, and she shared her database with them. In her interview, she says, "We don't need to talk about numbers anymore. We can take action. We need to move forward and start dealing with root causes."

Likewise, the report "Invisible Women: A Call to Action, A Report on Missing and Murdered Indigenous Women," presented to the House of Commons in March 2014, draws attention to this human rights travesty as one that is largely hidden from the general public. Moreover, the lack of accountability and transparency in the systems that should be protecting Indigenous women and girls speaks to their ongoing devaluing, which accepts and, through a violent silence, perpetuates this sociological phenomenon.

SOCIOLOGICAL PHENOMENON? CALLING IT WHAT IT IS!

> *There's something horrific going on here. It's not about individual cases and we need to understand that it's happening right across the country.*
> —Invisible Women: A Call to Action, A report on Missing and Murdered Indigenous Women

> *Lauretta Saunders was writing her thesis on Missing and Murdered Indigenous women when she went missing herself.*
> —Niki Ashton, MP, NDP critic for Indigenous Affairs

The film captures the above statements, which were delivered in the House of Commons to push for a national public inquiry. Also captured in the film is the then Justice Minister Peter MacKay throwing the papers documenting over forty reports on missing and murdered Indigenous women on the floor. The disorder that followed sent a clear message to Indigenous women across the country that our disappearances not only do not matter but are something to be made a mockery of in the eyes of those with political power.

It is this mentality that contributes to the sociological phenomenon that targets Indigenous women and girls. It is well understood within Indigenous communities that if these horrific numbers of women missing and murdered were happening to non-Indigenous women, there would be an immediate response. Indigenous communities and human rights advocates around the world, like Nick, "take issue with the prime minister of Canada stating that this crisis facing Indigenous women today is not to be viewed as some kind of sociological phenomenon." This message is effectively captured throughout the film as the global push for Canada to take action is documented in the headlines "Ottawa largely ignored 700 recommendations of Missing Indigenous women" (from *The Canadian Press*) and "UN report slams Canada's human rights record" (from *The Toronto Star*).

VOICES OF GRIEF: VISIONS OF HEALING

> *Once you listen to the families you are forever changed.*
> —Carolyn Bennett, MP

The film makes it clear that it is the families, those who are most deeply affected by the issue, who must have a leading voice in the direction of a national response. The politicians interviewed for the film along with the family members believe that the victims' families should have leading roles in the national inquiry. Their stories as presented in the film speak for themselves. They showcase the deep love felt by their families, as they speak out and push for answers and accountability. Here are their stories as shared in the film.

Linda John is the mother of Helyna Riveria, who was shot and killed by her boyfriend in 2011. Helyna was a mother of four young children, who now reside with Linda. As mentioned earlier, Helyna was a childhood friend to many of us in the Fort Erie community. Her mother Linda had just started to speak out publicly about this issue to bring awareness and hope. Her message "to teach our children to honour and to love" is expressed by Helyna's four children through the strength of spirit they carry.

Laurie Odjick is the mother of sixteen-year-old Maisy Odjick who went missing from the Kitigan Zibi reserve in September 2008, along with seventeen-year-old Shannon Alexander. Laurie expresses her grief and vision of healing in the film, "Maisy and Shannon disappeared off of the face of this earth, nobody seeing anything, nobody hearing anything. To this day, nothing." Maisy Odjick's mother has remained an advocate to find justice for her daughter. She created "Maisy's Foundation of Hope" in memory of her daughter. Maria Jacko, Maisy's aunt, describes her frustration with the police response, noting that "right away they thought they were runaways, so no need for an Amber Alert, no need to follow protocol. It's unfortunate because if protocol was followed maybe things could have been different."

Bridget Tolley's mother was struck and killed on the Kitigan Zibi reserve by a police cruiser occupied by two on-duty officers from the Quebec police force. In her mother's honour, Bridget founded "Families of Sisters in Spirit." In the film, Bridget notes the many mistakes made in the police report, which was initially withheld from her, including the time, date, and address. She also points out that the brother of the officer that struck and killed her mother was in charge at the scene.

John Fox is the father of Cheyenne Fox from the Wikwemikong First Nation of Manitoulin Island. His daughter's death was immediately ruled a suicide, but her father, family, and community believe otherwise. John Fox conducted his own research into his daughter's death and found that the police "failed, they failed my daughter, they failed me, they failed my family, and they failed the community."

Bridget Tolley and John Fox share a common frustration in the relationship between the police services and Indigenous families. As Nick articulates in the film, "Sadly Bridget's story is not uncommon, and many families are dissatisfied with RCMP and police involvement and corruption." Laurie Odjick also expresses this frustration noting that the police did not do their job. She points out that they are "very insensitive to the families and to the topic."

Laurie Odjick also discusses her disappointment in the National roundtable on Missing and Murdered Indigenous Women. As Nick points out in the film, only one family member from each province was invited to attend. Laurie was invited and had initially thought the family members were going to have an opportunity to share their stories. She notes that there was a preset agenda and that the family members did not have the opportunity to share.

As Nick stated, "This process and leaving out so many victims' families from the meeting is what pushed John Fox to hold a rally on Parliament Hill." Nick Printup and the film crew attended the rally, where they were able to record opening statements and also connect with Niki Ashton, MP. The following words from John Fox's welcome at the Rally showcase both the frustration felt by the families, but also their refusal to be silent:

> We are here today to make our voices known about the roundtable. We have a lot of concerns about what's going on with the whole process. We are here for a very specific reason for our beautiful women our children and the youth we are here to honour them with our presence.

Nikki Ashton also responded with the following statement:

> I stand with you in solidarity to call for action to put an end to the violence against Indigenous women and to call for an inquiry, a national public inquiry. And as John just said, one that based on Indigenous knowledge, one that is guided by Indigenous families by Indigenous women. People around the world are saying enough. But the only people that are not at the table to be part of the solution is the federal government and Mr. Harper the Prime Minister. So our message to Prime Minister Harper today is "if you are not willing to be part of the solution then you Mr. Harper are part of the problem." We can afford an inquiry that is done properly, but what we can't

afford is more women who are missing and murdered in our country!

When our families come together for rallies and demonstrations, there is a lot of grief that is shared. It is also a time for ceremony to bring healing. Often a healing or honour song will be song as we put our collective energies together to remember our sisters and support the families:

> *"Sister, Sister, I want you to know, you are so strong and beautiful. I got to know, where did you go? I think of you every day since you gone away."*

These words are sung by round dance singer Nikki Shawana. Her song expresses the love we collectively carry for our missing sisters. Her song is played during the film as the family's stories are shared.

THE NEED FOR PARALLEL ACTION

> *Families need answers. Families need compassion. Families need help.*—Maria Jacko, aunt of Maisy Odjick

One thing that sets this documentary apart from others is that it was presented through a well-rounded and holistic approach, which is effective in reaching a wide audience. It presents interviews of family members, Traditional Knowledge Keepers, academics as well as prominent politicians all immersed in the national dialogue. All of these individuals can shed light on the push for a national inquiry from the grassroots to the political arena. I asked Nick to share more about this approach:

> I knew that needed to be done. I critique a film in a number of ways as a viewer. If you look at Indigenous films, their films are popular among Indigenous community but not necessarily acknowledged in mainstream. I wanted the general public to understand this issue and knew that they needed to hear about the issue from someone that looks like them to be able to understand this issue

> more, and who better to do it then the people they elect to represent them.

This brought Nick and the crew to reach out to the Conservative, Liberal, and NDP offices. They tried contacting the Conservative government several times to be a part of this film but never received a response. The others were more than accommodating, although Nick noted the difficulty in trying to schedule interviews. Justin Trudeau was out of the country at the time, but the team was able to interview his wife Sophie Trudeau. The dialogue with the politicians interviewed for the film showcase their support for the national public inquiry. Moreover, as Nick stated, they help to reach a wider audience and in this way promote understanding among the non-Indigenous population.

The following statements, presented in the film, attest to the political support for more than a national public inquiry but also "parallel action" and family involvement.

> It needs to be done. To be able to solve a problem you need to understand all the levels and all the elements of one problem. There is also a need for a deeper structured database.—Sophie Gregoire-Trudeau

> The inquiry is an important step forward. It's not the only thing we can be doing. Absolutely not—there has to be parallel action.—Niki Ashton

> This won't work top down. This is community by community, and family by family, and urban setting by urban setting, and we are going to have to figure out how we do this, but it will only be by listening to people with the expertise and lived experience.—Carolyn Bennett

The film project inspired that parallel action by bringing together so many people in support of the call for justice. I asked Nick about the support that has helped them put the final product together. Nick began by talking about the support of his peers, the Fort Erie Native Friendship Centre, and the entire film crew. He noted the support of film executive producer James Crow, along with Trace Hyama, Veronica Wilson and Mitchel Corner in Toronto. He also acknowledged the support of the Kickerstarter supporters, who donated over twelve thousand dollars in only thirty days. These supporters were from all over the world—Canada, U.S., Germany, and South America. As Nick stated, "It was amazing that these people that I had never met before wanted to help for nothing in return. It speaks a lot to what people want to do for social issues."

Indeed there are many non-Indigenous allies ready to listen with an open heart and support the call for action. It was this support that prompted Nick to initially pitch this idea to his film class. His film crew being all non-Indigenous certainly had a lot to learn about Indigenous realities in Canada, and Nick and I talked about how this one issue of missing and murdered Indigenous women and girls in Canada is deeply interconnected to many other issues in our communities. I asked him to share a bit about the lessons that his film crew learned as they travelled to his home reserve for the interviews with the families. Nick responded with the following:

> I wanted the team to be aware of some of the things they might encounter going to a First Nations community. No one had ever been on a reserve before, which I expected, and I just made them aware of conditions. For example, housing conditions; I had never been in many of the families houses who we interviewed. I also wanted to be mindful and respectful. In my dad's community, you can't drink the water; there's too much mercury. This has been going on for twenty years, and it is only an hour from Ottawa. Our local reserve, Six Nations of the Grand River, is much more developed than many of the communities. It was important to make them aware of that. When we were at my dad's community, we had posted on Facebook that we would be at the youth centre, and we would be having a drum performance there. Someone in the community was able to see that and came to the centre because an extended family member had recently killed himself, and the community just became aware of it that day. That being their local drum—there are certain songs that you sing when someone

> passes and his nephew came to see if the drum group would sing these songs. It was eye opening to the crew because as we are filming this tragic issue, we had talked about other issues on the road trip there, so they knew suicide was a major issue that confronts First Nations communities. But here we are filming one issue, and this other issue comes up, and it just devastates everybody that night, especially me being a distant family member. Then the next day, we had to get on the road and leave the community, and the film crew was just speechless. Again, as non-Indigenous, this is not an issue that they face in their communities. They know it's an issue that exists everywhere, and we discussed that, but they were right there to experience it, and see it as a real thing.

Nick and I talked about the connections between these issues and the disheartening realities that are so close to home for us. As I write this, the community of Attawapiskat has just declared a state of emergency for the youth suicides that have recently took place while Canada sits idly watching. The issues that face Indigenous peoples today can only be understood by looking back to the history of colonization, as Nick articulated in the film. There is a need to understand more than just what was done to us, but why it was done, and consider what changes have been made. The dominant ideology that sought to break the spirits of Indigenous women and to kill the Indian in the child, in many ways is reflected in the ongoing colonization that persists today. It is echoed in the news reports that erase the identity of an Indigenous woman by only referring to her as a sex worker and not a mother, daughter, or sister. It is reflected in the opinion articles that refer to the North as a dangerous place that Indigenous youth must escape from. This mindset continues to inflict trauma on our communities today. The connections between these issues must be understood as we collectively work towards reconciliation. Through the film project, Nick's peers were able to come to these understandings. Their lessons speak to the power of experience in terms of promoting awareness and compassion. Through the film, their experiences serve as lessons for all by inspiring a holistic dialogue in the spirit of bringing healing to Indigenous communities.

As Nick stated, what began as a class assignment developed into something much more. "It was a class project that took on a life of its own." I believe education has a strong role to play in promoting social justice and human rights for Indigenous people, and the film is evidence of that. As Sophie Trudeau expresses in the film, "We need to have more empathy, collaboration, peace, and compassion between ourselves, and we have no excuse as Canadians to not cherish and foster these values." The *Our Sisters in Spirit* film is a tool for promoting those values and promoting an informed understanding of the violence against Indigenous women and girls in Canada.

To come full circle, I close with the words of Nick Printup from the end of the film that serve as a call to action and an expression of hope:

> *Change is possible. The hope for humanity to prevail and the hope for the dignity of women all women to be upheld lies in the wake of action, an action everyone can be a part of. This makes those who have been missing or who have been murdered our sisters in spirit, and it is our job as a society to ensure that they are not forgotten.*

WORKS CITED

Jacobs, Beverley. "Response to Canada's Apology to Residential School Survivors." *First Voices: An Aboriginal Women's Reader*. Eds. Patricia Monture and Patricia McGuire. Toronto: Inanna, 2009. 11–14. Print.

Our Sisters in Spirit. Dir. Nick Printup. (2015, awaiting official release). Film.

Shawana, Nikki, Golde Nish Records. "Sister Round Dance Song (MMIW Honour Song)." YouTube, 20 Mar. 2014. Web. 22 Apr. 2016.

IV.
TAKING A STANCE:
RESISTANCE AND SISTERHOOD

11.
Sisterhood on the Frontlines

The Truth As We Hear It from Indigenous Women

SUMMER RAIN BENTHAM, HILLA KERNER, AND LISA STEACY,
VANCOUVER RAPE RELIEF AND WOMEN'S SHELTER

APPLYING A FEMINIST ANALYSIS to men's violence against Indigenous women involves a critical examination of the power imbalances between men and women, between white people and Indigenous peoples, and between the wealthy and the poor. It compels us to understand how those in power maintain their power and control over the oppressed. All systems of oppression—sexism, racism, colonialism and capitalism—intersect in the lives of Indigenous women who experience men's violence.

THE COLONIAL CONTEXT OF VIOLENCE AGAINST INDIGENOUS WOMEN

From the 1870s to the late 1980s, the government of Canada stripped Indigenous women of their rights through the implementation and enforcement of the *Indian Act*. By 1850, there were already laws in place that defined an Indian, and the state had created reserves as a way to dictate where Indians could live. These laws shaped the *Indian Act* of 1876, which inserted a belief in the racial superiority of white colonizers into federal law and legalized the assimilation and eradication of the Indigenous population. The *Indian Act* contained particular implications for women; it entrenched patriarchy by transmitting Indian status through the male line, which, simultaneously, eroded women's traditionally held roles.

Under the act, Indigenous women who married non-Indigenous men or Indigenous men from other nations had their Indian status taken away. Loss of status meant that these women lost the right to live in their own communities. This sexist policy resulted in the uprooting and displacement of thousands of Indigenous women and damaged the ties to their families by denying Indian status to their children and grandchildren. Isolation from their communities, and the resulting loss of kinship support networks, forced Indigenous women to depend on their husbands. Sadly, for many Indigenous women this forced dependence meant staying with their male partners even in the face of abuse. The *Indian Act* was only partially corrected in 1985 and again in 2010. Indigenous peoples are still governed by this *Indian Act*, which continues to perpetuate racist and sexist discrimination.

Part of the intergenerational devastation of colonization for Indigenous peoples was the residential school system, which was operated by the church and state in co-operation. In 2015, the final report of the Truth and Reconciliation Commission of Canada opens by highlighting residential schools as a crucial element of colonial policy:

> For over a century, the central goals of Canada's Indigenous policy were to eliminate Indigenous governments; ignore Indigenous rights; terminate the Treaties; and, through a process of assimilation, cause Indigenous peoples to cease to exist as distinct legal, social, cultural, religious, and racial entities in Canada. The establishment and operation of residential schools were a central element of this policy, which can best be described as "cultural genocide." (1)

Indigenous children were forcefully removed from their families and communities and placed into residential schools, where their cultural teachings and practices were prohibited, they were denied the right to speak their traditional languages, and they were deprived of their traditional foods, clothing, and protocols. The children were often physically abused and sexually assaulted. Many did not survive.

The colonial legacy of forced child apprehension continued through the Sixties Scoop, which started in 1961 and continued into the 1980s. The common practice of the child welfare authorities during this time in Canada was to "scoop" almost all Indigenous newborns from their mothers who lived on reserves. At its peak, one in four status Indian children were forcibly and without consent taken from their parents and communities and remained in the "care" of the state. Records show that in 1951, twenty-nine Indigenous children were in provincial care in British Columbia; by 1964, the number jumped to 1,466. Indigenous children, who had comprised only 1 percent of all children in care, came to make up just over 34 percent (Bennett and Sadrehashemi). Federal initiatives, such as the Adopt an Indian Métis program, aggressively advertised Indigenous children to white adoptive parents. It is estimated that between 11,000 and 28,000 Indigenous children were removed from their homes and placed with white families in Canada, the U.S., and Europe during the "scoop."

Raven Sinclair, a university professor, describes how the Sixties Scoop continued the colonial policy and practice of aggressive assimilation through child apprehension: "The white social worker, following on the heels of the missionary, the priest, and the Indian agent, was convinced that the only hope for the salvation of the Indian people lay in the removal of their children" (67). It was not until 1980 that the *Child, Family and Community Services Act* required social workers to notify the band council if an Indigenous child was removed from the community. During this time, the government changed the child welfare laws so that bands could run their own social service, yet problems similar to those seen during the Sixties Scoop persist.

A 2008 report from the auditor general of Canada shows Indigenous children to be vastly overrepresented in care, citing that 51 percent of all children in care in British Columbia are Indigenous, even though Indigenous people comprise 4 percent of the province's population. The report further states that Aboriginal children in British Columbia are "six times more likely to be taken into care than a non-Aboriginal child" (2). In this context the term care is ironic, as the appalling lack of care given to Indigenous children apprehended by child welfare systems is now widely accepted. These examples are only just part of the devastating evidence of state-sanctioned discrimination against Indigenous peoples. Racism, poverty, displacement, child apprehension, and the dismal failure of the child protection authorities—all brutal legacies of colonization—conspire to make Indigenous women disproportionately vulnerable to men's violence.

THE TRUTH AS WE KNOW IT: FRONTLINE FEMINIST RESPONSE TO VIOLENCE AGAINST WOMEN

In 1985, an Indigenous woman, who was a member of Vancouver Rape Relief and Women's Shelter at the time, wrote the article "The Truth as We Know It" on behalf of the collective. The article states:

> It is overwhelmingly white men born into rich families who hold the positions of most power in this society. They make the rules and social policy for the rest of us, including the large numbers of the poor, women and people of colour. There is overwhelming evidence that men rape within the same class or race and down. Although we know that violence against women is perpetrated by men of every race and class, the jails are disproportionately filled with native men and poor and working class men.

Thirty years later, based on our frontline work with women, in particular with women of colour and Indigenous women, this statement is still very much the truth as we know it.

In Canada, Indigenous women—who are at the bottom of the sex, race, and class hierarchies—are victims of all men's violence. They are raped and beaten by their fathers, their domestic partners, and other men in their communities. Outside of their communities, they are raped, beaten, forced into prostitution, and killed by men of every race. Wherever Indigenous women turn, they are subjected to horrifying, and sometimes deadly, attacks from men, frequently white men. A sobering statistic reminds us that Indigenous women between the ages of twenty-five and forty four who do have status under the *Indian Act* are five times more likely than all other women of the same age to die as the result of violence (NWAC 14).

Exposing men for their violence against women is one of the most important achievements of the feminist movement. Starting in the late 1960s, women came together in consciousness-raising groups to reveal to one another their individual experiences of oppression. As Carol Hanisch explains "Consciousness-raising was a way to use our own lives our combined experiences to understand concretely how we are oppressed, and who was actually doing the oppressing. We regarded this knowledge as necessary for building such a movement." Through these discussions, women realized that violence against women is a collective experience that affects all women. Women also realized that this collective experience creates and reinforces the power relationships between men and women. This understanding was the catalyst for the creation of anti-violence feminist services, and it has been deepened and reinforced by the knowledge accrued by frontline workers from rape crisis centres, transition houses, and women's centres.

The accumulation of stories told by hundreds of thousands of women to frontline workers all over the country and in other parts of the world has created an invaluable knowledge on how men use their relative power as men—and often the relative power of their race and class—to attack women. It also exposed and crystallized how different patriarchal institutions, such as the church and the state, collude with men's violence by increasing women's vulnerability and by refusing to hold men accountable for their sexist attacks on women.

Since 1973, Vancouver Rape Relief and Women's Shelter, where we work, has been available to women who call the confidential crisis line to report and resist men's violence, twenty-four hours a day, seven days a week. Every day, women call our crisis lines to reveal their experiences of incest, rape, prostitution, harassment, and wife assault. Women tell us about violent attacks by men. We connect these individual women's experiences to one another and to our own, in a feminist anti-violence praxis that understands that no woman is free from men's violence or the threat of men's violence. Men's violence against women is a force that exploits and enforces all women's inequality.

We know that we cannot adequately respond to a woman who calls us until we understand the particular power of the man who has attacked her. We understand that sexism and racism reinforce each other, and, therefore, we ask every woman who calls us to tell us if her attacker is a white man or not and what her race is.

Because we ask about race, we know that Indigenous women are disproportionately represented among our callers and residents. In 2015, more than a third of the calls we received were from Indigenous women and more than a third of the women and children we housed were Indigenous. Indigenous women are subject to the violence that all women experience, and they suffer at the hands of men of all races, from all communities, in all locations.

In 2015, we heard from Indigenous women who were raped by their uncles, fathers, stepfathers, and grandfathers. One woman told us that she started sleeping with a hammer under her pillow when she was twelve. We heard from a grandmother whose granddaughter was raped by the adult son of the foster family that the Ministry of Child and Family Development placed her with. Battered women called us after they were criminally charged after defending themselves or after the children were apprehended when the police were called. Women assaulted by police officers have called us. One woman told us about being kidnapped from one province, brought to Vancouver, and raped. We heard from another woman lured from her northern community to Vancouver by an internet lover; she was then trapped and forced into prostitution in his downtown single-room occupancy hotel.

When Indigenous women tell us about the attacks that they have experienced from white men, it is very clear that these acts are a result of both racist and sexist hatred. Indigenous women battered by their white husbands have told us these men make it explicit that they are attacking them because of their race; one man frequently told his wife to "go back to the rez"; another called his partner a "piece of garbage"; and another told the mother of his child that she deserves his attacks because "native people are stupid." An Indigenous girl adopted into a white family had to endure racist slurs screamed at her during beatings. An Indigenous woman in street level prostitution was told by a john, while he was raping her, that she was "not the first pretty little native girl" he had chosen to attack.

We assure the women who trust us enough to call us, and tell us about the violence they have experienced that we are confidential and independent from the state. It is crucial that we can make and keep this promise because women are overwhelmingly reluctant to engage the state, particularly the criminal justice system, in their fight against the man who attacked them. Since the 1970s, 70 percent of women have consistently chosen not to report the men who attack them to the police (Lakeman 148, 153).

Women who engage with the state agencies responsible for protecting women from violence and for holding violent men accountable experience systemic, sexist discrimination. For Indigenous women, the colonial legacy of institutionalized racism exacerbates the state's failure to intervene or respond on her behalf.

Often, men who attack Indigenous women know and explicitly say that because she is an Indigenous woman, the police will believe him when he blames her for the attack or he says she is lying about it, especially if he is a white man. We also tell Indigenous women that we understand their particular reluctance to report to the police. We know from our own crisis work and from reports from the Highway of Tears in British Columbia and Val D'Or, Quebec, that police have been exposed for far worse than institutional indifference when it comes to their treatment of Indigenous women.

This past year, we supported a woman to make a police report about a white man who was using drug treatment meetings as a way to gain access to and rape Indigenous women who were struggling with addiction. This man has since been charged. We assisted her the way we assist all women who are considering reporting to police.

First, we are honest with her and tell her that, statistically, men rape women with no consequences or accountability from the criminal justice system (Johnson 632). Then. we tell her that despite this grim reality, we will call the police with her, wait with her for them to arrive, and sit beside her while she gives her initial report. We will advocate for a timely, adequate, and thorough investigation resulting in criminal charges. If the charges go to court, we will be with her when she is called to testify. We explain that we have made a deliberate decision to ally with every woman who chooses to make a police report about sexist violence and to claim her right to be equally protected under the law.

Often violent men face no criminal charges. The Vancouver Police Department failed to take a full statement when a woman who had been assaulted by a john reported at the hospital. She later decided she wanted to provide a full, detailed statement, but she did not know who was assigned to her case and did not have any success getting the attention of someone with the power to move the investigation forward. We used what we know about navigating the bureaucracy and the chain of command to get a direct line to the investigating detective and to argue that he ought to pay attention to this case, reminding them of their failure in the investigation of Robert Pickton. We argued that he should pay attention to this case of a white man attacking Indigenous women in prostitution in Vancouver's Downtown Eastside. The police's tendency to dismiss women by labelling them as "uncooperative" or "unreliable" is exactly what men count on. Although police officers were willing to take a statement about one assault, they dismissed the possibility of investigating and charging him for buying sex, for exploiting the poverty and desperation that drove this woman into prostitution. After taking her statement, the police recommended charges, but the Crown declined to prosecute the case, as it characterized her as uncooperative and her evidence as unreliable.

We fought with an RCMP detachment for three days to take a statement from a woman who managed to get her abusive husband out of their home and wanted to get a peace bond under section 810 of the Criminal Code of Canada. Officers attended to the home three times in three days, and each time, they told her that no crime had been committed and that her case was a matter for family court. The Crown has since approved the peace bond, and he can no longer contact her or be present at the home. However, paying for rent, food and other basic necessities on her own applies constant financial pressure, which is leading her to consider letting him back into the home.

Women who call our crisis line reveal that abusive men's threats to call the child protection agencies are an effective way to keep Indigenous women trapped and under their control, as we are all fully aware of the long history of the state-sponsored removal of Indigenous children from their homes. To counteract this threat, we raised money to pay for a lawyer to represent a young Indigenous mother who was charged with assault when she defended herself against her batterer, a much older white man.

Crown counsel wasn't asking for jail time so despite meeting the financial criteria, she was not eligible for a legal aid lawyer. She would have had to defend herself in court or bow to the pressure to plead guilty in order to avoid a trial, a potential conviction and a criminal record for domestic violence. As long as the charges were on the record, he continued to have access and control over her. He exploited her fear of losing her child by threatening to drag her into a custody fight that he claimed she would not win. Recently, after almost a year since her arrest, these charges were dropped and she can start to consider using family court to gain custody and a protection order.

We intervened to have a woman's children returned to her after they had been apprehended because she, apparently, "failed to protect them from their father's violence." We arranged for safe transportation to our transition house when the Ministry of Children and Family Development would not.

We took collect calls from a women's prison. The caller was a young woman who was apprehended from her family, raped in foster care, and ended up criminalized and jailed. When she was released at age nineteen, she was dropped off in the Downtown Eastside and prostituted out of a harm-reduction shelter for at-risk young women. We managed to arrange for her release to a treatment centre and accompanied her to have an abortion because she was pregnant as the result of a rape.

We have offered these women our empathy and our alliance, connecting them to us, and to each other. We provide peer-counseling, safe shelter, advocacy for the state to respond and, when necessary, for the state to back off. The increased impoverishment of women and the systematic dismantling of social welfare systems means that the remaining, unfunded independent women's centres, like our rape crisis centre, are pressured to tend to all the effects of women's desperate inequality including hunger, homelessness, addiction, and mental health.

PROSTITUTION AS SEXIST AND RACIST VIOLENCE

In addition to operating the twenty-four-hour rape crisis line and the transition house, we monitor media coverage and court cases related to male violence against women. Two striking and highly publicized cases of white men perpetrating deadly, horrific violence against Indigenous women are the cases of Robert "Willie" Pickton who preyed on and murdered women from Vancouver's downtown eastside, and Bradley Barton who was acquitted in the murder of Cindy Gladue. Less known, is the case of Martin Tremblay, a man with a lengthy record of violence against young Indigenous women in the lower Mainland of British Columbia.

Martin Tremblay is estimated to have assaulted 103 Indigenous girls between his releases from jail in 2001 until 2014. His past criminal convictions included

> Five convictions for sexual assault arising from incidents which occurred between the spring of 2001 and October 2002. [Wherein] Mr. Tremblay pleaded guilty to sexually assaulting five First Nations teenage girls on December 4, 2003. The convictions were based on videotapes made by Mr. Tremblay which depicted the assaults. The victims appeared to be drugged or passed out at the time of the assaults. (1, *R. v. Tremblay*)

In 2013, Martin Tremblay was charged with two counts of failing to provide lifesaving measure and two counts of administering a noxious substance in the death of two young Indigenous girls in Vancouver. In December of 2015, after continuous pressures from community groups and women's organizations, the Supreme Court of British Columbia classified Martin Tremblay as a dangerous offender and sentenced him to an indeterminate period of incarceration. The judgment described his targeting of young, Indigenous girls:

> He was a drug dealer and offered his home to at-risk youth, primarily female First Nations teenagers, for the purpose of partying. He was well known to [one of the victims] who referred to him as her "street dad." He provided gifts, alcohol, drugs, and a cell phone to her. She in turn, invited her friends to his residence where he gave them free alcohol and drugs. (1, *R v. Tremblay*)

This description of Tremblay's modus operandi is strikingly similar to what we hear from Indigenous women who call our crisis line and describe how they were lured into prostitution as girls.

In Canada, most prostitutes are Indigenous. We believe that prostitution exists because men believe that they have the inherent right to access the bodies of women and girls. Men's privilege, power, and entitlement to Indigenous women's bodies keep Indigenous women oppressed. People label Indigenous women as "survival" prostitutes. This is of no surprise to Indigenous women because no matter what Indigenous women do, they are always operating in a desperate state of survival mode. The brutal forces of poverty, racism, and inequality effectively negate women's ability to freely consent to engage in prostitution.

In Vancouver, prostitution is far worse for Indigenous women, now more so then ever. Harm reduction strategies have created a warehousing system for Indigenous women, which force them to reside in unsafe locations, where men access their bodies in exchange for money or drugs. We understand these strategies as enforcing and protecting the male demand to keep women in unsafe, unliveable conditions, which allows men to continue to commodify and objectify women.

Young women and girls of Indigenous descent are forced, trapped, tricked and entrenched into street-level prostitution in numbers grossly disproportionate to any other group. The intergenerational histories of having families torn apart by colonial state policies have forced a disproportionate number of Indigenous women and girls into extreme poverty, homelessness, and prostitution. In Vancouver, where Indigenous peoples make up approximately two percent of the city's population, studies estimate that 30 percent of women in street prostitution in Vancouver are Indigenous (Cunningham and Christensen). Often Indigenous women experience brutal and deadly violence in prostitution.

Between 1991 and 2004, 171 women involved in prostitution were killed in Canada; 45 percent of these murders remain unsolved (Shingler). Those who support the legalization of prostitution suggest that indoor prostitution will protect women from violent johns. We argue that yhis is false because violence is intrinsic to prostitution. Therefore, we believe that changing the location does not and will not alleviate the violence women in prostitution experience and that legalizing or decriminalizing prostitution will further increase the sexual violence that has contributed to the murders and disappearances of over 1,200 Indigenous women and girls across Canada.

Any attempt to move prostitution indoors creates a hierarchy based on race within prostitution itself. This hierarchy abandons Indigenous women who have little to no opportunity of exiting prostitution; they experience levels of violence that are hard to fathom, violence that is perpetuated by men, not only because she is a woman but because she is an Indigenous woman.

Male violence against Indigenous women is motivated by racism and enforced by societal indifference to the safety and welfare of Indigenous women. This indifference allows men to continue to escape accountability for criminal acts of violence against women. This increases the vulnerability of Indigenous women and has been exploited by Indigenous and non-Indigenous men who continue to carry out acts of extreme violence against Indigenous women and girls. Indigenous women face life threatening, gender-based violence, compounded by hatred and racism at disproportionate to any other race group in Canada. Denying Indigenous women the protection they are entitled to allows men to escape responsibility and accountability for their acts, which only perpetuates and reinforces their racist misogynistic violent behaviour and male entitlement. The cycle of male violence against women never ends for far too many Indigenous women and girls.

THE RESPONSIBILITY OF THE CANADIAN STATE

When it comes to violence against women, three federal and provincial mechanisms are directly liable: the criminal justice system, the welfare system, and the ministers responsible for status of women. We need an immediate and effective transformation of how these systems treat women.

The criminal justice system consistently fails women who look to the state for protection from violent men. Both the police and Crown prosecutors are to blame for the low number of men who ever face a judge for their assaults on women. We have adequate laws on sexual assault. Men know that they can commit violence against women with impunity, and they definitely know they will get away with their violence against Indigenous women.

We require the criminal justice system to exercise due diligence when responding to all reports of male violence against women. Men who attack women must face consequences. Men need to know that they will be stopped and that they will be held accountable for their violence by the state.

The welfare system all over the country controls people's lives while keeping them impoverished. The UN Committee on the Elimination of Discrimination against Women wrote in its concluding observations of Canada:

> The Committee is also concerned at reports of cuts in social assistance schemes in many provinces and at the resulting negative impact on the rights of vulnerable groups of women, such as single mothers, Indigenous women, Afro-Canadian women, immigrant women, elderly women and disabled women, who rely on social assistance for an adequate standard of living. (3)

In British Columbia, a single person on welfare receives 610 dollars per month. Women's poverty is a key factor of their vulnerability to men's violence. Women stay with abusive male partners because they have no prospect of economic independence. Women tell us they resort to prostitution sporadically or permanently to pay for rent and other basic needs they and their children have. We call for a provision of guaranteed livable income as a means for women to secure economic independence and to provide for themselves and their children without barriers or hoops to jump through.

The elimination of some of the provincial status of women ministries and the erosion of any meaningful substance at the federal status of women ministry level means that there is no entity in some provinces or at the federal level that is committed to the advancement of women, to women's equality and to the support of the independent women's movement in its fight to end violence against women.

We want independent, women-controlled transition houses, rape crisis centres, and women's centres in every community, including in remote and isolated areas. There are nearly 3,100 reserves in Canada alone; many of these reserves are not funded to provide any form of transitional houses for women and children escaping male violence. Women's services are a proven and effective method to offer women genuine safety, support, and advocacy, and they must be available to any women at any given moment. We also know that "Working to aid women after sexist violent attack is not enough. We must end the inequality of women and the use men make of it" (CASAC).

FEMINIST SOLIDARITY WITH INDIGENOUS WOMEN

In 2012, the largest-ever global study on violence against women concluded that "The autonomous mobilization of feminists in domestic and transnational contexts—not leftist parties, women in government, or national wealth—is the critical factor accounting for policy change" (Htun and Weldon 548). The women's movement is a crucial force in the efforts to eliminate violence against women. Since independent women's groups are the backbone of the women's movement, the Canadian government must provide core funding for national and local women's groups, including Indigenous-only women's groups.

Our solidarity with Indigenous women must be explicit and tangible. Non-Indigenous feminists must use their relative privileges of race and class to fight for substantive equality for Indigenous women. We need to promote Indigenous women's membership and employment in women's groups and services through affirmative action and a proven commitment to fight racism within ourselves and others. We are obligated to expose male violence against Indigenous women, to support with concrete means Indigenous women's survival, escape, and resistance, and to relentlessly demand fair treatment and full protection for them by all state agencies.

Indigenous women around the world are rising up, and we need to listen. We will continue to stand with and support our Indigenous sisters while they fight the system's intentional and cold-hearted destruction of them. Until women of all races and classes see our struggle as one—no women will be free.

As feminist anti-violence workers who understand prostitution as violence against women, we deliberately use the term prostitution and reject the term "sex work." For further discussion see: "Over 300 Human Rights Groups and Anti-Trafficking Advocates World-wide Weigh in on "Sex Work" Terminology In Media," Coalition Against Trafficking in Women, 4 Nov. 2014. Web.

WORKS CITED

Bennett, Darcie, and Lobat Sadrehashemi. "Broken Promises: Parents Speak about BC's Child Welfare System." *Pivot Legal Society*. Pivot Legal Society, 2008. Web. 11 Feb. 2016.

Canadian Association of Sexual Assault Centres (CASAC)."Constitution." CASAC, 2005. Web. 11 Feb. 2016.

Cunningham, L. C., and C. Christensen. *Violence against Women in Vancouver's Street Level Sex Trade and the Police Response*. Vancouver: PACE Society, 2001. Print.

Hanisch, Carol. "Women's Liberation Consciousness-Raising: Then and Now." *On The Issues Magazine The Progressive Woman's Magazine*. On the Issues,Winter 2010. Web. 9 Feb. 2016.

Htun, Mala, and S. Laurel Weldon. "The Civic Origins of Progressive Policy Change: Combating Violence against Women in Global Perspective, 1975–2005." *American Political Science Review* 106.3 (2012): 548-69. Web. 9 Feb. 2016.

Johnson, H. "Limits of a Criminal Justice Response: Trends in Police and Court Processing of Sexual Assault." *Sexual Assault in Canada: Law, Legal Practice and Women's Activism*. Ed. E. Sheehy. Ottawa: University of Ottawa Press, 2012, 613-634. Print.

Lakeman, Lee. *Obsession with Intent*. Montreal: Black Rose Books, 2005. Print.

Office of the Auditor General of Canada."2008 May Report of the Auditor General of Canada." *Office of the Auditor General of Canada*. Government of Canada, 6 May 2008. Web. 11 Feb. 2016.

Regina v. Martin Daniel Tremblay. The Courts of British Columbia.

Government of British Columbia. 1 Dec. 2015. Web. 9 Feb. 2016.

Shingler, Benjamin. "Prostitution in Canada: Pattern of Police Repression Makes Sex Work More Dangerous, Experts Say." *The Huffington Post*, 1 Feb. 2012. Web. 22 Apr. 2016.

Sinclair, Raven. "Identity Lost and Found: Lessons from the Sixties Scoop." *First Peoples Child and Family Review: A Journal on Innovation and Best Practices in Aboriginal Child Welfare Administration, Research, Policy & Practice* 3.1 (2007): 65-82. Web. 9 Feb. 2016.

Statistics Canada. *Measuring Violence against Women: Statistical Trends 2006*. Ottawa: Minister of Industry. 2006. Print.

The Truth and Reconciliation of Commission of Canada (TRC). "Honouring the Truth, Reconciling for the Future: Summary of the Final Report of the Truth and Reconciliation Commission of Canada." *The Truth and Reconciliation Commission of Canada*. TRC, 2015. Web. 9 Feb. 2016.

"The Truth As We Know It." *Vancouver Rape Relief & Women's Shelter*. Vancouver Rape Relief & Women's Shelter, 2010. Web. 9 Feb. 2016.

United Nations Human Rights: Office of the High Commissioner. "Concluding Observations of the Committee on the Elimination of Discrimination against Women: Canada." *United Nations Human Rights*. United Nations, 2008. Web. 9 Feb. 2016.

12.
Visualizing Grassroots Justice

Missing and Murdered Indigenous Women

VICKI CHARTRAND, MYRNA ABRAHAM, LEAH MAUREEN GAZAN, CHERYL JAMES, BRENDA OSBORNE, AND CHICKADEE RICHARD

Stop disappearing our women and stop disappearing the work of Indigenous communities.
—Leah Gazan, Visualizing Justice Conference, 2015

THE ISSUE OF missing and murdered Indigenous women across Canada has long been a concern for Indigenous communities, but it has only in the last few years been given significant media and public attention. In 2004, the Native Women's Association of Canada launched the public campaign "Stolen Sisters" to draw attention to the high numbers of Indigenous women going missing and being murdered. They framed the issue within a colonial analysis to draw attention to a violence against Indigenous women that is endemic to Canada. Although Indigenous women may experience violence on reserves or through intra-familial violence (Canada, Statistics Canada), what was unique to this campaign was that it highlighted the systemic and ongoing colonial violence experienced by Indigenous women not only within their communities but also off reserve, within urban centres, on the highways, and at the hands of strangers (Amnesty International; Native Women's Association).

More recently, many publicized grassroots Indigenous campaigns have highlighted and linked the murders and disappearances to the ongoing colonial violence experienced by Indigenous women. Despite this work and the current widespread national attention, the disappearances and murders remain largely treated as a domestic or partner violence issue or an Indigenous community problem (LaRocque; Bopp, Bopp, and Norris; Royal Canadian Mounted

Police). As a result, there have been few strategies implemented at the government or criminal justice levels to address the issue of missing and murdered Indigenous women through the lens of colonialism and as endemic violence. Many Indigenous women, families, and communities have taken up their own strategies to address the widespread disappearances and murders with their own resources. This is reflected in strategies such as the "Drag the Red" campaign, started after Tina Fontaine's body was found in the Red River of Manitoba and police refused to search the river for other missing bodies; the "Am I Next" campaign, initiated after the death of Loretta Saunders and consists of Indigenous women holding "Am I Next" signs and posting them on Facebook; the toolkit for missing persons developed by the Ka Ni Kanichihk non-profit organization; Operation Thunderbird, a grassroots group who uses crowd mapping to document the murders, assaults, and disappearances of Indigenous and non-Indigenous women in Canada and the United States; the Bear Clan Patrol group who carry out searches and support for Indigenous families in finding loved ones; the "Walk4Justice" and "Tears4Justice" walks across the country to raise awareness and connect families; the "We Care" campaign to support immediate action to address violence against Indigenous women and girls; and the "No Stone Unturned" concert and cultural gathering to honour Manitoba's missing and murdered women and children. To date, there has been little attention or research focused on these and many other existing grassroots strategies of Indigenous women, families, and communities to address the disappearances and murders of Indigenous women.[1]

Postcolonial and feminist research highlights the ongoing experiences of discrimination, racism, sexism, and colonialism experienced by Indigenous women and peoples in Canada today (Acoose; Chartrand; Ending the Violence Against Women, BC; Lawrence; Pratt; Razack; Samuelson and Monture-Angus) and the little public and media attention that the disappearances and murders of Indigenous women receive (Jiwani and Young; Gilchrist; Palacios; Strega et al.). Culhane defines this as a "regime of disappearances" given the historical, ongoing, and systematic regularity with which Indigenous women go missing and are murdered in Canada. Simply contextualizing the issue as "domestic" or "partner" violence or as an "Indigenous problem" erases the broader context of violence, race, and gender, while generalizing the issue to all women and placing responsibility on Indigenous communities. This creates the view that not only are Indigenous women and communities responsible for their own safety, but they are by extension ultimately responsible for the violence committed against them. This ongoing, pervasive, and largely unaddressed violence has resulted in women, families, and communities themselves having to address the disappearances and murders of Indigenous women, which has been largely invisible to the Canadian public. By highlighting the work of a conference panel, this chapter is part of a broader collaborative strategy working to make visible the important and overlooked grassroots work of Indigenous women, families, and communities as those with the greatest expertise and knowledge in the area.

VISUALIZING GRASSROOTS JUSTICE

This chapter presents the shared dialogue of a conference panel at the Visualizing Justice conference at the University of Winnipeg, Manitoba on May 7-9, 2015. The panel was made up of Indigenous women activists and family members and anti-violence scholars active in missing and murdered Indigenous women initiatives. The panel came together as the result of diverse grassroots collaborations and initiatives to promote spaces for Indigenous women to provide their wisdom and expertise and to share their strategies, solutions, and knowledge about the disappearances and murders of Indigenous women from their communities. This work not only contributes to a growing body of postcolonial and feminist literature that explores the ongoing racialized and gendered experiences of colonialism for Indigenous women and peoples in Canada today, but also highlights the important and often overlooked work and contributions made by Indigenous women, their families, and their communities. Many have been involved in this work for years and mostly out of necessity as they struggle to survive and fight colonialism, racism, and sexism. Each speaker brings a unique and different quality and perspective to the work against violence, but all collectively highlight the significance and importance of strengthening Indigenous communities, collaborations, and how the disappearances and murders not only affect families but also the health and well-being of entire communities.

VICKI CHARTRAND

I want to acknowledge the traditional custodians of this land and that we are in Treaty One territory. As a non-Indigenous scholar, it is important to recognize that violence is not an Aboriginal problem, but a Canadian problem, which has largely befallen Indigenous women, families, and communities. Just as we are disappearing Aboriginal women, we are also disappearing the great work that is being done in the communities. I first began this work in northern British Columbia, where I worked at a shelter for women and had met Gladys Radek from the Gitxsan/Wet'suwet'en territory. She was with the "Walk4Justice" campaign in 2010 and doing one of its six walks across Canada. Each walk was approximately 7,500 kilometres over the course of 105 days. Throughout her walks, Gladys has met many families and has collected the names of over 4,200 missing and murdered women and children across Canada, with a large majority being Aboriginal women and girls. Gladys and other supporters are pushing for a national public inquiry that will explore the systemic, colonial, gendered, and racialized realities of the disappearances of the women and inform the development of a unified national action plan. Since this time, Gladys and I have been co-ordinating other walks and collaborating at conferences and presentations. This dialogue is the result of these collaborations with Indigenous activists and scholars to recognize and listen to the important work that is being done at the grassroots level within Indigenous communities.

LEAH GAZAN

I am a member of Wood Mountain Lakota Nation, located in Treaty Four territory in the Province of Saskatchewan. In my work to end violence against Indigenous women and girls, I often wonder how many families are out there who have missing children but do not know how to navigate this patrilineal bureaucracy, which results in their loved ones becoming invisible in a justice system that often fails Indigenous women and girls. It has been disturbing to see how many Indigenous women are denied access to government meetings across this country where decisions are being made about their well-being—where only individuals who hold colonial titles are allowed to participate, excluding Indigenous women who have the wisdom of experience or traditional knowledge. Indigenous women from the grassroots often hold the knowledge that is necessary to address the colonialism, sexism, and patriarchal laws that have resulted in the crisis of murdered and missing Indigenous women. The "We Care" campaign was a social media campaign in which people would take a photo of themselves while holding up a sign labelled #WeCare and #MMIW to engage the broader public in supporting Indigenous women and families of murdered and missing women. At a certain point in colonization, Indigenous women were declared to be without souls and, therefore, no longer considered to be human beings,[2] which worked to legitimate the historical violence against our women and girls. Today, the racism is often hidden in new language, but the same judgements are passed on to our communities. For example, what was once referred to as the "Indian problem" is now called "Aboriginal issues" and violence, including the violence against Indigenous women and girls, is somehow an Indigenous problem. A cognitive dissonance has occurred, resulting in the public failing to respond and to do its part to ensure the safety of all Indigenous women and girls. Violence is not an Indigenous problem; it is everyone's.

CHICKADEE RICHARD

When I was younger, I was approached by a man who asked me if I wanted to make ten dollars for a blowjob. In that moment, I knew that I was asked only because I was an Aboriginal woman. It was also in that moment that I became very aware of my situation as an Indigenous woman and our situation as Indigenous people. I became aware, and I also became active in the struggle against violence and colonialism. I have a daughter. I did not want her to be harassed. It was at this point that a group of us decided to start the Bear Clan Patrol. It was a model that we adopted from work being done in Indianapolis, where the streets were patrolled to support women and keep communities safe. The Native Youth movement also became a part of the patrol, and we had discussions and educated each other on what was happening to Indigenous people and our women. At this time, no one else was talking about what was going on or what was happening to the women. The police was not very helpful, so we brought our own solutions forth. Starting in 1995, we began holding vigils in the north end of Winnipeg, where we would build a fire. Sometimes the vigils would run all night. No one was providing solutions so we made our own through finding our strengths and our gifts to do this work. The issue of missing and murdered Indigenous women is only now at the forefront of the public eye, unlike back then when we were making our fires and holding our vigils; we were already at the front of this. People are only now calling this grassroots, but this is a grassroots movement that started twenty-five years ago. I have been grassroots forever.

I was once appointed to the Indigenous advisory counsel for the chief of police by the Community Justice Department. At the end of the first meeting, I told everyone, including the chief of police that "I hope that I am not wasting my time here. I hope that you are going to hear what the community wants and you will follow through on their recommendations." I do not have time to waste. We need to put things in perspective and see how what is being done in those bureaucratic systems affect us as a people. I stopped going after two meetings. How can I go to a place where I do not trust who I sit with? I do this work because I care, and if I care other people will care as well. I know first-hand what it is to sit and share and give moral and spiritual support and friendship. I know first-hand some of the things families experience on a daily basis, such as going without food or transportation. We do not have money or an organization, but we give what we have because others do not have and because we do care. We do not need a government working from the top down to tell us what to do. The systems that exist today have been there for a long time to oppress us, and they are not helpful. They operate an abuser—an abuser of our people. From the grassroots level looking up, we see what these systems do not see: we see the problem, we see the wrong, and we can take of our communities. We have clans that, historically, always took care of their communities. Our communities were thriving, but colonialism and the Indian Act shattered them, along with our government structures. We are bringing back the clans, such as Bear Clan, to rebuild healthy communities, and people will know that we are out there protecting and healing our communities. But we cannot do this on our own. Our communities need support. As an Indigenous mother and grandmother, I take it very personally when one of our women or children goes missing. They are taking away from our community and the strength of our community and all the potential of our women.

CHERYL JAMES

Forty years ago, when I was nine, my mother was murdered. My dad remarried, and some years after they separated, my stepmother was murdered by a white woman and was left on the ice of the Assiniboine River. For many years, my sister was sexually exploited and heavily drug addicted. I helped raise her children as she was healing. She is now clean and back in school. Growing up, I could not understand why all of this was happening, and I was so angry and confused. So, I also went missing a lot. One time, I was with my sister at the ice rink, and two men came up to us and began to rub themselves against us. I could not imagine what they were thinking to believe that they could do this to Indigenous women. When I came back home and with some time through school, I began to learn about colonialism. I then understood what these men and others had learned; they learned behaviour long ago brought by the settlers when they first came here.

My life really started to turn after my brother became involved with Children of the Earth. I could see the leader that was growing in him, and I was inspired. Today, I am currently in my fifth year of a postsecondary education. There was a time when I was taught, and I believed, that school and I did not go well together. Not long after, I began to think about my mom who was murdered. In honour of her memory, I would go on walks and started singing and drumming. It is through the drum that I found my voice, and

I began to help raise awareness about our women. Through the drum, I could also give voice to losing my mom and my stepmom. It was also at this point that I met Gladys Radek and was moved to join the walk in 2011. With every step, I would pray for every family member. It was a spiritual time for me as I healed and grew. These traditions and medicines help our people and our families to heal.

MYRNA ABRAHAM

When my older siblings were taken into boarding school, my mom started drinking and as the alcohol took over, she forgot about us. As babies, we were starving. Our aunties took us home and fed us teaspoons of water and sugar until we were stronger. I do not remember how old I was when I was first molested. My sister Sharon was once raped by twelve men. I remember my mom was once stabbed in the head by my stepfather. I remember my sister being crushed between two beds. I remember when I was six or seven, I started to fight back. I remember when my stepfather came home drunk it was the first time we fought him off. I remember another time when my mom was drunk, a man climbed on top of her, and I beat him off with the leg of a table. For us, life was violent. We had to fight to survive. When I found out Sharon was a victim of Pickton, I went to the trial. I learned that the only way they knew she was on his farm was because they found her DNA on a dildo and gun. Sharon said she would be a Jane Doe when she died. Except Sharon was my hero. She would fight beside me. She inspired me, and I loved her.

BRENDA OSBORNE

I am Brenda Osborne. My daughter Claudette is missing. Helen Betty Osborne, who was murdered here in Winnipeg, was my cousin. I remember even though my aunt was old, she would walk for my cousin. No one seemed to take notice. Six months later, we found parts of my cousin's body in the Red River. It was then that my daughter Claudette asked me, "If I ever go missing, will you come looking for me?" When my daughter first went missing, I was able to find her. She was at the hospital nine months pregnant and haemorrhaging. She lost the pregnancy and was arrested because she is a drug user. All everyone sees is an addict and sex worker. But this is not the point. She is my daughter.

When my daughter went missing again, I spent days looking for her. I made food for some of the girls on the street and asked if anyone knew where she was. The police saw me looking for her and pulled me over to ask what I was doing. I would tell them I was looking for my daughter. "Who else is looking for her? Who else is asking questions?" I asked. They told me they were doing their job and to stay off the streets or I could be charged with prostituting. They talked to me as though she were missing because of my parenting. But we had money back then; we had a car and a house. But since then, it has been taken away. I decided that instead of driving, I would walk and hang posters. We always helped ourselves.

In 2008, I started walking to raise awareness for the missing and murdered women. Too many think we are trying to get money from people instead of seeing the good we are doing in raising awareness. I do not ask for money. When we walked to Ottawa, no one was there to meet us. Stephen Harper was hiding when we arrived. It is 2015, and still nothing has changed. Not since I started walking or since my auntie started walking. No one is hearing us.

EPILOGUE

These voices form an important and vital piece of Indigenous grassroots knowledge to rethink how the families and communities are central to addressing the endemic, racialized, and gendered violence experienced by Indigenous women in Canada. Each presentation not only paints a picture of the struggles and challenges faced by the women, families and communities, but also reminds us of the important work that they carry out, the knowledge they share, and the many ways they give. Any plans to address the violence that is endemic to Indigenous women must flow from the families and communities, who need to be at the forefront of any discussions, recommendations, or plans of action. Indigenous peoples stand witness to their ancestors' histories, bear the experience of

Canada's settler colonialism, and hold the wisdom to know what their communities need. We, therefore, conclude this chapter with the drumming wisdom of Shannon Buck from the Keewatin Otchitchak (Northern Crane) Traditional Women Singers who shared her teachings of the drum with us at the conference.

The crane is one of the birds that return to the earth in the spring. When she returns, her feet touch the earth four times before landing to awaken the spirit of the earth. This is one of the medicines crane brings to the people—an awakening of our spirit and a love for one another. The drum calls people together—she is a place of healing for women and community through her heartbeat. Her medicine is also the teaching of our connection to one another and our connection to earth. Our drumming and our songs do not have words to express what we carry in our hearts. They are songs from our hearts and what words cannot express. This is a grandmother drum for the women to drum at in prayer and ceremony. The drum wears a skirt like we do that represents our responsibility and rights as women. It is like the covering of Tepee and standing in the truth of who we are—keepers of the home and community. Colonialism is hurting our women. The destruction of the earth and water is so closely connected to what is happening to our women. The drum reminds us that we are sacred and precious and that we can stand in the truth of who we are as leaders, teachers, healers, and decision makers. She reminds us that we are much more than what society has taught us that we are as women. When women sit at the drum, the drum gives them strength, the drum gives them healing power. That is also her medicine.

Meegwetch.

ENDNOTES

[1]European colonizers adopted the papal bull of Pope Alexander VI, *Inter Caetera*, May 4, 1493 that stated representatives of the monarchy (Portugal and later Spain), could declare lands for the Crown if they were occupied by heathens—non-Christians.

[2]Grassroots here is understood as non-government funded and non-academic bodies, which are directly and indirectly affected and involved in the issue (see Stewart, Hunt, and Blaney).

WORKS CITED

Acoose, Sharon Leslie. *An Arrow in My Heart: A First Nations Women's Account of Survival from the Streets to the Height of Academia*. Vancouver: J. Charlton Publishing, 2015. Print.

Amnesty International Canada. *Stolen Sisters: A Human Rights Response to Discrimination and Violence against Indigenous Women in Canada*. Toronto: Amnesty International Canada, 2004. Print.

Bopp, Michael, Judie Bopp, and Julian Norris. *Mapping the Healing Journey: The Final Report of a First Nation Research Project on Healing in Canadian Aboriginal Communities*. Ottawa: Solicitor General Canada, 2002. Print.

Canada. Statistics Canada. "Violent Victimization of Aboriginal Women in the Canadian Provinces, 2009 (Juristat Article)." Ottawa: Statistics Canada, 2011. Print.

Chartrand, Vicki. "Tears4justice and the Missing and Murdered Women and Children Across Canada: An Interview with Gladys Radek." *Radical Criminology* 3 (2014): 113-26. Print.

Culhane, Dara. "Their Spirits Live within Us: Aboriginal Women in Downtown Eastside Vancouver Emerging into Visibility." *The American Indian Quarterly* 27.3/4 (2003): 593-606. Print.

Ending the Violence Against Women, BC. *Increasing Safety for Aboriginal Women: Key Themes and Resources*. EVAW BC, 2011. Web. 15 Oct. 2015.

Gilchrist, Kristen. "'Newsworthy' Victims? Exploring Differences in Canadian Local Press Coverage of Missing/Murdered Aboriginal and White Women." *Feminist Media Studies* 10.4 (2010): 373-390. Print.

Jiwani, Yasmin, and Mary Lynn Young. "Missing and Murdered Women: Reproducing Marginality in News Discourse." *Canadian Journal of Communication* 31.4 (2006): 895-917. Print.

LaRocque, Emma. *Violence in Aboriginal Communities*. Ottawa: National Clearinghouse on Family Violence, 1994. Print.

Lawrence, Bonita. "Gender, Race, and the Regulation of Native Identity in Canada and the United States: An Overview." *Hypatia* 18.2 (2003): 3-31. Print.

Native Women's Association of Canada (NWAC). *What Their Stories*

Tell Us: Research Findings from the Sisters in Spirit Initiative. Ottawa: Native Women's Association of Canada, 2009. Print.

Palacios, Lena Carla. "Racialized and Gendered Necropower in Canadian News and Legal Discourse." *Feminist Formations* 26.1 (2014): 1-26. Print

Pratt, Geraldine. "Abandoned Women and Spaces of the Exception." *Antipode* 37.5 (2005): 1052-1078. Print.

Razack, Sherene H. "Gendered Racial Violence and Spatialized Justice: The Murder of Pamela George." *Race, Space, and the Law: Unmapping a White Settler Society*. Ed. Sherene H. Razack. Toronto: Between the Lines, 2002. 121-156. Print.

Royal Canadian Mounted Police (RCMP). *Missing and Murdered Aboriginal Women: A National Operational Overview*. Canada: RCMP, 2014. Print.

Samuelson, Les, and Patricia Monture-Angus. "Aboriginal Peoples and Social Control: The State, Law, and Policing." *Marginality and Condemnation: An Introduction to Critical Criminology*. Eds. Bernard Schissel and Carolyn Brooks. Halifax: Fernwood, 2002. 157-173. Print.

Stewart, Wendy, Audrey Hunt, and Fay Blaney. The Implications of Restorative Justice for Aboriginal Women and Children Survivors of Violence. Ottawa: Law Commission of Canada, 2001. Print.

Strega, Susan, Caitlin Janzen, Jeannie Morgan, Leslie Brown, Robina Thomas, and Jeannine Carriére. "Never Innocent Victims: Street Sex Workers in Canadian Print Media." *Violence against Women* 20.1 (2014): 6-25. Print.

13.
Personal Political Pedagogy with Respect to #MMIW

MAXINE MATILPI

I LIVE ON A SMALL ISLAND off the east coast of Vancouver Island, and my work as an instructor at Vancouver Island University takes me on the road several times a week. I don't often pick up hitchhikers, but when I do, I only pick up First Nations people. By now, almost everyone in this area has heard of British Columbia's Highway of Tears, and the Pickton farm, and some of us have read Amnesty International's 2004 report, *Stolen Sisters*. The story of missing and murdered Indigenous women is now part of everyday conversations in my circles. But long before these stories reached public and political consciousness, along with my Indigenous and non-Indigenous students, I began exploring the colonial history and current reality at the root of these emerging stories.

The intensity of this work has changed my personal thoughts, actions, and feelings, so now if I see a First Nations woman alone on the side of the road, I worry for her safety. If I see a First Nations man, I worry other drivers will be afraid of him and won't want to pick him up. Also I think, "That could be one of my relatives; I ought to help."

Over the last fifteen years, there's one First Nations man I frequently see hitchhiking on the Island Highway between Victoria and Campbell River. He's roughly fifty years old, a big scruffy guy, with long hair, heavy black boots, a jean jacket, and a black leather vest. He looks like he could be a biker. Years ago I picked him up just south of Parksville. "Gus" and I talked as we drove to Victoria about the "word on the street;" there were fifty women missing from Vancouver's Downtown Eastside. We discussed the number of the day: five hundred missing or murdered Indigenous women across Canada. We talked about how, up and down the coast, the families of these women were trying to get the attention of the public, the press, and the police, but there was a deafening silence with respect to these women, who'd been labelled as drug- or alcohol-addicted sex workers, making bad decisions, and choosing risky lifestyles. There seemed to be widespread indifference, maybe even hardened hearts, with respect to these women. The police suggested that maybe the women didn't want to be found—as if to try and explain why they did nothing—and the very real concerns of friends and families weren't, and still aren't, taken seriously.

Gus and I talked about how it's not just Canada where Indigenous women were disappearing. "Hell no, it's Mexico, and Guatemala, South America," he said. All over the world, Indigenous women are being targeted. At that time, folks on the Moccasin Telegraph were saying, "Forget about the number 500. It's more like a thousand."

I told Gus about Bernie Williams's and Gladys Radeck's "Walk-4Justice" and how the previous summer, in 2008, a group of Indigenous women had walked from Victoria to Ottawa to draw attention to the issue. That spring I'd heard Gladys speak in Victoria about how these disappearances were connected to organized crime, human trafficking, and organ harvest. "Holy shit! Human trafficking and organ harvest? Doesn't that only happen in far away places, like where there are no laws or judicial systems to protect people? And isn't trafficking about people trying to get INTO Canada, not OUT?" I told Gus about Gladys telling us she'd received anonymous phone calls threatening her to "Shut up and quit talking about this stuff. You don't know who you're messing with."

But this *is* the word on the street, and I worried that in the same way the Moccasin Telegraph turned out to be right about those first fifty missing women from the Downtown Eastside, the Moccasin Telegraph may also be right about organized crime, human trafficking, and organ harvest, and the numbers, even the RCMP are now using a number in the thousands.

Gus tells me it's not just women any more: Indigenous men are also being targeted; hitchhiking isn't safe for anyone. He tells me gruesome stories about some young men last seen hitchhiking outside of Campbell River.

I don't know what to think; the whole thing is horrifying. The Moccasin Telegraph has "street cred," so this news is F'in freaky.

Gus's information about the danger to men as well as to women and girls gets me stirred up, worried for my sons, and I tell Gus he'd better be careful. He reassures me that he knows how to look after himself, he learned that in jail, and also, as he pats the side of his belly, that he packs "protection." He's not specific about what he means by "protection," but I imagine a gun or knife and think I, too, ought to be careful.

Years later, I was invited to "Ab Camp" in Tseshaht Territory, near the city of Port Alberni. Ab Camp, aka Aboriginal Awareness Camp, is an opportunity for first-year law students from the University of Victoria to build community, to connect with their whole selves, their classmates, and local people, and to learn and talk about what's important from an Indigenous perspective. I'd been asked to facilitate a Talking Circle with a focus on concerns of Indigenous women. A Talking Circle is a powerful tool for building community through deep listening, bearing witness, and engaging not just our heads, but also our hearts. I start the circle as I always do following Indigenous protocols, acknowledging we're on Tseshaht territory and identifying my family and community. I'm Scottish-English on my dad's side; on my mom's side, Kwakiutl/Ma'amtigila, part of the larger group of Kwak'wala speaking people, known as Kwakwaka'wakw. Our territory is located a hundred miles north of Campbell River on the eastern tip of Vancouver Island.

These protocols, which embody and express the value of family and community, provide opportunities to recognize, build, and maintain relationships, but they also provide credibility and are an assertion of Indigenous laws. The protocols are also important to me personally because with my skin and hair colour, I don't always look Indigenous, and I want people to know who I am and my cultural, linguistic, and community connections.

In the previous two years I had spoken numerous times about gendered and racialized violence—violence against Indigenous women—here in western "Kanata," a land inhabited by millions of Indigenous people for ten thousand years, but who were, and are still, dealing with the effects of systematic attempts to remove us from the landscape.

I'm a bit of a one-trick pony, speaking over and over about the same things: the importance of gaining a broader understanding of this violence and the reality that violence against Indigenous women is nothing new. Indeed, our peoples have been the victims of colonial violence for hundreds of years. A broader and intersectional understanding of violence, oppression, and colonization is essential to contextualizing the story of missing and murdered Indigenous women.

I studied with the late Trish Monture[1] for eight intensive weeks at the Summer Program of Legal Studies for Native People, at the University of Saskatchewan, so I have been highly influenced by her presence and ideas and have read and taught her work. Trish reinforced how there is violence in being colonized, in having your lands taken and occupied, and in resisting these systematic attempts. She reminded us about the violence of having your children taken, as Indigenous kids were, to residential schools, and later into the social welfare system during the Sixties Scoop, when they were put into white foster homes or adopted by white families.

There's violence in not having access to an economy with your own resources or in having your resources taken or destroyed by government-endorsed corporations. There's violence in not being allowed to practice your spirituality, in the banning of ceremonies such as the potlatch or sundance, as was the case in Canada from 1885 to 1951.

For a few of the law students in the Talking Circle, this perspective comes as a surprise. Most of them are highly accomplished with undergraduate degrees, and law school admission is competitive, so they're a bright bunch, confident and poised. Even so, through open-hearted circle magic, some of them become undone, unsettled, teary-eyed, and we pass around a box of Kleenex. We all acknowledge the difficulty of doing this work.

For Indigenous and non-Indigenous students alike, there's a kind of violence in learning these histories, in hearing about smallpox-infested blankets, the effects of the *Indian Act*, residential schools, and stories of Helen Betty Osborne, J.J. Harper, and Donald Marshall.

As Paulette Regan argues, learning about Canada's colonial history, and even teaching it, is downright unsettling. Every year, I remind my Women's Studies students that over the semester, they should expect to be both an insider and outsider to the course material and that this unique experience of working together and of having both insiders and outsiders in the same class can be challenging but also rewarding. I follow the advice of Dr. Serena Patterson (a former teacher) and encourage students to be patient with one another as we "blend and exchange perspectives, practice respectful listening across the divides." Sometimes class discussions are tense, and we find ourselves in those places where the most profound learning happens, those moments of disequilibrium, when our world is shaken out of past paradigms.

For sure, there's discomfort for all of us, for me as the teacher, for the students who feel as though they've been lied to through omissions and silences in their prior education, and for the Indigenous students who feel the (re)opening of colonial wounds.

Although I used to be impatient with them, I've come to empathize with the students who have not had the opportunity to learn a more complete colonial story and who, as a result, minimize the significance of systemic racism in Canada. Racism, most people would like to believe, is something that happens in the American south, not in Canada. Canadians like to think of themselves as nice, or fair. In my classes, I'm often astounded by the number of my students who know little of the truth about Canada's colonization, and who find it hard when we dispel lies or "deconstruct the peacemaker myth" (Regan).

Even as recently as 2013, when the Truth and Reconciliation Commission (TRC) held major and well-publicized events across the country, I still had students who hadn't heard of residential schools. That September one student held up her hand to admit she had no idea what the TRC was. She bravely admitted to not knowing what I was referring to when I used the phrase "residential schools." As a recent grad of a BC high school where she had been an "A" student, she had taken all the courses the school counsellor had told her to take to ensure her success in university, yet she knew nothing of Canada's history of residential schools. She confessed to feeling duped by these institutional omissions.

Sometimes when we dispel lies and deal with the omissions from their prior education, non-Indigenous students tell me that they would rather we didn't spend so much class time on colonization or racism; they find it uncomfortable and frustrating, even irritating. I suspect they would prefer we discussed or learned Indigenous women's crafts, weaving or "maybe even learn to do beadwork" (Chrystos). I have written about these tensions and offer suggestions, such as transformative embodied pedagogies, for bringing differing viewpoints together (Matilpi 221). I am a mom, and these students are the ages of my children, so I try to see them as someone's baby. I've learned to tread carefully with this information, to aim for gentle correction, not wanting to break their spirits. For me, pedagogy and process take precedence over product, the journey more important than the destination.

An element of Indigenous pedagogy is reciprocity, so in our classes the information flows both ways. I'm constantly learning from my students. For example, most Canadians know about the December 6 memorial event for the fourteen women who were murdered in Montreal in 1989. In 2002, one of my non-Indigenous students pointed out that when those fourteen white women were murdered, there was a lot of action and public response with respect to violence against women and the initiation of the National Day of Remembrance and Action on Violence against Women. The student pointed out that this was around the same time that women began to go missing from the Downtown Eastside in Vancouver. So it seemed to her that white women could see their own faces in those classrooms in Montreal but not in the streets of the Downtown Eastside. Poor Indigenous women–especially those who were sex workers and addicts—were not the "poster girls" for violence against women. December 6 became another in a list of feminist events, such as International Women's Day and Person's Day, that do not adequately acknowledge colonial violence and the scope of that violence against Indigenous women.

Early morning November 2004, I've driven down to Halalt Territory, about halfway between Nanaimo and Victoria. Filmmaker Christine Welsh was about to start working on Finding Dawn (2006) and had chosen to start the process with a ceremony to remember and honour the women who would be profiled in the film. A group of about forty have been invited to witness this ceremony. The morning is grey, damp and cold, and we're gathered in a grove of large maple trees, their yellow-brown leaves dripping in the heavy fog.

A table had been specially built for this ceremony, and we were asked to witness in silence. We stood watching as a banquet was carefully laid out by three "workers," the woman leading the ceremony, "See-co," and two men. At each of the twelve places, the workers set a plate of food and a beverage. Large baskets and platters of other food, bread, pasta, shellfish, and salmon were also placed on the table so that there was clearly much more food than what would be needed to feed twelve people. The table was beautiful, with flowers, twelve cans of Lucky, a pack or two of smokes, a lovely banquet for twelve with plenty of other food for whoever else might choose to attend.

When the table was set, the workers pulled out boxes of wooden matches and lit the paper and cedar kindling that earlier had been stuffed underneath the wooden table. Everything went up in smoke.

Huge billows rising through the maples.
Cedar crackling.
Cakes melting,
cans of beer hissing,
salmon bubbling.

It takes a long time for this kind of a fire to burn so we stand on the wet maple leaves witnessing the work, silent, watching, listening, waiting.

Holding the space.

As the fire died down, See-co described to us what she had seen during the burning. She described "those girls," "our loved ones," hovering above the maple trees, coming to partake in the feast but hesitating at first because they didn't feel safe. There were men among us, and "those girls" were reluctant to come closer because they didn't trust men; some of them had been badly hurt by men.

But then they could see that not all men were bad, that there were good men amongst us, and they felt safe—safe enough to invite other "girls" to come along. See-co described how the girls thought nobody cared and how they were now feeling at peace because they could see our concern through our presence at the burning.

Afterwards, we were reminded by the ceremonial leaders that our work on this matter of missing and murdered women would sometimes be hard, sometimes we might feel like giving up, but that we should feel we're being guided by the spirits of the women we were honouring; we should always remember they're watching over us, protecting us as we do the work.

Our Indigenous communities have many beautiful traditions surrounding death. For example, many Indigenous cultures practice the burning of clothing and food for loved ones. In my Kwakiutl community, one of our traditions is a mourning ceremony, which generally takes place early in the day before a potlatch. Women who have lost family members are invited by the host Chief to come to the front of the Bighouse and dance while a "Cry Song" is sung.

By the solemn presence of these dancing women, the entire community acknowledges the families connected to these women who have experienced loss, and everyone is given an opportunity for the washing of their own tears. I remind students of the simple personal-is-political fact that those statistics about the high mortality rates in our communities are connected to real human beings—mothers, sisters, aunties, daughters. Because our communities experience perpetual, repetitive, relentless tragic loss, these ceremonies are important demonstrations of love and support. The public expression of being fully present and witnessing grief is powerful, as it connects us to community and ancestors.

There's real beauty in people coming together in this way. When my mother died, our small Kwakiutl community hosted several hundred people for her funeral; our family could feel their respectful loving presence. Later at a memorial potlatch, while I sat and then danced with other women at the front of the Bighouse while a "Cry Song" was sung, I felt this connection with community.

Because they recognized the uniqueness of the violence towards Indigenous women, Downtown Eastside activists choose to mark their difference from other feminist groups, to emphasize the effects of racism and colonization. They held the first Valentine's Day March on February 14, 1991. I consider this event to be like a "Cry Song" because it is a respectful and public acknowledgement of the murdered and missing women and of the grief experienced by their families. This public acknowledgement of grief is important because it is a way for others to bear witness to the loss. But it's much more than that: it's also a day to celebrate resistance, solidarity, and survival, and to protest against racism, poverty, and violence against Indigenous women. I've encouraged my students to participate and have reminded them of the importance of bearing witness, of bringing their whole selves to the work, of being fully present, and of integrating it into their lives. The Downtown Eastside Memorial is also a day where stories inspire personal and political action and a desire for change.

My teaching involves creating space for stories and more and more, I aim for action-oriented pedagogy. I recognize that "I'm blessed with life" (Chrystos 14) and that I feel a personal responsibility to use my privilege and try my best to model action both in and out of the classroom. I have learned to be an opportunist and to take advantage of every opportunity to spread the word. Sometimes, this means building awareness and solidarity with others, such as practising and performing a three-minute ballet with the ladies in my ballet class exploring loss and love or pulling together words, languages, art, movement, music at the local Writers and Readers Festival with a performance art piece, "Living Memory and a Graceful Spreading of Eagledown." I've answered requests to facilitate community screenings of *Finding Dawn*, and even, with the help of my husband, white-washed and repainted the neighbourhood graffiti fence.

I appreciate the power of grassroots unfunded projects, such as that of Christi Belcourt. During that wondrously energized winter of 2012 and 2013 when Idle No More burst onto the streets and into shopping malls, Métis artist Christi Belcourt put out a call over social media asking for contributions of moccasin tops for a memorial installation honouring missing and murdered Indigenous women. Each pair of intricately beaded, quilled, or embroidered moccasin tops would represent the unfinished life of an Indigenous woman or girl in Canada. This collaborative art project would later become the foundation for a memorial, a ceremonial bundle for "Walking With Our Sisters."

The following summer in 2013, I was teaching "Human Rights and Indigenous Legal Traditions" at Winnipeg's Canadian School of Peacebuilding (CSOP), and I wanted a project to help students connect their hearts—as well as their heads—to this national issue. My hope was, as Velcrow Ripper describes in "Fierce Love," for students to learn and act "from their hearts, to take their parts in creating change, with a spirit of positivity, compassion, love and a balance of interdependence and self-determination" (Ripper). I encourage my students to "be the change" and to go out into the world and change others. The process and pedagogy are more fully described in my article "Imagining Peace" but, suffice to say, that summer, I witnessed students fully engaged: beading, sewing, helping each other, teaching, learning, listening, and using teamwork to accomplish goals. We all become conscious of adding our energy to the collective energy initiated by Christi. When we set aside our needles and thread to watch Christine's film, *Finding Dawn*, students were struck by the significance of our work together. Afterwards, we moved our chairs into a Talking Circle to debrief and consider motivation and empathy. One story creates space for another, and our hearts become deeply connected through this shared experience of working together. Before we package and post our eighteen pairs of moccasin tops to Christi, we complete our work together with a ceremony.

Two summers later in 2015, the Walking with Our Sisters (WWOS) memorial comes out west to Vancouver Island. I was excited about reconnecting with the eighteen pairs of moccasin tops our class submitted two years earlier. I was offered another opportunity to "walk the talk" through an invitation to work with the organizing committee. By early spring 2015, the task of hosting the memorial reveals itself to be huge. At times, the work is tough, and relationships become strained. Despite the guiding principles of "Love, Kindness, Respect, and Generosity" set out in the WWOS handbook, our meetings seem brusk and business-like, disappointingly unceremonious. There are frustrations over decision-making processes, disagreements about how to fundraise, and even whether or not we're engaging in lateral violence. Some of us worry there isn't enough focus on the spirits of the women. Sometimes I feel discouraged, like giving up, and I wonder if it's possible to make things right. I regret we hadn't used a Talking Circle or started with a prayer or ceremony. Then I recognize *my* personal "response-ability," my ability to respond, and wish *I* had started with a prayer or Talking Circle or ceremony—except I feel like I don't know how to do this properly.

I remember the words of my colleague and friend John Borrows: "Sometimes when you don't know a ceremony, you have to make or dream it up." I remember the burning with Christine and the spirits of the women watching over and protecting us and think: if you do it with the right intention, there's no way you can do it wrong.

March 17, 2015

I make an

Early morning fire
Outside,
Peaceful water
Burn beautiful elk stew
Smoke
Sizzle, calm
I'm sorry we didn't do this sooner
I'm sorry I didn't do this sooner
Breathe
Look for a sign
Longing for a sign
Sky soft, clouds calm
Creator: Give me a sign.
Nothing.
Just the sizzle of elk, steam rising
Then,
the barking of sea-lions
a jet above the clouds, and
Ha! The words, "Bring it to today's world."

And another,

April 2, 2015.

Burning this morning with food prepared by my students for yesterday's WWOS event...

Sunny morning on the beach in Campbell River
Melting cupcakes
Sizzling spaghetti
Burning chocolate
small fire
Me, holding the space, protecting a cheese stick from being taken by my circling relatives,
Seagulls hovering.
Reminding me that even those closest to us can be problematic.

And another, going deeper.

April 6, 2015

burning Saturday night. This time,
Full moon
High tide
in the dark
alone
at Village Point, site of old Pentlatch village, Denman Island. Just me and the
Sea lions,
a single loon,
many frogs.
Offered popcorn,
Put my ear on ground, on the midden,
warm soft ear-lobe flesh on cold sharp shells, bits of crusty dry seaweed,
Listening, waiting for instructions.
Listen to animals, birds, dance, burn food.

When you don't know how to do a ceremony sometimes you have to make it up.
Or dream it up.
Magical three minutes dancing remembering laughing playing trying tipping daring
That place.
That place where I'd watched the sun go down and the moon come up, did my own private and safe listening, hearing sea lions and getting my instructions:
Dance,
Listen to animals (and birds)
Make a fire
Feed the fire
Pray

I remind myself the focus of the work is not me, or any of us on the organizing committee; it's about those women and girls, their grieving families. I gain important insights on marginalization, the politics of privilege and moral intelligibility—the importance of bringing our whole selves to the work, using our brains, our bodies, our hearts and spirits, talking to students, friends, kids and partners, changing minds and public discourse, changing hearts, and even governments.

A small group from within the big group comes together, and we build new relationships with more good-hearted people.

We drink tea,
break a fast with a Unitarian ("living her faith"),
make circles and ceremony,
get brushed with cedar,
Try to walk the talk on a daily basis, acting on moral responsibilities.

In the end, we set aside differences for the sake of the project, and over four thousand visitors experience the memorial as deeply profound. Some are changed and gain new perspectives.

Monday morning October 2015. There are close to 300,000 kilometres on my old car, and I have an appointment later in the day for an oil change. The car dealer is located on the outskirts of Campbell River on the stretch of highway where four lanes turn into two and where Indigenous hitchhikers often stand. Sometimes when I stop to pick them up, I learn they're on their way to the same potlatch, funeral, or ceremony as I am, so we chat on the two-an-a-half-hour drive up the island.

As I dress for the day, I'm thinking about leaving my car for servicing and considering what to wear. I'll be dropping off the car and will have to walk that stretch of road. What to wear? It's a perfect autumn day, sunny and no wind or rain, so maybe I'll wear the beautiful cape my cousin made for me. The back of the cape features a Kulus. A Kulus is sometimes known as baby thunderbird and is connected to one of our Ma'amtigila creation stories and is easily identified as an Indigenous design. It occurs to me that as much as I love this cape and its Kulus, I'm not sure I want this design on my back as I walk up this stretch of road—the same stretch of road where hitchhiker Gus described the gruesome stories taking place. I worry the Kulus might make me feel as though I have a target on my back, and I wonder then if my visibly Indigenous students feel this on a daily basis.

As I say, I'm a one-trick pony. I talk about this stuff a lot, in my work, in my play, and in my spare time. It fills my head and my Facebook page, even takes up my creative energy. For me, this is what it means to "walk the talk," to bring my whole self to the work, staying committed to process and ceremony, living my values, and trying to bring others along using art, theatre, poetry, dance, and Indigenous and contemplative pedagogies in both the university and community classrooms. There are opportunities for learning and teaching everywhere, every day.

The story of missing and murdered Indigenous women is not just an Indigenous story: it is part of the story of colonization and for Canadians, is part of our collective story. This is Indigenous land and we belong here, but this land is haunted by the violence of colonization, genocide, and disrespect for our humanity. The planet will benefit when we work together, understanding the intersections between justice and love, Indigenous rights and women's lives, and, as Lee Maracle explains, the connections between violence against women and the connections with violence against the earth. We all have a right to justice and to a decent life.

I used to think there was widespread Canadian indifference to this story of missing and murdered Indigenous women. But social change is always slow and, maybe, at times it's so infinitesimally slow and we're so close to it that we just can't see it. When I step back, reflect on the astounding numbers of people who've contributed to and attended WWOS events, when I hear politicians talking about a national inquiry, I think, hope, and pray that maybe the discourse has changed.

I hope this story of how I've been inspired by the work of people, such as Gladys, Christine, and Christi doesn't sound like I'm tooting my own horn. My hope is that somehow my story will help someone else. In the same way that sometimes one student telling her story will create an opening for another to tell her own story, maybe this story of how a political story became part a personal story might inspire a desire for action, deep engagement.

Bring your body, bring your heart, bring your whole self. Be the change; maybe inspire the change in others along the way.

Ha-em!

ENDNOTE

[1]Patricia Monture-Angus

WORKS CITED

Borrows, John. Personal conversations. Ongoing

Chrystos. "I Am Not Your Princess." *Not Vanishing*. Vancouver: Press Gang Publishers, 1988, Print.

Maracle, Lee. "Connection between Violence against the Earth and Violence against Women." *Idle No More*. N.p., 2 Mar. 2014. Web. 20 Apr. 2016.

Matilpi, Maxine. "In Our Collectivity: Teaching, Learning and Indigenous Voice," *Canadian Journal of Native Education* 35.1 (2012): 211-220. Print.

Regan, Paulette. *Unsettling the Settler Within: Indian Residential Schools, Truth Telling, and Reconciliation in Canada,* Vancouver:

University of British Columbia Press, 2010. Print.
Ripper, Velcrow. "What is Spiritual Activism." *Fierce Love*. WordPress, n.d. Web. 20 Apr. 2016.
Welsh, Christine, dir. *Finding Dawn*. National Film Board, 2006. Film.

IV.
VOICES OF HEALING:
NARRATIVE AND POETRY

14.
Little Sister

TASHA SPILLETT

Little sister
I see you even if you have yet to see yourself
Even if you mask yourself in fragments of untruths of you
Even when you cloak yourself because somewhere, sometime, someone has made you feel that to hide is safer than to shine as you were meant to
Little sister I wish to speak into your mind sacred words of you so loudly that they are like the Thunderbirds when they come to visit and wash everything away
I wish to make you a crown of sage to show to all that rest their eyes on you, that you are made of medicine and of royalty
Little sister I will sing you songs until your voice remembers it was meant to dance
I will pray into being all that is needed to remind you, that you are where beauty and strength come together to embrace
I will dance medicine into the path that we walk on so that is again worthy of you
Little sister
I see you

Note: *This piece is a demonstration of love for young Indigenous women who are finding themselves in a world that was not created to honor them. This piece has been published in a youth magazine but all rights remain with me.*

15.
She, Remembers, Warrior

partner abuse

TASHA SPILLETT

She remembers the day he got the word warrior tattooed across his broad shoulders
The ink linking his Sundance scars together forming a constellation across his back

She remembers standing behind him
Reaching up to heal his freshly wounded skin

He, a warrior and she, the medicine that he insatiably consumed

She remembers reading that word

Warrior

the moment her eyes no longer betrayed her
She watched the black ink flow into dark blues and purples

dancing like northern lights across her own esh and seeping into the unseen of her
She remembers

Note: *This piece speaks to the partner abuse that so many Indigenous women survive and, despite it, thrive. It also seeks to redefine the construction of* warrior, *held within our Nations. The warrior, is indeed, she.*

16.
What I Learned from Walking With Our Sisters

GILLIAN MCKEE

I volunteer ahead of time to help lay the vamps. I go to the opening ceremony. I go see the installation on my lunch hour. I go see the Thursday night showing of "Highway of Tears." After that, I think "I don't know how much more of this I can take." This sad weight that overcomes. Because I have the luxury of walking away back to work, back to my life. What I learned from Walking With Our Sisters is that I am at the end of a long line of non-Indigenous people who have walked away—not walked alongside.

~~~

I want to look at each and every pair of vamps—the images of mother and child, the flowers, the rainbows, the butterflies, the shooting stars. The vamps of beadwork more delicate than a pencil sketch, a smudged, wobbly daisy drawn on a rough black paper cut out, vamps of seal fur, birchbark, soapstone, Métis braid. We walk alongside on a red cloth laid over sage past the coloured cloths hung on the wall to represent the grandmothers. A silent row of vamps arranged around the outside edge is turned looking in toward us. I want to look at each and every single pair, as unique as each of the women it represents, and say—I see you.

~~~

I go one last time Friday at the end of the day just before the exhibit closes. I want to make sense of it. How could this have happened? How could we have allowed this to happen? Because we did—it was my people who, not just let this happen, but made it happen.

Not only because there was an Indian agent among my ancestors, but just by virtue of living as the colonizers. I don't make any sense of it. There is no sense to be made. This is not in the realm of analysis and problem solving. This is loss, grief, anguish, shame, fear that whispers among us in the room walking our slow silent prayer around the circle of unfinished lives.

~ ~ ~

The Elder says to me—that sadness you feel—know that this is what our communities, our families are feeling. She comforts me when I should be the one holding her up. How can she forgive me and my kind? The fear I feel is personal—for my own Indigenous daughters—and what if that were magnified a thousand fold for my own nation's mothers and daughters? I want to say I see each of you as beautiful and loved. I want to imagine a strong, proud daughter standing in each one of those moccasins.

~ ~ ~

Not a hundred feet from the door of the centre where the Walking With Our Sisters installation is in its final days of honouring the missing and murdered Aboriginal women, where I can almost smell the smoke of the sacred fire as I walk to my car, a young native woman sits on the gravel dirt beside the street. An RCMP cruiser is pulled up, angled, door open, the officer standing feet apart, hands on hips, looking down at her. She sits cross-legged in front of a metal power box, twiddling dead grass in her fingers. The bubble gum pink fluffy headband, the necklace, the nice sweater looks like she had plans other than sitting here looking vacantly at the stony dirt in front of her. The officer looks at me over the top of his sunglasses, and we exchange a look. He wants me to see everything is okay here. But this scenario is not okay. My mind flits to the centre. Should I run to the sacred fire and say, can someone of her own people please help her, take her home? I return his look. I see you, and I see her, and I am watching. I want to trust you. I have talked so much with others over the past two weeks about being in solidarity, about walking beside our Aboriginal women. I walk past. I leave the girl and the officer. In my car, I weep. Too late I know what I should have said: "you take care of her." Because I know that it is not just for them, or for him, but for all of us to not let her become another of the missing and murdered. To keep her safe.

Note: *Walking With Our Sisters is a commemorative art installation for the missing and murdered Indigenous women of Canada and the U.S. It toured to Whitehorse in April 2015. It is an installation of moccasin vamps "that represent the unfinished lives of murdered and missing Indigenous women exhibited on a pathway to represent their path or journey that was ended prematurely." For more information please visit: www.walkingwithoursisters.ca.*

17.
To My Sister I Have Never Met

SHERRY EMMERSON

We are not related by blood, nor have we ever met
Still I call you sister
Your sorrow is my sorrow and your happiness is my happiness
Your story is my story for we are all interconnected
Sadly we will never meet as I am still here and you are gone
Your life taken carelessly by someone who could not see your worth
I see your worth
I see a strong and brave Indigenous woman
Capable of rising up and changing a nation
As a daughter, mother, wife, aunty, sister, friend and most importantly a human being with purpose
Not as a whore or just another easy squaw who asked for it, a victim of your circumstances
A guise they use to justify the cruel treatment you received
Nothing you did warranted the inhuman treatment you experienced during your final moments here on mother earth
Fear not sister for your death will not be in vain
We are standing here thousands strong telling your story
Screaming it out for the world to hear
Ensuring no one forgets you died a death that should have outraged a nation
They are starting to hear us now and can no longer deny the justice you deserve
You are not alone
You are not voiceless
We hear you sister

18.
If One More

SĀKIHITOWIN AWĀSIS

if one more of my sisters
is touched non-consensually
her mind made to warp
a righteous relationship with
her own skin and body
made to think she is
less than
not part of the land
part of a rib that came from
someone more complete than
she is
the life giving force that breathes

speak this!

what every one
of the human species
needed
what all life came from
for once
look into her eyes
and see us

because there's already been
more than one of my sisters
since we've begun

pushed up between a wall and the finger
of a friend's friend who made her
I've had enough
there is not a day without a reminder
that women weep in discomfort
as if it is her own bones that betray her
while it was he who had his way with her
I'm beyond rage
I am danger
because it is not just strangers
it's so called comrades
men we know
who are supposed to be brothers

we've had enough
will shame you for what you've done
loudly and publicly reprimand you some
take to the streets, your neighbors
demand all but none

as much and as long as you degrade her
be it a lifetime or more
because these are our sisters
don't doubt us
cut out or try to prove wrong us
while perpetrator pals are brought closer

she is the only doorway into this world
respect her

19.

Take Back the Night

SĀKIHITOWIN AWĀSIS

land rights extend to body autonomy
I'm anti-exploitation, pro-First Nations sovereignty
reclaim your voice; your presence is relevant
root yourself, but acknowledge your settlement
our cities are what remain of fur trade
day dynamics, not much has changed
it's still our lives at stake
Indigenous sisters missing with no action by the state
it's still lower wages we make
but another world is ours to create
so let your voice pierce the sky
your kind heart and spirit fly

we are the ones
this is the time
the love we have stuns
let your inner fire shine
through pitch black night
as fierce as the now
take your fist
and raise it proud

all your life
you've been fighting this fight
it's what rapists call "nature"
and survivors "strife"

who's left and who's right?
whose land? we've lost sight
we're taking back our bodies
taking back our right
led by grandmother moon
take back the night

taking back our land + right

20.
Accomplice

ALYSSA M. GENERAL

How grisly this game of hide and seek has become.
Body instead of a being.
Still childish in believing our hiding spots will be unveiled, recovered.
To hear the shrill glee in our surprise instead of the attack and decay of a vacant timbre.
The sharp exhalations that grieve our names.
Like childhood nightmares
The monsters are faceless, nameless,
Kin to the dark.
Protected,
And somehow we are in hell.

Did we inherit this statistic?
Our vices pre-determined?
Does the colour of our skin depreciate the worth of our blood?
Either way it is red,
And we have paid our ransom.

And those that spew that apathy,
That these are just crimes,
That the one in five that could be you, my sister, my mother, my niece,
my daughter.
That these numbers have no value,
Their hands are thick with red.
I cannot expect a number to convey the loss,

To absolve the weight of grief or the empty space consumed by the echoes of our absence.

One is too many.

I look at my daughter,
And I hope she will be different,

I will rally, I will empower, and I will challenge
The definition.
I will let her imagine her future differently,
so she will have vision.
I will teach her our ways,
so she may know where she comes from,
and so she may define her own path.

Like our women,
Who fell into seafoam,
Who shaped the earth,
Who birthed balance,
Who became the moon,
Who married and killed the serpent,
Who changed the world by changing her mind.
These women are our ancestors,
Our blood,
We must remember the strength we come from
Because it is the strength we still carry
And our women,
They deserve more than a name, and face on a wall.
They deserve future.

21.
Moving Forward

A Dialogue between D. Memee Lavell-Harvard, Gladys Radek, and Bernice Williams

D. MEMEE LAVELL-HARVARD, GLADYS RADEK
AND BERNICE WILLIAMS

A nation is not conquered until the hearts of its women are on the ground. Then it is done, no matter how brave its warriors or how strong its weapons.
—Cheyenne Proverb

THESE WORDS RECOGNIZE the central importance of Indigenous women in the interminable struggle for the survival of our families, communities, and, in fact, our people. Land claims settlements and the recognition of treaty rights become hollow victories, rendered meaningless, if there is no one left to exercise these rights. This reality is not only well understood but in fact embraced by the colonizer. Its logic has shaped the official policies and practices for generations now. As Mary Eberts points out, the Canadian state has been actively engaged in orchestrating the extinction of Indigenous peoples, openly admitting their goal was to "continue until there is not a single Indian in Canada that has not been absorbed into the body politic, and there is no Indian question, and no Indian department" (148). Indeed, if the "band ceases to exist," the land reserved for that band is taken by the Crown, and the band exists "only so long as there are members" (Eberts 148). In so far as the goal was, and apparently still is, the eradication of Indigenous peoples (and the continual reminder of the shameful foundations of the Canadian state), each new life brought into our world is a symbolic and literal act of resistance. The birth and nurturing of yet another generation is a battle won in the longstanding war against our Nations.

According to studies on the topic, women "formed the very core of Indigenous resistance to genocide and colonization since the first moment of conflict" (Jaimes and Halsey 311). Our very existence not only signifies the success of such longstanding political resistance, it also, simultaneously, evidences the continued failure of the colonial project. It is, therefore, not surprising that Indigenous women and girls have been targeted and subjected to the racist and sexist vitriol, ignited and fueled by our refusal to be subjugated, assimilated, or eliminated. The disproportionate levels of violence, and the appalling numbers of missing and murdered Indigenous women and girls, must be understood as both integral to, and the outcome of, the historical process of dispossessing Indigenous peoples from our traditional territories. It was with this purpose in mind—to create awareness and understanding—that we set out on this journey. We have been fighting violence since the very beginning. This is why the Native Women's Association was created over forty years ago; this is why Bernie and Gladys started the Walk 4 Justice. Our women warriors came together to speak out against the oppression of our women, to speak out against the discrimination, and the injustice.

Memee: People often ask why I decided to become involved in the Native Women's movement, in human rights activism, and I realize that it was not a conscious decision at all. I feel like it just sort of happened to me. Maybe I naturally evolved into the role, because my mother was an advocate for Indigenous women's rights and an activist for as long as I can remember. She went all the way to the Supreme Court back in the 1970s fighting the discrimination in the Indian Act after she lost her Indian status through marriage. When the other mothers were making cookies and knitting sweaters, we were making protest posters and banners, and when we did bake sales it was to raise funds to go to Ottawa to protest something. Standing up against injustice was just a part of our daily lives. That was just how I grew up, right from birth, being an activist before I could even walk. But that is what happens. You cannot help but be political when your every waking minute is a lived reminder of injustice. You can't just ignore it.

Bernie: Exactly. We are living this every day. When you are down in the streets of Vancouver you can't just turn a blind eye and ignore the suffering. So we decided we were going to do something about it. We started on the Highway of Tears in 2006, when we walked from Prince George to Prince Rupert to open the symposium. We got the idea from one of the family members out there because we felt that nobody was listening. I said "let's stop talking about it and let's do it." We needed to create some awareness. It seemed like everything else was more important than our women. We didn't know what the outcome was going to be, so we started compiling the stories, compiling the data, we gathered thousands of names of missing or murdered girls. Then it became more of a reality, it actually shocked even the families.

Gladys: I was looking for Tamara, my niece. She went missing in 2005. We waited for years and nothing happened. During the Robert Pickton trial and the BC inquiry, we had no answers. The cops wouldn't share any information with me. The only thing they did was come around and threaten me when I tried to get the answers for myself, to do the job, their job, because they weren't doing it. The only time they talked to me was when they wanted our list because it was much larger than their list.

Bernie: We just felt that there was not enough media or attention, women were going missing and still being murdered; the police weren't doing anything, and nothing was changing. There was no public help or anyone to try to push this. That is why we took this journey. It is going to get worse before it's going to get better. How many more women have to die? How many more children have to go into care? I don't understand it. It shouldn't have taken over three thousand of our women to go missing, and people still don't see it. This is genocide.

Gladys: They have been trying to control our women for generations. Think about it. If Indigenous women have on average five children, and these RCMP reports are admitting to almost twelve hundred missing or murdered Indigenous women, that means we are missing out on six thousand members from our future generations. That is genocide plain and simple.

Memee: This is why we have fought so hard for a national public inquiry because we want those questions answered to determine what is going on here. We know in academic text book terms that this is about racialized, sexualized violence, but what is not as well understood are the many ways in which this plays out in the daily lives of Indigenous women and girls in Canada. When you are in a country where Indigenous peoples have been degraded and dehumanized as part of the colonizers efforts to steal the territory, to oppress and eliminate the Indigenous peoples for economic reasons, and at the same time they brought patriarchy over from Europe, and the belief that women were inferior, that they were essentially the property of men, when you put those two ideologies together you end up with a situation where Indigenous women simply don't matter. They become disposable.

Bernie: We are just not that important. All I hear are negative things, even the policing hasn't changed. Really nothing has changed. I know that they are supposed to have cultural sensitivity as part of their training, but here on the [Vancouver] Downtown Eastside, it really hasn't changed. They still have their attitudes. They are still beating up our people and still throwing us in jails. Things just haven't changed. When there is a family member that goes missing ... we were asked to go out a few weeks ago, a group of us, four women, went out looking, she was just a young girl, like sixteen or seventeen. I know there are those groups that work closely with the police, and they praise them, but they are not down here, doing what we are doing, on the front lines. We check everywhere, go through the bars, through the alleys, we go through some of the sleazy hotels and some of them won't even let us in. We show pictures.... So no nothing has changed, and I get really disheartened when I see so many of our young people who are constantly in a fight at ground zero here just to survive.

Gladys: We have seen this time and time again where the attitudes come out, the police officers who don't bother investigating when our girls go missing, or worse yet don't even bother taking a report because they have been raised to be racist. They fully believe that all our people are drunks or addicts, or prostitutes, and it's not worth their time to go looking, that they have better things to do. The coroners are just as bad as the police are. They don't do any investigation.

Bernie: So many families they don't have closure because if you try to question to police they just brush you off. They just say no this is the way it is and sorry for your loss. They think it was just another Indian. So much of that happens here, from every level down here, all across Canada families have a lot of questions. They aren't getting answers. There is just so much....

Memee: I am tired of the cops blaming our women for their own victimization. You see the reports that blame the victims, blame the women for their own situation. They say it was because they had high-risk lifestyles, it was because they were in the streets, because they were hitchhiking. But nobody hitchhikes just for fun. They hitch a ride because they have no other choice, because they are in a community with no transit, and they don't have enough money for a car. They have no other choice. If they need to get into the city for an appointment, they have no other choice.

Gladys: She shouldn't have had to be hitchhiking first of all, and I feel that way about all the girls that went missing on the highway of tears. If they had a transportation system, maybe Tamara wouldn't have been out there hitchhiking. Maybe Nicole wouldn't have been out there, none of those girls. They wouldn't have had to be hitchhiking or walking home along those highways.

Memee: We have actually seen how the police and the justice system have put our women in danger. They transport our girls, sometimes hundreds of kilometres from their community into the city for court, and then if the judge says "Okay, you are free to go based on time served," she is just released, cut loose in the city with no thought to how she is going to get safely home. Even in my own territory, and we are not a remote First Nation, the closest bus stop is over an hour away, and it is not even a real bus station.

They just pull over, and the greyhound bus lets you off at the gas station. There is no taxi service, so you would have to hitchhike for another hour to get home. So in these cases the system has put our girls in danger, but if she was to disappear between that bus stop and home everyone would be blaming her. They would be saying she should have known better. She shouldn't have been hitchhiking. So yes I agree our women are often in high-risk situations, but when you look at the facts, our women are being placed in high risk situations by the system. You look at the fact that we have First Nations where people are living in Third World conditions in the middle of one the richest countries in the world because of hundreds of years of broken treaties, exploitation, abuse and oppression. If our people, our communities had access to even a portion of the profits that come from the resources extracted from our lands, we would be self-sufficient, but those resources have been taken to make some private company shareholders rich while the people in that area starve. Many don't even have clean water, or hydro ... that shouldn't be happening in a rich country like Canada but it is. Nobody believes this is happening.

Gladys: Unless the government starts putting some money where their mouth is and starts providing services for our women, we are not going to get anywhere. Those women are still going to be coming into the cities in droves, and they are not going to have anywhere to go, not going to have any education, not going to have a counsellor to talk to about the abuse they have suffered. They are not going to be able to find a home because it is virtually impossible for anybody to afford a home here in the city these days. There is no affordable housing anywhere. Even a working class couple can't find a place to live. What about all those single moms with five kids and no place to live.

Bernie: I see the young girls being brought in, whether it is Edmonton or Seattle. We figured out how they are getting these girls across the borders, out in White Rock they have the train lines, so they go out and party on Crescent Beach and they party up on top of the train boxes, and those trains leave in the morning with those girls passed out on top. Then they are gone. That's how they are getting the women out of here.... We stopped them once. I overheard a conversation and I got on the phone right away, told them how these three young women were going to be trafficked. They had someone who was going to pay ten thousand each, so they get the girls totally wired, and there was supposed to be three girls coming from Edmonton in exchange. I just happened to overhear the conversation, and we called a friend who called the police, and it was stopped. But those girls didn't have a clue what was about to happened to them. It is a business. It is sick, and it is sad. The women I have talked to, I asked them straight out if there was a place for you to go, to get out of here, would you go? But you would have to detox. They all said "yes, this is not what we want." They get these girls high, give them free dope until they are addicted, then you owe them. These girls come to the city to go to school. They go out on a weekend, and now they are stuck down here. They are just really wired, then the gangs get a hold of them, and they are putting them out on the street corner. That is not part of our culture. There was never even a word for prostitution. That was brought here and it is a business, and huge business.

Gladys: Those groups that say they advocate for the rights of sex trade workers to help them, if you were to do anything to heal those women and actually help them, those pimps would be out of a job. Plain and simple, it is all about the money. They don't want to help these women. Why should they? They are getting government funding to keep these women in the streets, just like those 237 organizations in the downtown eastside of Vancouver. It is a million dollars a day to keep them going. It is a multi-billion dollar industry. We are commodities. Our girls keep going around the revolving doors and keep them in business.

Memee: I find it really interesting to see how both *The Globe and Mail and The Toronto Star* have taken up this cause, and started looking into it themselves instead of reproducing the usual racist portrayal of Indigenous women. Very often in the past, if one of our women went missing it didn't even make the news, and if it did it was an extremely racist, blaming the women kind of portrayal that has contributed all along to the problem. The fact that both of these major voices in the media have taken the initiative, and invested their own resources into finding the truth of this story, has made a huge difference. Canadians are talking about it. Now there is a change in government, and this inquiry is going to shine a light on the systemic factors, the corrections issues, the policing issues, there are very clear connections to the child welfare issues. Once we shine a light, and expose the way that racism and sexism have made our women unsafe, then we will be able to take concrete actions that will make a real difference. In the ten years Harper was in power, there was not one conversation. He absolutely just shut the door. He wouldn't even talk to us because he didn't want to hear. He didn't want to know what was happening, and he wanted to keep it that way. At least with the new government they are willing to listen, willing to start the dialogue.

Gladys: I've gone through the Harper regime where virtually nothing happened because he showed such an obvious racist attitude towards our women, and now we have a prime minister who is very young and good at finding tears, but there are still no resources out there to alleviate the problems. Every single day I hear about another girl who has gone missing or been murdered. Here we are in the spring of 2016, and those of us who work out on the frontlines know we are preparing for an influx of youth hitting those streets in every major urban centre in this country. They have no resources to address the new influx of girls that are being trafficked through all the cities, and I don't see any resources going into mother's centres or shelters. They are going to be hitting the streets from here until the summer and by then it will be too late. Schools are letting out, and these girls don't want to go home, then they slip through the cracks.... And why don't they want to go home, everybody knows ... they are suffering from severe poverty and now addictions.

Bernie: If it was me calling the shots, I would say we need to set up things for our women: health, healing and wellness places for them. Our chiefs need to step it up too. We understand about the funding and all that, but for our homeless, we need proper housing. It's the same thing that we have been saying for all these years. We need education. Why do we have to scramble just to get the crumbs, to go to school. Our youth are dying on the street. Honest to God, I have never seen so many kids on these streets and it just breaks my heart. There is nothing to sustain them. They leave their homes, and end up down here, and it starts the whole cycle all over again.

I think these chiefs, all our leaders, need to start making better choices, to take care of their people, to stop playing the blame game. I ask them why can't we have proper housing, and schools, and jobs and health. There is so much money coming out, but it goes to these organizations that are going to try to fix us, but it's not going to help. We need exiting programs to help get these young women out, off the streets, before they fall through the cracks. But programs that have culture as the base, I really believe that it is the culture that is going to save them. We can't change what happened in the past, but we can work together to come up with strategies now. Our kids are dying on these streets, dying at high rates. I see more kids than I have ever seen before and it just breaks my heart ... I wish there was something more I could do.

Gladys: Having been across Canada, we have seen a lot of lateral violence ... sometimes when you speak your truth it hurts a lot of people. But then there are others out there who are jumping on the cause, but they have no idea what it's actually like to be a family member, to loose someone to this kind of violence. Our family members know what the flaws are in the system, they know from first-hand experience. They know what would have protected their loved ones.

Bernie: These organizations too, I hold them accountable for it because they want to keep our people oppressed down here, to keep these people here. That's where the money comes from. I think the money needs to go somewhere else.... Giving them methadone and crap, it's a Band-Aid because nobody wants to deal with the real issues. Everyone understands about the residential schools, but we need to step it up now. Our families are broken and handing out money isn't the answer we need to get to the root of all this.

Memee: Exactly, our women are in unsafe situations because of the racism and sexism, the challenge is to get people to see how hard it is to survive in the streets. If you had to spend a day in the life of an Indigenous woman on the streets in any city in Canada, you would see that they have to be smarter and tougher and stronger just to stay alive. They are not in the streets because they are too lazy to get a job, in fact far from it. Surviving in the streets is exhausting. It takes a tremendous amount of effort to survive. People don't understand the amount of work it takes just to survive when you are in an environment that works against you. They have to be warrior women just to get through the day in these streets.

Bernie: Oh god yes, I have to believe that before it is my time to go I hope and I pray and there has to be something that is going to shift this around. Stop these people that are hurting and killing our women, that are trafficking our girls. The whole justice system needs to change. As long as these guys are getting picked up and put in jail and then let go again. This is the place they bring them to. Nobody wants them in their community, so they dump them right back here in the Downtown Eastside. But the leadership has to stand up. We already know how the system has failed us. We gotta stand together for our future generations, like my little grandbabies.... I worry myself sick about them. Being a mom you understand that.

Memee: I think that is the worst part ... on the days when it all becomes too much to handle, I remind myself that those babies are counting on us. That we can't give up, that we have to carry on and continue the struggle, not only for our own children but for the next seven generations to come. In fact some of the young people now believe that the seventh generation has just been born, and they will be the ones to finally break the cycle. They will not just survive but finally actually see our nations thrive.

WORKS CITED

Eberts, Mary. 2014. "Victoria's Secret: How to Make a Population of Prey." *Indivisible: Indigenous Human Rights*. Ed Joyce Green.

Halifax: Fernwood Publishing, 2014. 144-158. Print.
Jaimes, Annette, M. with Teresa Halsey. "American Indian Women at the Center of Resistance in Contemporary North America." *The State of Native America: Genocide, Colonization, and Resistance*. Ed Annette M. Jaimes. Boston: South End Press, 1992. 311-344. Print.

About the Contributors

Myrna Abraham is from Sagkeeng First Nation. She is the sister of Sharon Abraham, whose DNA was found on Robert Pickton's farm in Port Coquitlam, British Columbia. She is a support worker in Winnipeg and also carries out walks to honour the families who have lost and are missing their loved ones.

Brenda Anderson teaches Women's and Gender Studies and Religious Studies at Luther College at the University of Regina. She studies the impact of colonialism on women, with an emphasis on the theoretical and activist processes of decolonization. Co-chairing a conference on missing and murdered Indigenous women led to co-editing *Torn from our Midst: Voices of Grief, Healing and Action from the MMIW Conference* in 2008, and a second edition with updated and new material is in process. Brenda is co-researcher on a nationally funded project examining Muslim women's usage of digital technology for interreligious dialogue and faith activism.

Sākihitowin Awāsis is an Otipemisiw and Anishinaabe Two-Spirit land defender and spoken word artist of mixed descent. Her research focuses on energy justice and the Enbridge Line 9 Pipeline reversal. As a writer, she has contributed to the book *A Line In The Tar Sands* as well as *kimiwan* zine. Her work at Atlohsa Native Family Healing Services draws connections between the health and well-being of Indigenous families and the earth. She is continually inspired by acts of decolonization, resurgence, and community healing.

Summer Rain Bentham (Costaslish, Squamish Nation), **Hilla Kerner**, and **Lisa Steacy** are frontline workers at Vancouver Rape Relief and Women's Shelter, which is a feminist collective operating a rape crisis centre and a transition house in Vancouver, BC.

Carrie Bourassa is a Professor of Indigenous Health Studies at First Nations University of Canada. As an Indigenous community-based researcher, she is proud to be the successful nominated principal investigator on two Canada Foundation for Innovation Grants, which funded the Indigenous Community-based Health Research Lab in 2010 and the Cultural Safety Evaluation, Training and Research Lab in 2016 at the First Nations University. She is a member of the College of New Scholars, Artists, and Scientists of the Royal Society of Canada. Her research interests include the impacts of colonization on the health of Indigenous people; creating culturally safe care in health service delivery; Indigenous community-based health research methodology; HIV/AIDS, HCV, among Indigenous people; end-of-life care and dementia among Indigenous people; Indigenous Water Governance and Indigenous women's health. Carrie is Métis, belonging to the Regina Riel Métis Council #34.

Jennifer Brant belongs to the Tyendinaga Mohawk Nation with family ties to Six Nations of the Grand River Territory. She is a mother of two boys and is currently completing her PhD in Educational Studies at Brock University. Jennifer is the recipient of a doctoral fellowship from the Social Sciences and Humanities Research Council. Jennifer teaches in the Indigenous studies program and is currently employed as the program co-ordinator for the Gidayaamin Indigenous Women's Certificate Program at Brock University. Her work is driven by her passion to contribute to Indigenous community well-being. Her research interests includes Indigenous maternal pedagogy, Indigenous women's literature, and the advancement of ethical space for Indigenous scholarship.

Vicki Chartrand is an Assistant Professor in the Sociology Department, Bishop's University Québec. She has over fifteen years of experience as an anti-violence worker and advocate. This includes working directly with women and children, Indigenous communities, and prisoners in an advocacy and outreach capacity.

Caroline Fidan Tyler Doenmez received her MA from Columbia University in 2015, where she studied under Audra Simpson. Her master's thesis project, which included fieldwork in Nova Scotia and Manitoba, interrogated the right to life of the murdered and missing Indigenous women and girls in Canada. Caroline will be starting a PhD in socio-cultural Anthropology at the University of Minnesota in the fall of 2016.

Sherry Emmerson is an Anishinaabe-kwe from Chippewas of Nawash Unceded First Nation located in Neyaashiinigmiing, Ontario. She is a graduate of the Addictions and Community Service Worker program from Everest College as well as a graduate from the Aboriginal Adult Education Bachelors of Education program from Brock University. She is currently working as an addiction services initiative caseworker on her reserve. She is a wife and a mother of two, who actively advocates for her people by using the knowledge she has learned to bring awareness to the injustice that her people face and showcase their resiliency and strength.

Thomas Fleming, Professor of Criminology at Wilfrid Laurier University, has taught at the University of Alberta, University of Toronto, York University, Ryerson University and the University of Windsor. He served as the first graduate director of the MA in criminology, and designed the criminology program at Laurier. He received the Leadership in Faculty Teaching Award (LIFT) from the province of Ontario for his contributions to the field of criminology, and is a member of the Laurier Teaching Hall of Fame. Dr. Fleming is a fellow of McLaughlin College, York University. He has published twelve books in the field of criminology, numerous articles and book chapters, and has presented fifty papers at international scholarly conferences.

Leah Maureen Gazan is a member of Wood Mountain Lakota Nation, located in Treaty 4 territory. She is currently teaching in the Faculty of Education at the University of Winnipeg. Leah's career has focused on community capacity building and development, and supporting the advancement of First Nations across Canada. Leah has been an active participant in social movements, including Idle No More and is a founder of the #WeCare campaign. Leah was also recently selected to present at the Standing Committee on the Status of Women in Ottawa to testify about how the federal government has fared in addressing the issue of violence against Indigenous women and girls. Leah recently completed a TedX Talk titled "The Eye of the Colonial Storm."

Alyssa M. General is an artist, poet, and resource developer from Six Nations of the Grand River Territory. She has created illustrations for the Kanyen'kéha children's show, Tóta tánon Ohkwá:ri, and has collaborated with other Mohawk speakers on a series of short, educational films in the language. She also received national recognition for her poem "Enkonte'nikonhrakwaríhsya'te."

Anita Olsen Harper is a member of the Lac Seul First Nation in Northwestern Ontario; her first language is Anishinaape. As a post-doctoral student at the University of Manitoba, she studies traditional land use mapping. She enjoys work in Aboriginal education and training, anti-violence, health and well-being, Indigenous knowledge translation and history-heritage representation. She sits on the Advisory Board of Unama'ki College of Cape Breton University. She was recruited to the Indigenous Health Advisory Committee (IHAC) for the Royal College of Physicians and Surgeons of Canada (RCPSC). In 2014, she was elected trustee, Zone 5 of the Ottawa-Carleton District School Board (OCDSB).

Cheryl James is from Roseau River Anishinaabe First Nation. She is a member and manager of Keewatin Otchitchak (Northern Crane) Traditional Women Singers. She is also on the Bear Clan Patrol council. She is currently a student at the University of Winnipeg. Formerly, she was a youth support worker, mentor, community helper, and administrative assistant at Ma Mawi Wi Chi Itata Centre.

Wendee Kubik is an Associate Professor of Women's and Gender Studies at Brock University, as well as an adjunct professor at the University of Regina. She is a member of the Environmental Sustainability Research Centre and Social Justice and Equity Studies program at Brock University and a member of RESOLVE Saskatchewan. Her research interests focus on women's health, violence against women, farm women, food and water security and sustainability, women's work, and gender analysis.

D. Memee Lavell-Harvard, Ph.D., was elected president of the Native Women's Association of Canada in 2015. She is a proud member of the Wikwemikong First Nation, the first Aboriginal Trudeau Scholar, and currently serves on the Independent Advisory Board for Senate Appointments. Ms. Harvard is a full-time mother of three girls. Since joining the Ontario Native Women's Association as a youth director in 1994, Ms. Harvard followed in the footsteps of her mother, Jeannette Corbiere Lavell, advocating for Indigenous women's rights, and the empowerment of Aboriginal families. She was co-editor of *Until Our Hearts Are on the Ground: Aboriginal Mothering, Oppression, Resistance and Rebirth* and *Mothers of the Nations: Indigenous Mothering as Global Resistance, Reclaiming and Recovery*.

Maxine Matilpi, J.D., LL.M., is Ma'amtigila and Kwakiutl, and also of Scottish and English descent. A former chief negotiator for the Kwakiutl First Nation, she teaches First Nations' Studies and Women's Studies at Vancouver Island University in Snuneymuxw Territory and is also project lead for RELAW (Revitalizing Indigenous Law for Land, Air and Water) at West Coast Environmental Law. Her research and scholarly interests are Indigenous and contemplative pedagogies and Indigenous feminisms. She is also a dancer, an artist, and a soccer mom.

Gillian McKee is of Scottish, Irish and English descent whose ancestors were settlers seven generations ago on Huron and Six Nations territories. She is the mother of two Indigenous daughters. Twenty eight years ago she moved to the Northwest Territories and sixteen years ago to the Yukon and has learned much from the First Nation, Métis, Inuit, and Inuvialuit people of Canada's north. Her writing comes from her personal journey of finding her place in relation to Canada's Indigenous peoples.

Rosemary Nagy is Associate Professor of the Department of Gender Equality and Social Justice at Nipissing University. Rosemary has published extensively on Indian residential schools and Canada's Truth and Reconciliation Commission, with the support of a SSHRC standard research grant. As a non-Indigenous Canadian, Rosemary is interested in settler responsibilities to redress the ongoing violence of colonization, and argues that reconciliation must be a process of decolonization. She views the missing and murdered women as being in many ways a direct legacy of the schools, and Canada's refusal to acknowledge its role in violence against Indigenous women is an obstacle to reconciliation.

Patricia O'Reilly, JD, is a barrister, solicitor and mediator who practised in the area of poverty law for many years. She is a lifelong social activist and law reformer. She is an Assistant Professor in Law and Society at Wilfrid Laurier University and teaches in the Criminology Department. She was previously a professor at Grant McEwan College and instructor and community education organizer at Goldsmiths College in London, England. Ms. O'Reilly's pedagogy embraces a feminist, anti-oppression approach. Ms. O'Reilly has co-edited two books, *Youth Injustice: Canadian Perspectives* (2008) and *Violence in Canada* (2016). Her research interests include First Nations Peoples and the law, media and crime, violence, assault on workers, and the sociology of law.

Brenda Osborne is from Norway House Cree nation. She is mother of Claudette Osborne who has been missing since 2008. Brenda has lost other loved ones including her cousin Helen Betty Osborne to four non-Aboriginal men from The Pas who kidnapped, assaulted and murdered her. She is an organizer of annual walks and ongoing searches.

Isela Pérez-Torres is Mexican journalist. She was born in Ciudad Juárez, where she wrote about violence against women. In 2009, she left México, and she was granted political asylum in Spain in September, 2010. She is currently a PhD student at Universidad de Alcalá.

Nick Printup belongs to the Onondaga Nation Beaver Clan; his family comes from the Sour Springs Longhouse located in Six Nations of the Grand River. Nick is also from the Algonquin Nation and a community member of Kitigan Zibi Anishinabeg First Nation. His Haudenosaunee name is Hi:Honh'Donh:G-wus meaning "He Opens The Door." His Anishinabe name is Gaahgii Gehjewan meaning "Forever Flowing Water." In 2015, Nick graduated from Niagara College's three-year broadcasting program, majoring in Film Production, where he won best documentary, best short film, and best music video. In August 2016, Nick will graduate from an International Business Management Post-Graduate program. Nick is a published a writer, who before returning to school was a social worker primarily working with at-risk First Nations.

Gladys Radek belongs to the Gitxsan Wet'Suwet'En Nation, Laxilu, Small Frog Clan, and is from Moricetown, BC. Gladys co-founded the Walk4Justice in 2008, a campaign to raise awareness and seek justice for victimized women. Her own niece, Tamara Chipman, disappeared in 2005 along Highway 16 in northern British Columbia. In 2011 Gladys made it to the top ten for the Champions of Change, a CBC contest to honour volunteerism in Canada.

Chickadee Richard is an Anishinaabe Elder of the Bear Clan. She is the founder and council member of the Bear Clan Patrol. She has served on the board of the Indigenous Environment Network and is a spokeswoman for environmental issues and matters related to reducing violence against Indigenous women and girls.

Jessica Riel-Johns is an Anishinaabe-kwe (Ojibwe) from Batchewana First Nation located in Sault Ste. Marie, Ontario. She is a graduate of the Criminal Justice program at Sault College and is currently graduating from Brock University, with a Bachelor's of Education. Her research interests include Indigenous women's pedagogy, Indigenous feminism, Indigenous epistemology, and ontology. She is a public speaker on social justice issues involving Indigenous people. She is a mother of five, a wife and a social advocate.

Josephine L. Savarese is an Associate Professor in the Department of Criminology and Criminal Justice, St. Thomas University, Fredericton, New Brunswick. In the fall of 2015, she served as the Acting Coordinator of Women's Studies and Gender Studies. While in that role, Josephine organized a series of events including presentations by Elders, a guest lecture and the installation of the Redress Project by Jaime Black to bring an Atlantic Canadian focus to missing and murdered Indigenous women. Her chapter is dedicated to the women, children, families and communities impacted by the stories told in this collection.

Tasha Spillett is Nehiyaw and Trinidadian. She is an Indigenous educator in Winnipeg, currently teaching in the Department of Native Studies at the University of Manitoba, and in the Faculty of Education at the University of Winnipeg. Tasha has a master's degree in Indigenous land-based education from the University of Saskatchewan. In her work as an educator, Tasha calls on Indigenous traditional knowledge as a framework for both her methodology and her pedagogy. She looks forward to continuing her academic studies, which will include an exploration of international Indigenous land-based education as an intervention to ongoing colonization.

Bernice Williams also known as Skundaal from the Haida Nation has been carving for almost 40 years and her pieces have been sold all over the world. She is the first and only woman to apprentice under the late world renowned artist Bill Reid. Her work includes a traditional Button Blanket, "The Dance of the Eagle" that was given to Rigoberta Menchú Tum upon receiving the Nobel Peace Prize, a 30 foot totem pole for the Vancouver School Board, a 47 foot canoe commissioned by the city of Richmond's village of Steveston in 2000, and the "Homeless People" totem pole in 2010 at the First United Church. Her work can be seen in the great halls of museums, and in the U.S. for Senators,

Congressmen. Her greatest passion is teaching youth living a high risk style by reconnecting them to their culture, as she believes culture saves lives.